Love Song to the Plains

Books by Mari Sandoz published by
the University of Nebraska Press

LOVE SONG
TO THE PLAINS

Mari Sandoz

Illustrations and map by Bryan Forsyth

UNIVERSITY OF NEBRASKA PRESS • LINCOLN / LONDON

Library of Congress Catalog Card Number 61-6441
Copyright © 1961 by Mari Sandoz
All rights reserved
Manufactured in the United States of America
International Standard Book Number 0-8032-5172-6

First Bison Book printing September, 1966
Most recent printing shown by first digit below:
11   12   13   14   15   16   17   18   19   20

Bison Book edition published by arrangement with Harper and Row.

∞

For Van

Teacher and friend of a writing lifetime

Contents

Foreword

On my wall, wherever I am to be for some weeks, hangs an old cowboy hat, stained and plainly no John B. Stetson. Years ago, far from home and preoccupied with an old Indian site, I was trapped in a sudden shift of wind by a prairie fire sweeping in too fast to escape on my borrowed horse. I tied my jacket over his eyes and set a backfire for a bare spot for us, using my hat to control the flames.

I don't recall where I learned that piece of Plains lore. Many old-timers stopped at our home near an ancient crossing of the Niobrara: Indians, breed descendants of the fur men and *voyageurs*, old buffalo hunters, sky pilots, Texas trailers, broken-down gamblers, road agents and hideouts from the cattle wars. They told stories, stories we could all hear so long as we kept silent. When I was seven or eight I liked to climb to the top of Indian Hill overlooking miles of the river and beyond, to where I hoped to see far places in the shimmering mirages, perhaps even Laramie Peak, as old-timers promised. The gravel under my bare feet was black from Indian signal fires, and just below me was the place where our father had led a vigilante gang that hanged a man and let him down alive.

I didn't see the hanging but I had seen birth and dying long before either was a shock, and the hardship, the violence and gaiety of homestead life. Unfortunately, even in my earliest writing, I found ordinary words poor saddlebags to transport my sense of these things. I began to maneuver for special relationships, special rhythm patterns, the strings of words perhaps as abrupt as a cut bank or vagrant as a dry-land whirlwind; as gentle as a June morning, or harsh as blizzard snow, driven in endless, twisting drifts.

But I never learned to say how Laramie Peak might look in a mirage.

M. S.

I Pathway to the Southern Sea

The place called the Great Plains spreads southward from the upper Saskatchewan River down to the Rio Grande—a high country, a big country of vast reaches, tremendous streams, and stories of death on the ridges, derring-do in the valleys, and the sweetness and heartbreak of springtime on the prairies.

Half of this region was the old Nebraska Territory that lay like a golden hackberry leaf in the sun, a giant curling, tilted leaf. The veins of it were the long streams rising out near the mountains and flowing eastward to the Big Muddy, the wild Missouri. The largest that cut through the center of the Plains was the broad, flat-watered Platte, usually pleasant and easygoing as an October day, and below it the Republican, deceptively limpid but roaring into sudden gullywashers that flooded all the wide valley and could sweep away even the most powerful of the wilderness herds.

North of the Platte River the determined Niobrara cut a deep, three-hundred-mile canyon across the tablelands, the swift clear waters an eternal rebuke to the sullen gray of the Missouri that had to accept them. Beyond these streams, but still within the region that was a whole in nature before the foolish little lines of the white man cut it awkwardly this way and that, lay such rivers as the White, the Cheyenne, the Grand and the Cannonball, the Belle Fourche, the Powder and the Yellowstone. True, these names were from the late-comer, the white man, but they carried the song of far horizons within them, and the tremendous breadth of sky open to all the winds —winds that could sweep in great bloomings across the prairies, yellow, blue and purple-red, or white as summer snow, the brush-lined spring gullies and waterways white too, fragrant in plum and chokecherry, followed by the tumbling pink of the wild rose. Millions of ducks, geese, cranes and gleaming white swans made their annual flights over the plains so conveniently laddered by the east-flowing streams, while on the rolling prairie the great buffalo herds grazed into the cyclonic winds in their own migratory rounds, their millions moving dark as vast cloud shadows over the earth, whether in the greening of spring or the expanse of blizzard snow. And following them was a scattering of brown-skinned men, the reach of their arms extended by weapons of stone.

So the seasons passed, as the ages and the aeons had moved over the region, leaving the history of their moment behind in the Crinoidea of the great limestones. The later creatures vanished into their own stony graveyards: the sea monsters, the silurians, the mammoths and mastodons, the camel and the tiny eohippus who, tiptoeing like a ballet girl through geologic ages, lost all his five toes but the center one as he grew into a horse, and vanished from the region that proved so friendly when he returned. And when he did come back it was not alone but bearing the carpaced, gold-seek-ing Spaniard up that ladder of streams that flowed across the Plains, for even this bearded, palefaced man, godlike in his self-created image, had to move from water to water as the buffalo moved, and the pursuing wolves and Indians.

Coronado found no golden cities, only the unbelievable distances, the few habitations the most contemptible—skin, grass or the lowly earth. He found nothing of the Quivera whose stories he had accepted so eagerly, nothing of the land where even the common people supped from golden jugs and bowls, where a stream six miles wide bore great canoes with golden eagles at the prow, a river with fish large as horses. If Coronado had gone as far as the Missouri he would have seen great canoes, not, it is true, prowed with eagles of gold but perhaps carrying live eagles, live golden-headed eagles, the pets of an occasional warrior. And if Coronado could have waited two hunderd and fifty or three hundred years he would have seen craft more fabulous than even his most glorious hope churning their fiery way up and down the Missouri current, carrying tangible wealth beyond any he could have dreamed.

There were great fishes too, perhaps not as large as his horse but good-sized pike and many catfish as heavy as the Spaniard himself. As for a river six miles wide, in spring flood the old Missouri spread two, three times that distance wherever the valley opened her bosom.

The disappointed goldseeker wreaked his scornful anger upon the Indians whose stories he had hungered to believe, not understanding what one less bitten by avarice would have known: that some stories are told to be believed and some are not; of those intended for belief, only a few are true, the rest either unconscious lies and misapprehensions or deliberate falsehoods, told for advantage or from necessity, such as saving one's skin, or hands and eyes and tongue.

The stories believed by Coronado weren't the last tall tales told about the land that hid Quivera from him. First there were those of great exploits and derring-do that the Spaniards brought back to cover up their failure to return loaded down with gold. Oñate, whose expeditions in the period 1598-1601 reached far up the buffalo plains, is quoted as saying he had succeeded in reaching the city of Quivera, on the north bank of a shallow river, which sounds very much like the Platte, or the Arkansas, the Cimarron or the Canadian. One story tells of a fight with the Escanzaques, in which Oñate killed a thousand Indians, which would have made a substantial hole in any tribe of the region, but then if all the Indians reported killed by the white man in the trans-Missouri country had actually died there would not have been one red man left to face Custer at the Little Big Horn. Always the authorities at home had to be appeased, face had to be saved, and the superpatriots and the hero worshipers satisfied—worshipers willing to blow up any fleeting glimpse of an enemy into a bloody slaughter.

But the ring-tail roarer, the real tall tale of the Spaniards on the middle Plains, was not put together until two hundred years after its supposed occurrence, and tied to one Don Diego de Penalosa, who, according to the story, reached the Platte and Loup River region in 1662:

> Here they found themselves within sight of a vast settlement or city situated in the midst of a spacious prairie, and upon both banks of the last mentioned stream [the Loup]. This was the city, or one of the cities of Quivera. It contained thousands of houses, mostly circular in shape, some two, three and even four stories in height, framed by a hard wood which seems to have been walnut and skillfully thatched. It extended along both sides of this second river for more than two leagues, at which distance a third stream flowed into the second. Beyond this the city again stretched out for many miles; just how far is uncertain, for the troops never reached its ultimate boundary. The plain upon which the huge village lay was some eighteen or twenty miles in breadth.*

Unfortunately there seems to have been no such army out of New Mexico at all, but the story, if published earlier, would have been a fine forerunner of the voluminous fiction-called-fact that take the Plains area for their locale—the often repeated account of Portugee Phillip's lone winter ride into Fort Laramie with the news of the Fetterman Massacre in 1866; the report of 3,000 Sioux killed in the Wagon Box fight near Fort Phil Kearny in 1867; the stories of Wild Bill Hickok, Wyatt Earp and Bat Masterson as law men; Buffalo Bill Cody as an Indian killer; Eddie Burgess as the Yellow-Haired Boy

---

* Judge James W. Savage, pamphlet, 1885, based on article by John Gilmary Shea, supposedly inspired by a manuscript in Madrid, using actual names and places in a fictional account.

Chief of the Pawnees; Calamity Jane as a scout or the beloved of anybody at all; and a hundred other such elaborations.

The early French to the Missouri country came in no gaudy metallic expeditions. In June 1673 the slender craft of Jolliet and the back-garbed Marquette passed the mouth of the river of the Oumissouries, whose rapid waters rushing eastward in full flood tide astonished Father Marquette, who hoped by means of this river "to make the discovery of the Vermillion Sea or California." True, there was La Hontan's account of a supposed journey to the Missouri in 1689, and frankly written to please rather than to inform, but most of the early French came very quietly, often slipping westward on Indian moccasins, in twos and threes or alone, carrying powder, bulk lead and the beaver traps. They paddled when they could, portaged from one watershed to another and walked over wide prairie stretches if necessary. Instead of gold they followed the richer if less heady and inflaming musk of the beaver.

Often the Frenchmen remained out in the Missouri country and beyond, taking native wives and, through the matrilinear custom of the Indians, becoming members of the woman's tribe, as a Sioux who married a Cheyenne woman became a Cheyenne. This custom was so deeply rooted that when early explorers asked about white men in the region, it seldom occurred to the Indians to mention those married into their people, perhaps their own families. The *coureurs de bois* and the early French traders with Indian wives and living in the villages were fellow tribesmen, brother Indians. Although Bienville reported in 1704 that Canadians were working the Missouri in parties of seven and eight, Lewis and Clark, in 1804, were sometimes told they were the first white men to the region, perhaps by descendants of the same Frenchmen of a hundred years ago.* Or perhaps of Spaniards, who had penetrated toward Canada

* Several old buffalo-hunting Oglala Sioux of the author's acquaintance called themselves full bloods although their grandfathers or great grandfathers were white men. Even now a man obviously more white than Indian will say he is a full blood because both of his grandmothers had Indian blood, even if only a fraction.

very early. Practically all the tribes had stories of much earlier white men come among them, often men with eyes like the fallen sky, even bluer than those of the Mandans of the upper Missouri, adding to the legends of Madoc's Welsh sailors landing on North America in about 1170. It was claimed that Madoc's men, drawn or driven inland, left Welsh words from Ohio to the Yellowstone valley.

In more recent times stories grew up of traces left by the Vikings as far west as Minnesota and the Lake Winnipeg region. Some of the Teton Sioux had stories of three yellow-haired men who came with the northern Indians to the ancient trading fair at what later became Horse Creek, emptying into the North Platte near the Nebraska line. This was long before any winter count, the Indians said, back when they lived near the great sweet-water seas.

That old trading ground had long attracted the far-traveling young men of good family—a place of general truce where all the tribes could meet in peace for one fine summer moon, hear the news, see what was being made and discovered. Adventurers and traders and visitors came from the Pacific slopes, from Mexico, and from the country of the snowy wolf. They came for barter and for the ceremonials, for entertainment and the competitions: races, wrestling, dances and the great show-off feasts. Here southerners brought their elaborate featherwork, raw copper, piñon nuts, medicinal plants, armadillo shells, turquoise and other handsome stone to be traded for the fine quillwork of the Chippewas and the Sioux, the red pipestone, the ermine, white wolf and fox, and for tools and ornaments made of elk, moose and caribou horn, for the strong northern bows and the deep-furred robes. There was always some special arrow material too, such as obsidian and the rose quartz, to be chipped into the delicate little points for birds and small animals. After the Kiowas passed through on their migration southward, they returned in large numbers each summer, their pack dogs loaded down with goods —the real peddlers of the prairies.

Back when the Teton Sioux were still around the Minnesota region, three young men of prominent family making their customary youth tour had joined some others for the journey to the summer fair, more than six hundred miles away. They carried strong bows for the hunt and for defense through wide enemy country, with the new French knives at their sides and all the trade goods they and their big pack dogs could manage on a fast trip.

More than three hundred years later the descendants of these three men still told of the dusty-haired, travel-lean youths in moccasins and breechclouts with their rough-haired wolfish dogs hurrying toward the camps strung out along the trading creek, the blue smoke of the cooking fires hanging in the evening air. Suddenly they had stopped, as one of their younger dogs broke into a barking and noise at a great dog-man creature charging toward them so fast it was useless to run. The Indians set their arrows, ready to make a stand, but some distance off the man creature lifted the left hand, palm out, in the sign of friendship.

The first young Sioux to regain his head shouted "Big-dog!" and ran forward to see, the others at his moccasin heels, for this must really be one of the big-dogs they had heard about from the southern vistors, the creature that the French called *le cheval*.

While the gayer, the flightier ones of the party danced, waited at the water path for the maidens, took part in the footraces and betting, the wrestling and target shooting, the rest looked at the long knives, the swords that the southerners had, and the guns. Such things they had seen among the French, with even a couple in their home village. But the young Sioux warriors could hardly pull themselves away from the horses, only a few here, and carefully guarded. They forgot all the instructions of the women at home, given most explicitly, and with unease that their fine handwork must be trusted to such giddy and adventuresome youths.

"Bring the green and blue feathers, the round copper moons that can be made to shine like the red sun, and the far herbs for the ailments," one woman had checked off on her fingers. "Three things."

"Perhaps also one of the feather capes from the deep canyon people, and the stone that is blue as the sky with streaks of the cloud," another added.

But now at the trading all this was forgotten, and when the fair broke up and the Indians moved away, east and west, north and south, in large and small parties, mostly afoot, strung out to become little shimmering specks in the heat dance of the wide plain, a couple of the young Sioux were riding the big-dogs. The others trotted along side in admiration and impatience for their turn, amused at the complaints of the chafing where a good rider must grow callouses.

With mirror flashes they signaled their approach to the village, from far off, and much sooner than the people expected. There was a great outcry and excitement. The foolish young men must have been waylaid, lost all their goods, were fleeing home. Then, when they appeared, there was another alarm, and an excitement running through the village like fire in tall pine. Only the women who sent the goods were angry, cheated that everything they had made and even the guest gifts that the men must surely have received as important young strangers from far off, and an iron-hard shield and a sword that they won at gaming—all gone for the two big-dogs.

It seemed a very poor bargain to these women standing with folded arms against the foolish young men, even when it was pointed out that they had acquired a stallion and a mare, already with foal—the foundation for a great herd such as the southerners told about, and with it an important place in the band, the tribe. Besides, the work of everyone, the women, too, would be greatly eased. The women met this with Sioux skepticism. They would believe these things when they came. In the meantime some of the men stood off to jeer the returning youths, noticing that their thighs, nearly horizontal under the direct rays of the sun on the long ride home, had become very dark, much darker than the rest of the skin.

"Burnt thighs!" one of the wags shouted, and all the others saw that it was true, even the French trader among them. "*Brule*," he said. "*Brûlée cuisse*."

As the fame of the horses spread, their owners became known as the Burnt Thigh men, their people as the Brules, the Brule Sioux. They called the creek of the summer trading fair the River of the

Horses, or Horse Creek. Later it was part of the final hunting grounds of these Brules—hundreds of years later.

The *coureur de bois* was often a self-sufficient man, one able to go out into a strange land, among a strange people, and perhaps never return to his own. A most unusual one was Bourgmont, educated, a writer, and so capable that early in 1706 he was made commandant at Fort Detroit. The post was besieged by the Fox and in 1712 a party of Missouri Indians went to help the French. After the siege was broken Bourgmont went home with these allies from the far wilderness for a visit. He became the idol of the tribe, left his post, married into the Missouris and wrote of them, and their country, their stream, including the statement: "Higher up the river, one finds the Large river, called Nibraskier by the French and the Indians." This was perhaps the first printed use of the word that was to become the name of a vast region, a territory and finally a state.

Rumor, stories carried on the wind, told of rich mines up the Missouri as well as over toward New Mexico, and of a passage to the western sea for those with the initiative to find it, and beyond, to the fabulously rich trade with China and Japan. Because no one knew much about the great western wilderness, it became a fertile cave to breed the wildest winds of rumor. For a hundred and fifty years after Coronado the Spaniards received disquieting accounts of the French penetrating their vague borders, as the French heard of Spaniards far up the foothills of the Rockies nearly to Canada.

After the Pueblo rebellion of 1680, Spain turned her attention toward her natural enemy in America, the French. Some, it was said, had already passed the western mountains on their way to the South Sea, while others were pushing hard toward New Mexico, both overland and up the Red River, aiming for the trade and the mines of the Southwest, and surely for the ultimate ouster of Spain from the region.

In 1699 a Navajo war party, raiding the Pawnees well within Spanish claims, captured French carbines and powder flasks. In 1719 Bienville, governor of Louisiana, sent Du Tisne to expore the Missouri country and to tie the Indians to the French traders and to France. On his way to the Pawnees Du Tisne stopped at the Padouca village and erected a cross with the arms of the king of France. Historians offer several locations for this village, depending upon their identification of the lost tribe. Those who consider them Comanches put it down around Oklahoma, although the well-known Padouca village was above the Pawnee country near the mouth of the Niobrara River, its activities spreading as far up the Missouri as the Arikaras in the Cheyenne and Grand River region. Some consider these Padoucas of the upper Missouri an Apachean people who probably swung off into the sandhills of Nebraska under pressures from the whites and Indians as they pushed westward. As late as 1830 a few Padoucas came to Laboue's post on a little fork of the Snake River of the sandhills, a truce ground where Poncas, Sioux, Cheyennes, Pawnees and even occasional Kiowas traded in peace.

When the Spaniards heard of Du Tisne's penetration they acted. Although the story of De Penalosa's march to the Loup Rivers in 1662 was a tall tale in the best Plains tradition, Villasur was sent on a similar expedition in 1720, one a little more warlike and yet also looking for trade. With perhaps forty or forty-five soldiers, some settlers and traders and about sixty or seventy Indians (some accounts say 300), and a priest he pushed northeastward. The official interpreter was the Frenchman, Archeveque, who had helped kill La Salle, but apparently he assumed that no French among the Indians would know of his part in the murder. Optimistically he took along ten horses and six mules loaded with trade goods.

Villasur reached a junction of the Platte River in August, either at the Platte forks or the mouth of the Loup River. The stream was shallow in the dry summer heat, the sand quiet, and the crossing easy. From there the stories vary considerably, mentioning attempts at parleys, perhaps through a Pawnee, a man who spoke Caddoan (the linguistic stock of the Pawnees) or a Spanish-speaking sign talker. According to one account they found a large village with earth fortifications, but the Indians refused Villasur's request for a conference. The Pawnee interpreter, sent out to locate the village center, perhaps, or at least make overtures for a talk, came fleeing back, shouting that the angry Indians had lifted their war axes against him. Next morning Villasur moved out, halted opposite the village and sent an interpreter back across the river with presents of knives and tobacco for the chiefs. The man did not return but another one, whom the Spaniards could not understand, came. Villasur, determined to snoop out any Frenchmen around, prepared to move across to the village but the Indians still refused a conference, perhaps not understanding or perhaps because they or the Frenchmen among them recognized the Spaniards as enemies.

The next dawn, before he could advance, Villasur's camp was swept by a hot fire of lead and arrows that stampeded the horses through the bivouac. The commander fell, the priest too, and the murderer of La Salle. Most of the Indian allies escaped, ran, it seems, as from a battle that was not theirs. When the dust and the stink of powder smoke cleared away the ground was littered with dead. Only thirteen Spaniards got back to Santa Fe.

The version of the fight preferred by those who consider the Pawnee wily, the Indian generally treacherous, has Villasur welcomed with a big dance and feasting. According to this story the soldiers were quietly surrounded and then struck down at a signaling yell and pistol shot. Four reached their horses and two of these were killed while trying to whoop the mule herd away. Only two of the sixty or more proud Spaniards dragged back to the plaza at Santa Fe.

By any account Villasur's expedition ended in the largest single killing of white men between the regions of Bloody Kansas and upper Wyoming. More Indians would die in a tribal battle, and from soldier guns, but this was the only real manuring with white-man blood that this soil ever received.

Probably, as the survivors claimed, there were Frenchmen in the village; perhaps it was Spanish pride refusing to accept defeat from the uncouth savages of the Plains, as many other white men would refuse later. Certainly the arms were largely French, and it is inconceivable that as late as 1720 there could be a large Indian village on the Plains or perhaps anywhere in beaver country without a trader or two at home among them even if not present at the fight. The delighted Pawnees got fancier arms from Villasur than any they had ever seen—guns, pistols and swords elaborately chased and silver-mounted. They chopped some of the men out of their iron shirts, as the Indians called the armor, got a pack train of goods, and some excellent Spanish horses, without the trouble of raiding or trade. Their herds were famous all the next hundred and fifty years from this fine blood.

After this the Nebraska region was apparently overrun by expeditions, its fame varying but widespread. Bourgmont, in Paris with a group of western Indians that included a chief of the Missouris, his young daughter, and an Oto from up the river, helped spread the romance abroad. Trade grew too. By 1732 *voyageurs* were so common on the Missouri River that the eleven Frenchmen killed there by Indians discouraged no one. Next year a Frenchman who had lived some years with the Pawnees near the Platte went up to their relatives, the Arikaras, and returned with the news that he had found silver mines—a nice piece of passing fiction that did not depend upon the struggle for power in the New World for its interest.

Among the explorers to the trans-Missouri region were the Mallet brothers, who spent the winter of 1739 not far from the mouth of the Niobrara and then went across to the Pawnee village on the Loup and along the South Platte toward Santa Fe. As was to be expected, they were captured by the Spaniards, who, like the gentlemen they were, merely detained these brother gentlemen until spring, then permitted them to return. One remained; he had married there.

By this time practically every canyon and pocket of the upper Missouri country had been penetrated by fur hunters. Some of this was augmented by the search for the passage to the western sea. Adventurous man, still driven by that curious urge that kept sending him westward with the sun across vast continents, went for political expansion this time, for the great profits. Every trapper or trader back from the West was questioned, and possible routes were platted in the mind, in the dust with weed stalks, on paper. As usual missionaries followed on the silent heels of the trapper, sometimes with a secular eye on profits and politics, in addition to the divine's hunger for souls. They also queried the Indians, who, as in Coronado's time, wished to please and, hoping for presents and advantage, built up fantastic pictures of the West. Compared to these the trapper answers were often discouraging and so dismissed as from men perhaps jealous of the isolation of their domain, from men whose eyes were always down, looking for beaver sign.

One Frenchman with an overwhelming ambition to discover the western sea was La Verendrye. To finance himself, he acquired a monopoly of the fur trade north of the Sioux region and, with a son and a young priest interested in the Mandans, he pushed out in 1738. From accounts gathered up the Missouri, La Verendrye decided the south sea could be found. In 1742 his two sons headed southwestward from the Mandan village and located Indians who spoke Spanish. At what they called the granite mountains they turned back, swinging around past the Arikara village, where the brothers found another man who spoke Spanish—much too deep in French trade territory.

It was inevitable that the rich fur trade should build a commercial center for itself, a city that was to be the most important of the West for many generations. From this base all the region to the Pacific coast was to be taken over within seventy years; the entire destiny of a nation not yet born in 1763 would be influenced. This city, to stand for a time as the philosophical center of the world, was St. Louis, built on the Mississippi between the river's two great outstretched arms, the Ohio eastward and the Missouri northwest for thousands of miles.

Pierre Laclede, the founder, came up from New Orleans in 1763 with a broad charter for his new company to select the site of a post. When he heard of the Treaty of Paris, which gave the east bank of the Mississippi to the British, he settled on the west side, apparently unaware that France was out of North America and he was on Spanish soil. He sent out a warm welcome to Frenchmen everywhere, particularly to those now under the scorned Britisher, and named his village St. Louis for the king of France.

It was seven years before the Spanish officials came to visit and even then their influence was magnanimous and far away. The town grew and prospered, particularly under the added roweling of competition and conflict with the British traders of the Missouri country. Auguste Chouteau, who had come up at thirteen with Laclede, began to spread a name and a dynasty like a great tree whose roots followed the waterways across the arid plains. For eighty years the Chouteaus fanned out west and north over the stony mountains and deep into the Southwest too, becoming for a time the actual rulers of the vast domain. Two hundred years after Auguste arrived at St. Louis, the Chouteau name was still common on western maps and had been carried into the ballet by an exotic-throated part-Indian ballerina, Yvonne.

Such men as Auguste Chouteau were not to be hampered greatly by political changes an ocean away or, later, in the United States Senate. Although France had been expelled, the French hunter and trader was to hold a powerful position in the fur business under first Spanish and then American rule, and both with and against the powerful British-backed outfits. The Hudson's Bay Company was the old-timer, charted in 1670, eighty years before Auguste was born. In many ways it was the sovereign government of the wilderness, empowered to wage war against pagan peoples, and without boundaries, even national, that must be recognized. To avoid extermination of the fur-bearers, the Company favored pelts from the Indians over those from its own professionals, who practically cleaned a region of beaver, young and old, and then moved on. To the Indian trapping was incidental to his hunts and his tribal life. He harvested the mature male and when in best fur, avoiding, when possible, the half grown and the female heavy with young or in milk.

But the lack of established boundaries encouraged the old French traders of the upper lakes to organize into a loose combine, largely

dominated by a few Scottish merchants from Montreal. Trade revived after the violence of the French and Indian War ended, but
individual competition and the smallpox scourge of 1782 cut down
the profits. In 1783-84 the loose elements formed the North West
Company, one of whose members, Mackenzie, pushed his explorations to the fabled south sea, the Pacific. Next the company extended
its operations to the upper Missouri and the mountains, forcing the
lethargic Hudson's Bay outfit to active rivalry. Fur posts were dupli-
cated to stare at each other across the wilderness rivers. Some were
burned, the property confiscated, trappers and traders killed.

The violent men of this rivalry between the British companies
penetrated clear to the Platte and below, and brought open conflict
with the St. Louis traders all the way up to the Yellowstone. The
Spaniards were alarmed by the English threat approaching their rich
Southwest and the Pacific coast, fearing an easy conquest of all of
Louisiana too. The governor was particularly concerned over the
loss of revenue from the fur trade. The merchants of St. Louis protested that the British were corrupting the Indians with an abundance
of merchandise, and at prices the Spanish regulations and taxes pro-
hibited. Reluctantly Spain granted some relief to the trade, including
price control; preference for white employees over Negro, breed or
Indian; exclusive trade rights to all the country above the Poncas, at
the Niobrara River; and the exclusion of foreigners, meaning the
British.

Now all the St. Louis traders had to do was expel these Britishers.

The Company of Explorers of the Upper Missouri, always called
the Missouri Company, was organized, and a prize of two thousand,
later three thousand dollars was offered the first Spanish subject to
reach the South Sea by way of the Missouri. In 1794 an adventuresome schoolmaster named Truteau with a pirogue and eight men
headed up the river to build a fort at the Mandan village, estabish
an agency, fix prices, regulate trade, wean the Indians away from
the British and find the Pacific. It would have been a sort of all-
time tall tale if the schoolmaster had succeeded. In August Truteau
was overtaken below the Platte by D'Église, who was making his

third trip up the river. This time he was equipped for fast travel with his trade goods, and although Truteau, becoming a little dubious about his venture, pleaded that they join forces, D'Église hurried on. The Arikaras, anxious to keep his powder and guns from their enemies, detained him until the river froze over—which meant all winter.

The slower and inexperienced Truteau, with his small force, had even more trouble. In addition to the intertribal strife and the unwillingness to let arms reach an enemy, a general covetousness was growing up among the chiefs, and a fondness for bribes, such as the British paid them to harass and delay the St. Louis traders. Truteau was finally stopped by the Teton Sioux, who helped themselves to his goods. Eager to get on to the Arikaras, the Rees, he cached what remained and struck overland through the rough, broken country, by-passing the river Indians, for the Arikara village. He found the Ree village deserted, the Indians driven out by the constant raids. Disgusted, Truteau returned to his cache and on down the handsome October river, seeking a wintering place. He ran into other traders held up too, and angry as starving wolves. Most of them finally holed up with some tribe, made the usual compulsory presents, married into a warm earth house and a secure place to trade. The Indians bargained shrewdly but Truteau managed to get some furs, to be sent to St. Louis as soon as the river broke up. Then he headed back north, and, once more failing to get through to the Mandans, sent a messenger to the Frenchmen living among them. He ordered them to stop all trade in the name of Spain and the Missouri Company, which would supply all the necessaries to the Indians of the upper Missouri in the future. There must have been some lusty bearded laughter up there when the messenger arrived. The North Company had already built a fort near the Mandans and orders from the Spanish regions were no more than loons calling in the night.

Assuming that Truteau was installing his Mandan post, the Missouri Company sent out a strong expedition to reach him early so he would "be able to go overland to the Rocky Chain [Mountains] whither he has orders to go without delay in order to reach, if possible, by next spring, 1796, the shores of the Sea of the West."

That expedition was pillaged by the Poncas and reports that more British traders were entering the upper river were overshadowed, in a way, by the disquieting news that the Mandans and other northern tribes were in communication with Spanish traders from the Southwest. These the men of Spanish St. Louis could not expect to fight openly, only to outwit in secret.

The unlucky Truteau was displaced and by a Scotsman, because no qualified Spaniard could be found. The energetic James Mackay had worked for the North West Company, deserted the British and become a Spanish subject. Characterized as honest, intelligent, diligent, and familiar with the region, he was hired to drive his old colleagues from the Mandan villages and to destroy all their forts in the upper Missouri country. Armed with a pocket full of medals to hand out to the chiefs, and with the cynicism of experience, he started north, taking four pirogues of trade merchandise, one to buy his way past the Sioux, one for the Arikaras, one for the Mandans and the fourth to help him build any necessary forts against the British and to get him across to the Pacific. Because this was recognized as a lengthy undertaking, he was given a six-year passport.

Mackay and his thirty-three men reached the mouth of the Platte by the middle of October. The corn and squash of the Otoes had ripened, the Missouri valley was a marvel of golden autumn, the evening river reflecting the vast harvest moon, the air full of geese and cranes coming in from the north, the clouds of skimming ducks riffling the river as they lit. Just above the Oto village Mackay built a small fort, to be equipped with swivel guns later. He left a few well-armed, well-supplied traders there to toll the Indians away from the British. Then he went on to the main Omaha village, handed out gifts and medals to the headmen and erected a stronger fort. During the long winter days he made friends with the chief, Blackbird, and showed him where cannons would be placed to protect him and his people. In return Blackbird promised to punish the Poncas for their depredations against the St. Louis traders. He sent runners up to the

Sioux, the Arikaras and other tribes, asking them to visit Mackay for talk and gifts, and requesting an unhampered and peaceful passage for him.

The river froze over without word from the Arikaras, only rumors of more intertribal wars. In February Mackay sent his trusted lieutenant, John Evans, on ahead. Evans was a hardy Welshman, in America for information about a tribe of Welsh Indians. Mackay instructed him to look for "an animal with only one horn, on its forehead" in the Rockies, and Chouteau, familiar with the upper country, assured him that the Pacific could lie no great distance from the Missouri's source. So Evans started, eyes open, prepared to take possession of all territory he crossed for Spain and the Missouri Company.

In the meantime Mackay made the first comprehensive map of a part of Nebraska. While with the Omahas, 1796-97, he heard that British traders with twelve horses heavily packed had cut across to the Platte while another party was striking for the headwaters between the Colorado and the Arkansas—a bold venture with Spain and England just declaring war.

Mackay headed northwest from his fort to the mouth of the Niobrara, across the present South Dakota line and west, seeing many white (grizzly) bears. He crossed the Keyapaha River, found a large fossil thighbone, marched to the Niobrara near the present Valentine and down through the sandhill lake region to the head of the Calamus, describing the route on his map as "a great desert of drifting sand without trees, soil, rocks, water or animals of any kind except some little vari-colored turtles of which there are vast numbers." Now, a hundred and sixty-five years later, the little turtles are still there, but the soil is known to be deep, the grasses so luxuriant and long that the section has become one of the great cattle-producing regions of the world, as any good Scotsman should have realized at a glance.

Mackay swung down the Calamus and around east from its mouth, back to his fort with the Omahas. His route was a shrewd one, for it is in this section of the Niobrara country that the old Sioux recalled the first French traders living with their wandering villages in Nebraska, long long before the Scotsman came. Apparently Mackay left no account of the exploration, only the map with its notations—no mention of Indians or Indian sign although his route through the lakes and down the Calamus was surely on or near an Indian trail that was very ancient even in 1796. There is no evidence that he kept an eye out for the Hahitannes, a wandering bald-headed people that Truteau mentioned as occupying all the country beyond the "great river Platte as far as along the banks of the Arkansas River." Perhaps they were gone with the golden cities of Quivera and the one-horned creature of the stony mountains.

The Missouri Company had been reviving an old idea, a string of forts from the Otoes to the tribes above the Mandans "which it plans to continue gradually until it reaches the South Seas," to be maintained by a hundred militiamen. For this the Company requested 10,000 pesos annually, which would enable them to "succeed not only in driving the English from the Missouri but keep them away." The royal treasury would collect over 30,000 pesos a year from customs on the export and import of trade. A welcome addition would be a patrol of the Missouri with one or two galliots, flat-bottomed and armed with six two-pound cannons, some swivel guns and twenty sailors. There would be flags too, a lot of flags to pop in the wind.

But Europe was involved in the Napoleonic Wars, the market for castor pelts, to be made into beaver hats in France, was practically gone, the Indians angry at the falling prices. Only the Americans were untouched by war, and burgeoning with the urge to expansion.

But war came between England and Spain, and out on the Missouri an important man died, the first outstanding character of the region in historic times. Not for a hundred years would there be another native so widely known as Blackbird, chief of the Omahas.

While there was considerable maneuvering in any tribe for power over the traders and their goods, through favor and fear, no other chief ever achieved the tyranny of Blackbird. Whenever a trader

reached the main Omaha village—a wide cluster of rounded earth
houses dominantly overlooking the broad Missouri—Blackbird, who
had been watching from the high hill, drew his blanket about him,
and ordered the goods carried to his dwelling. Ostensibly this was
for protection and as a sort of testimonial to the tribe, common
where there was no regular post or permanent trader. Blackbird,
however, overrode all protest and boldly took everything he wanted
as his bounty, selecting tobacco, powder and lead, knives, hatchets,
kettles, red and blue flannel cloth, beads and hawkbells, paint and
whisky, and now and then a new gun. When these things were safely
put aside, he sent the village crier to call the Indians with their furs.
They came, crowding around the low entrance of the dark room,
loaded down with beaver, otter, mink and ermine, and the painted,
quilled and beaded robes made by the women who pushed in to see
the trader's utensils, the finery, in the flickering firelight. Prices at
Blackbird's lodge were always high, high enough to make a profit at
least five times the value of the goods the chief took, with no
haggling permitted.

By this system Blackbird and the traders grew rich in the days
when fur animals were disappearing along the river. The people
complained, as was their right, for any chief could be thrown from
his high place if enough were displeased. Many were, and several
stories are told of what happened. One says that a trader gave Blackbird a good supply of arsenic, with which the chief became a
prophet, foretelling the death of anyone who opposed him, even to
the exact date. It seems these men died in violent agony, which sug-
gests that the poison was probably not arsenic, common in frontier
trade for wolfing and to improve the shot that was made by dropping
hot lead some distance. Strychnine, also a common wolf poison, is
much more horrible in its effect: convulsions, back-arching of the
spine and withdrawal of the lips, exposing the teeth and gums in a
fierce, wild animal snarl.

Whatever the truth of these stories, Blackbird continued as powerful an ally of the Missouri traders as he had been a ruthless warrior
and war chief, taking horses, furs and scalps from the tribes around.

When some Poncas raided the Omahas, sweeping off a horse herd and capturing several women, Blackbird gathered his warriors "to eat up the Poncas" who, outnumbered, had taken refuge in hastily thrown up breastworks and sent a messenger out with a peace pipe. Blackbird shot the man down and the second one too, but when the Ponca chief sent the pipe back a third time in the hands of his beloved young daughter, dressed in her finest white buckskin, Blackbird accepted the pipe, smoked it for peace and made the girl his favorite wife, with great influence over him for years. Finally in one of his great rages, some say a whisky rage, he struck her dead with a large trade knife. In his grief he covered his head with a buffalo robe and sat beside the body day after day, not eating or drinking, until the tribe was convinced he would die right there. Finally one of his favorite warriors brought his young child, laid it on the ground and put the chief's foot upon its tender neck. The sorrowing man was touched; he rose and took up his duties for his people again.

Such a man cannot die an ordinary death, not with the storytellers. Some accounts say that in his remorse he took a dose of the poison himself, but the most commonly quoted tale is perhaps the one told to Father De Smet when he came through in 1838. The pious little Belgian priest had a zest for a good story, and for any heathen worth the sacrifices and hardships that life in the wilderness demanded of the man of God. According to this good Father's story, Blackbird was finally overcome by the guilt of his sins and starved himself to death.

It seems that Blackbird did die a gaunt and emaciated figure, but it was apparently not from deliberate starvation. He died of a white man's poison contained in no bottle or vial. In 1800 a most powerful enemy attacked the Omahas, one that no courage, no magic of Blackbird's could overcome. Smallpox struck the tribe and two-thirds of them died in the horror of the spotted sickness, in flight and in panic. Helpless, Blackbird had to see this happen before the disease found him. He asked to be buried on the great hill that overlooked the Missouri for thirty miles, up and down—the hill where he had seen both enemy and friend approach, and watched the strings of beaver-filled round bullboats bob on the spring flood toward St. Louis. Here, later in the season, the slower, goods-laden pirogues and longboats worked their way painfully up the river current, bringing the fine, useful things of the white man. Here too he had often stood with his blanket about him, waiting for his beloved Ponca wife to return from the visits to her relatives.

To this hill the Omahas carried Blackbird, moving in a long, slow file, the women keening the passing of a great man. They buried him on his standing horse, piled sod and soil up around them in a great mound, and set a pole in the top with the chief's pipe and fringed tobacco pouch, his scalp-trimmed shield fastened to the tip, the eagle feathers fluttering in the wind.

With him an era died, and soon a flag was to fly from the pole of his grave, not the Spanish, or the French or the British, but the banner of the arrogant young revolutionaries from the East.

II A New Flag

It is curious how well the Plains resisted the iron step of the Spaniard
clanking over the vast reaches. He claimed the region for over three
hundred years, more than two hundred and fifty years from the day
Coronado climbed up the sun-scorched prairies seeking his Quivera.
A few Spanish bits, stirrups, buttons, knives and a sword or two were
found, mostly from the Pawnee defeat of Villasur, and the coat of
mail that the Cheyennes still had in the 1850's. True, there were the
fantastic tales of the golden cities and fabulous creatures, but these
and the fact of good Spanish blood spilled on the sod of the Platte
country were soon lost, for fabulous tales are like the wind, and the
memory of the grass is short.

Even during the years that the Spaniards tried to make furs a
substitute for the gold they never found, their traders were mostly
French. In the entire license period there was only one Spaniard,
Manuel de Lisa, and one mestizo. All the rest were French and the

real riches of the Missouri country had been drained northward to Canada, whatever the flag over it, through the long-established French traders and hunters, including their breed descendants, all a part of the tribal life by birth or marriage. Often the white blood of the father or grandfather was forgotten except as it showed itself in the bearding of the male descendants, and if this was slight it was plucked out. Eventually there might be a blueness of the eye, as among the Mandans, which was perhaps from the blue-eyed Vikings or, less probably, from the shipwrecked Welsh.

In all his years on the Plains the white man, whatever his origins, had made no settlements, yet his powder and iron and his horse had revolutionized the life of the Stone Age natives, mounted them for long travel and migrations, for war and, most important, for the hunt. He had extended the accuracy and reach of their killing arms, first with iron tips for the arrows and lances and gradually with guns for the chase, bringing an unimaginable flexibility to the tribal economy. The precarious food supply, the desperate struggles for hunting grounds good enough for stone weapons, and, among the agrarian tribes, good corn lands and their constant vigilance and defense against predators had demanded a very tight, a communal society.

"The warrior and the hunter belonged to everybody, and so long as anyone had meat, all could eat," was the way the old Indians tried to explain it to those who knew no such interdependence, such common responsibility.

But with the white man's coming the Indian extended his hunting and trapping far beyond actual subsistence, the surplus going into trade for the new goods. Almost from the first these were the private property of the Indian, who had owned almost nothing except his most personal items: his clothing and regalia, his bow and the arrows with his mark upon the shaft. Now he could claim his share in the family horse herd built up by trade, by capture in raids or from wild stock and by breeding. He owned everything he bought with these horses and with his furs and the robes tanned by his women. This included his traps, his gun, and all the wolf poison he wished to put out, perhaps enough to destroy many, many animals never found, and thousands of birds that fed on the poisoned carcasses—magpies, crows, ravens, buzzards and even eagles. He could own whisky, enough to destroy himself, which might be very little.

The Indians of the Plains had no intoxicating brews of any kind and lacked the tolerance that perhaps twenty-five or thirty thousand years of imbibing ancestors had given the white man. A tin cup of frontier whisky, even with a finger's width of hard buffalo tallow in the bottom, could drive an Indian crazy although it would not stir much warmth in a white man, at least not the trade whisky made up-river—one gallon of raw alcohol to ten of water.

To the white man the Missouri country was a region to be drained of its surely eternal wealth of peltry, and a pathway to the even greater riches in the spices, silks and other luxuries of the China trade. Few saw the river as a great and noble stream rolling across much of a continent, from the ancient glacial snows to its destination in the mother sea. They were not amused by the stream's willfulness—like some tyrannical old *grande dame* of the provinces having her way. They saw no magnificence in the spring ice going out of practically twenty-five hundred miles of river, breaking up with the sound of artillery bursts in a canyon, to pile in great jams at the bends and in the mouths of tributaries all the way down. They scarcely noticed the pale fire of spring burn the tips of the willows and cottonwoods to gold where the fawn and the moose calf would soon stagger after the mother, the yellow buffalo calf buck awkwardly, the swan move on the water among lesser fowl, all in quiet preoccupation with their young. High above the far reaches of the river the hunting eagle circled, a fleck of black against the thunderheads climbing, rose-tinged and burnished, in the lowering sun. Perhaps in the soft dusk the courting flute of a young Indian cried out his yearning because he was a son of man, the only creature whose mating must wait upon other urgencies than its own.

The traders waited impatiently for the gray flood of the Missouri to run free of ice, so they could launch their strings of bullboats like great tubs rounded with beaver hides to ride high over the river's snags and bars and buried islands. The long files of fur boats fastened together loosely with rawhide strips required skillful maneuvering to get them past the great dams piled up by the flood: mammoth torn-out trees, their roots, trunks and branches catching lesser timber, brush, and the bloating buffaloes and smaller creatures that went through the winter's ice or were caught in some swift rise of the flood. Under the deceptive flow of the current might be sawyers, old uprooted trees, head-anchored in mud, the trunks and jagged roots rising and falling with the power of the flood waters over them. Somewhere a high bank or a whole point of land might suddenly shake and tremble from deep undercutting and then thunder into the stream. With a heavy growth of trees it might close off the river bed entirely, sending the rising waters into a new cut, into what would some day be another county, another state. And as the last furs of the winter trade reached the lower river, the flood waters were receding, the snags, bars and mudbanks more treacherous every day.

By this time the stream was full of craft headed upriver in the race to get the first goods to the trade regions, the ascent hopefully timed just after the most overwhelming power of the flood and before the river became meandering shallows of summer between mudbanks and sandbars, new snags and stumps pushing up by the hour.

"Too thick to wade and too thin to walk on," the river men called the Missouri, in one language or another.

Working their way painfully against the current that might be so swift, and yet so devious, the *voyageurs* sometimes put in days cutting out one impassable obstruction after another, particularly for the heavily loaded barges, while the lighter, less profitable pirogues might pass right through the obstruction's narrow outlet that boiled with the whole river's current. But sometimes the passage demanded tremendous bending to the oars, and for all the frantic effort it seemed the slender pirogues barely held their places, clinging to the gray flood like awkward, uncertain dragonflies. At any moment they might be tossed to one side or the other, piled up and crushed on the snags and torn logs, or forced around broadside by the rolling waters and swept over, the goods lost, perhaps the men too.

In places the *engagés* swam to shore with ropes in their teeth, the lines to be thrown over a stump or a root and the boat worked painfully from one tie-on to the next. Gradually towpaths were worn for long stretches. When keelboats came in, they were walked up the river in the smoother stretches, rows of men at each side of the boat thrusting their long poles down deep at the bow, leaning into them and toeing the narrow-slatted walkway firmly at every step toward the stern. The men marched in time, close behind each other, and hurried back to start over—two continuous lines working the boat against the current and over the shallows, their legs like cogs. Often the men on the walkways or on the tow or cordelle lines sang to keep the rhythm, and to ease the long laborious miles up to the Yellowstone. The songs were usually French-Canadian with a smattering of Indian words and English coming in gradually. Some were two-part, called palavers, perhaps with meaningless syllables and words, the whole sung back and forth, one section against the other, to the firm, deep-dug steps. A later, less bawdy version of a palaver went:

> Old Joe have wart on nose,
>   Old Joe, Old Joe
> Old Joe have two wart on nose,
>   Old Joe, Old Joe
> Old Joe he steal my girl,
>   Old Joe, Old Joe.

But sometimes they had to drop the oars or the rope for guns to stand off hostile Indians, plain robbers or some young warriors who had obtained a little whisky and wanted more immediately. As the rivalry with the British grew, and between competing American companies, ambushes became more common. Sometimes entire small parties disappeared.

Looking back, it is possible to wonder why the American Revolution was not followed by a great national bloodletting as the French had to endure only a short time later, and finally the Russians. Perhaps it was the absence of an anger nurtured by a thousand years of despotism, of massacres, dungeons and torture chambers, of ears, scalps and tongues torn away. Besides, America had no great castles with fabulous wealth in gold, satins and jewels blinking invitation to pillagers from the windows in the evening sun; no wealthy cities to sack, no vast armies to take over; no neighboring states to subject; no hope of a fat exchequer and the power it would bring; no vast landed privileges to be fought over. In fact land, territory free for the taking was the only real wealth of the entire American continent, its resources not only crude but undiscovered—a wealth that would demand a different, and a long and patient, ruthlessness of courage and daring, the only foreseeable reward obscure privation and hardship. Yet for a hundred and twenty years territory and its resources would be the American conspirator's goal, legally or illegally.

There had been rumors of plots for power from the first stirrings of independence—plots for straight raw power, implicating Conway, the French-educated Irishman who came to fight against England. He was given a brigadier generalship and within a year was accused of conspiring to put Gates into Washington's place as commander in chief, and who could say what next if he succeeded. The Conway Cabal included the tale-peddling Wilkinson who would be in one conspiracy or another the next thirty-five years, usually territorial, and generally working both sides, taking pay from both.

In 1800 Louisana was returned to France and the whole array of panoplied Spanish names connected with the faint, faraway shadow of government over the Missouri country seemed gone forever except in the eyes of a few conspirators. Some of the old southern families were certain that the crude and violent young men of the unstable American nation were practically kicking in the door with their cowhides. It was true that the guns of the revolutionaries had scarcely cooled when men like Jefferson looked westward again, this time with purpose and power. In 1783 Jefferson had tried to interest

George Rogers Clark in exploring the region from the Mississippi to California, but Clark, out in the Ohio wilderness that still had to be made secure from the British and Indians, had been turning his face southward for some time, preoccupied and involved with the Spanish governor and the governor's beautiful sister. The affair with Teresa, some said, was unfortunately dying in the tangle of Clark's finances. Unable to collect pay for his long military service to Virginia and the nation, he could not set up a Spanish lady properly. Then there were the charges of conspiracy by, and with, Wilkinson, depending upon where the allegiance, the power and the pocketbook of the accuser lay. At least Clark's acceptance of a military commission from France while an American citizen was true, as was the cloud of alcoholism settling over the man who had saved the Northwest Territory—a cloud common to many dashing war heroes not lucky enough to get killed in battle.

There were romantic stories told of Teresa, who, it seemed, finally tired of waiting after her brother died, apparently of poison, and "with bowed head to a convent hied."*

Dr. James O'Fallon, another Irishman come to join the Revolutionaries and soon deep in conspiracy himself, had been more successful, temporarily, in his alliance. He had married a sister of the Clarks. Wilkinson also made good connections early, marrying Ann of the rising Biddles, a sister of Clement and a cousin of Nicholas, who would one day, as head of the Bank of the United States, stand against Andrew Jackson.

These were some of the men with post-revolutionary plans for the opening West.

By 1793 Jefferson was instructing Andrew Michaux, the French botanist who was apparently also a spy, to explore the nation's western boundaries. He was to cross the Missouri above the Spanish settlements and seek out the largest streams leading most directly and by the lowest altitude to the Pacific. The American Philosophical

---

* From "His Spanish Love," a song of a general who lived "Where the deep Ohio flowed," and brought by Scotch-Irish homesteaders from Kentucky to northwestern Nebraska.

Society solicited money for the expedition. Hamilton contributed $12.50, Washington $25, Morris $20, Jefferson $12.50, and by April 1800 they had a total of $128.25—for the vast undertaking, perhaps vaster than most Americans knew.

April 30, 1803, Napoleon, needing money, signed Louisiana over to Jefferson at four cents an acre, about $15,000,000, a preposterous sum, many thought then and for years, particularly after Major Long labeled the vast heart of the Louisiana Purchase the Great American Desert. There were still some in the 1890's who could have agreed—those struck by the drought and ten-cents-a-bushel corn, if any grew, and those who considered the Populists and even William Jennings Bryan mortal menaces.

Congress, not consulted until the purchase was completed, wasn't alone in its surprise and resentment. The more leisurely French and Spanish residents of Louisiana were angered too, those less aware of the danger from their long-time enemy, England. But many welcomed the promise of prosperity under these enterprising Americans, with freedom from monarchal restrictions and regulations in religion, industry and commerce, and hoped that the weak nation could hold her quarreling rabble together. When Jefferson appointed the dubious Wilkinson to the commission receiving Louisiana from France, some called it a brazen announcement of expansionism by every possible means, an open threat to England and perhaps to the Spanish Southwest, even though Wilkinson had taken an oath of allegiance to the king of Spain in 1787 and accepted a Spanish pension. Conspirators must conspire—a warning with pertinence long after Wilkinson was forgotten.

There was other advice that the young nation might have heeded. Shortly after the return of Louisiana to France, Vilemont sent some suggestions to Talleyrand for good French relations with the Indians. The conduct of most of the Spanish governors and intendants toward the savages had been "the height of absurdity." Consequently the Indians avoided the Spanish traders in peace and met them with scalping in war while they bore a deference toward the English and showed a venerable attachment to the French. Why? Because "the French had the custom which the English observe with great care today; that of sending agents, honest and of a certain character, to visit the hordes, learn what was going on and make them affectionate to their protectors; while Spain had . . . only rude and inept men much more suitable to excite among the Indians scorn for their sovereign. . . ."

But now the Americans were coming.

The Louisiana Purchase was, next to the discovery of America, the most important event in the history of the Plains. Jefferson realized that few understood this and that he would have to dramatize the acquisition of this vast territory to the public as well as announce the change in government to the men at the remote fur posts, particularly the British-tied traders and the Indians themselves. His Lewis and Clark expedition dramatized the romance but produced little else of importance except the domination of the entire beaver and Indian country, vast as an empire, by one family and its in-laws for over forty years. They managed this through their control of the upper Louisiana Territory and its Indian affairs and thereby all traffic and trade within the region, even that of the sutler stores of the farthest posts. They controlled everything except the entrenched British traders and they worked hard to get these expelled.

Even the geographic and commercial information Lewis and Clark brought back could have been picked up by anyone at the St. Louis waterfront, by anyone willing to listen to the rough, bush-bearded men in from the upper Missouri, perhaps augmented by traders formerly at Hudson's Bay's Brandon Houses or from the North West Company. In the general murkiness and ignorance about the western regions a lot of tall tales floated up like preposterous mirages, many to be kept alive for one purpose or another.

Early in 1803 Loisel of the Missouri Company had been sent out by the lieutenant governor at St. Louis to explore the upper river for France. Late in May 1804, after St. Louis was transferred to the

Americans, Loisel reported that one might "travel by water in a certain manner, from Hudson Bay to the chain of mountains in Mexico which surrounds Santa Fe with the exception of a small portage overland of one-half league. . . ." He added that the Platte River rose west of Santa Fe and flowed between the mountains bordering the new Kingdom of Mexico. Surely Loisel knew these were gross canards but he was still trying to prove that he was the proper man to wean the Indians from the Americans, "who will imbue them against the Government, and perhaps against the Spanish settlements. . . ."

By this time Jefferson's expedition was headed up the Missouri and for the Pacific. He had selected his private secretary, Meriwether Lewis, the nephew of Fielding Lewis, who was married to a sister of George Washington, as coleader with William Clark. William was the younger brother of George Rogers Clark, who had been in private school with both President Jefferson and his Secretary of State, Madison. Before that the three were playmates at the Virginia estate of the Clarks' grandfather. Their common feeling against the British strengthened the old ties and determined the make-up and purpose of the expedition.

The two explorers and their forty-five men started when the Missouri current seemed tame enough for the long keelboat of twenty-two oars, accompanied by two open pirogues. All three craft carried sails, push poles and towlines. There were two horses aboard for emergencies and to hunt and to scout the country. There was plenty of wind for the sails, but the seaboarders Lewis and Clark soon found that the Missouri was so full of sharp bends, rising mud flats, flood piles and dangerous snags, visible and submerged, that the canvas was practically useless for anything beyond astonishing the Indians hurrying up to watch the winged boats. Even the push poles weren't very practical so early. Much of the trip proved a backbreaking matter of towing, cordelling.

Although most of the fur craft had roared down on the flood waters, the expedition met many traders with cargoes of beaver

from far in the high mountains, the men with their muskrat caps
turned up from their ears in the June heat, their long, winter-shaggy
hair tangled with their dark beards, their greasy clothing torn, fire-
burnt and mud-crusted. Some were maneuvering runs of the round
skin boats fastened together with strips of bull hide. Usually the
boats, looking like strings of dark and vagrant beads from far off,
were led by a fast pirogue that was to keep them out of whirling
eddies and off the shallows and obstructions.

Here and there a swift canoe passed the expedition, the blades
cutting the water, even the muddy droplets from the paddles spark-
ling in the sun. Some might stop, with warnings of robbery by
warring Indians, the tribes plundering anyone who traded with an
enemy if they could. Some traders had been ambushed, perhaps by
rival fur outfits or ordinary river thieves come up from the old
Ohio River holes. But most of the losses were to the competition, to
the encroaching British and their Frenchmen long with the tribes.
Furs were going north on trails worn very deep, and new ones
appeared every season.

Ah, yes, the British. The whole expedition was a warning to them,
feasible now that Washington was dead and the pro-British Feder-
alists defeated. Some of the traders understood these things very
well, but the rivermen were concerned with the dangers these soft-
fingered greenhorns to the Missouri would face, warning them that
the difficulties would increase with the summer's ripening, when the
stream drew back upon herself, exposing bars, sawyers and snags
like torn bones, so that cordelling was often necessary even going
down. Upriver was always bad.

The old Frenchmen with Lewis and Clark shrugged their shoulders, still bowed as under the tow line. Starting north late was bad,
but pulling even a light pirogue against the angry current just broken
free from the winter's ice was beyond the strength of fifty men on
the bullropes in those spillways through the obstructions and in the
narrows up the river.

An old *engagé*, too old for the wild spring journeys, drew a loud breath through his graying tangle of beard. True, but those early floods brought the plews down very fast, the boats racing on the water like dry cottonwood chips.

Lewis and Clark took two months to reach the Nebraska coast from St. Louis. July 15 they tied up near the mouth of the Little Nemaha. They reported what hundreds had noted there before, great quantities of wild fruit: grapes, still small and hard as bird shot; two kinds of plums that would be rosy sweet and flavorsome later, the Indians said; two kinds of wild cherries; gooseberries that must have been purpled and drying by then; and hazel nuts.

July 21 they reached the mouth of the Platte River. Here they suffered a couple of desertions, not uncommon with northbound parties heading into the raw and dangerous country. The Platte's bad reputation held to 1867, when up near the Forks a handful of General Custer's deserting troops ran for the river and were ordered shot down.

Farther on Lewis and Clark collected some Oto and Missouri chiefs to a point overlooking the broad Missouri bottoms and the lazy summer current that shifted from side to side among the sand bars, "like a glistening silver riband blown from a dandy's peruke," the moody Lewis was reported to have said.

The point, which they called Council Bluff, was high and west of the river and therefore seldom reached by mosquitoes against the summer's prevailing western winds, as every Indian knew. Here, August 3, on what Clark in his journals called "Hansom Prarie," they opened the first United States parley with Indians west of the Missouri. They made the meeting as impressive and pleasant as possible under the large sail raised like an awning against the hot sun, and with a little military parading for the Indians.

The hunters had brought in deer, wild turkey and fat geese, probably fat young ones, and with these and catfish from the river, well roasted over the cooking fires, they made a feast. Then they settled down to smoke and council. The two leaders told the Indians of the new government here now, of their President and his wishes, advising and instructing them in the proper conduct. (Scolded them like the whites do their children, some of the old Otoes said years later.) Flags, paint, red cloth and other presents were distributed and then the chiefs rose, one after the other, to make their orations that always opened with the greatness of their country, their warriors and their wise ones. But sickness and troubles had come with the good things the white man brought—sickness and a growing scarcity of game. Now they were pleased to have this Great Father their friends had come to bring here, one upon whom they could depend.

Then the medals for the headmen were given out, medals carefully graded to the recipient's importance. The canister of powder and the bottle of whisky were perhaps more appreciated, and in gratitude the women brought their best gift: ripe watermelons, cool and sweet.

Before they started up the river again, Lewis and Clark began what was to be a regular practice in the Indian country for eighty years. They lifted certain amenable men to the position of government chiefs, the first chiefs ever put over these people by anyone but themselves—men who now had reason to be grateful to the whites for more than the medals they were also awarded, a gratitude and an allegiance turned against their own people.

Lewis and Clark stopped a short time on Blackbird hill and left a flag for the man who had been buried on his standing horse. Farther on they called a council with some Sioux, the first of hundreds with the various divisions of this tribe in the Missouri country during the next eighty-five years. These councils involved much of the upper Plains, including the world's most productive gold mine—the Homestake of the Black Hills—and continued long after the last Indian was pushed to a shrinking reservation. But that summer of 1804 no Sioux anywhere could have imagined selling one bow's length of hunting grounds. They watched Lewis and Clark go north and then went to make their summer buffalo surround. Two years later the explorers returned. By then the Pacific had been reached and one route there, the most difficult, was mapped. The Sioux paid little attention. It was time for the summer hunt again.

Perhaps from the day the Rockies broke the shell of earth, tilting the region later called the Plains, all the area has been drained of soil, leached of water-soluble mineral. Since the coming of the white man the peltries have gone down the rivers. Now began a long period of new drainings by government officials, either for profit or as vantage point. By the time Lewis and Clark returned, Upper Louisiana had a new governor—the James Wilkinson who swore allegiance to the Spanish king less than twenty years before, who had intrigued to split off the western settlements of the United States and bring them under Spanish influence, and who received a substantial pension from Spain right into 1800, although as usual he was working for the other side too. In 1791, in spite of the foreign pension, he had been given a lieutenant colonel's commission in the U.S. army, some said to keep him out of mischief. Others believed it was because Ann Biddle's husband must have a steady and passably respectable livelihood even though small, at least enough so her sons could be taken to Philadelphia to school, away from the Kentucky wilderness against which she complained with un-Quakerish impatience. Now, as governor at St. Louis, Wilkinson could afford his coach and four, and the two servants on the block.

With the governorship and command of areal troops, Wilkinson felt secure enough in his hold on President Jefferson to enter into an agreement with Aaron Burr to conquer the Mexican provinces of Spain, and to send the twenty-seven-year-old Lieutenant Zebulon Pike out to explore the best route there. Pike had married the daughter of John Brown, the U.S. senator also accused in the Spanish conspiracy. As a further gesture, Pike was to take James Biddle Wilkinson, the governor's son and aide, along.

Connections were truly important in the take-over of the Plains.

Pike was to explore the headwaters of the Red and the Arkansas rivers and to treat with the Comanches, make allies of those raiders of the Spanish settlements. Perhaps to put a better public face on the expedition it was announced that Pike would escort fifty Osage and Pawnee Indians home, and arrange a peace talk between the two warring tribes. He camped near Lisa's post for the Osages and then cut across to the Pawnee village on the Republican River, where he found a sun-bleached Spanish flag flying over the chief's earthen doorway and Spanish medals hanging on the bare glistening breasts of the headmen. Pike talked them into exchanging the flag for the brighter, newer American one.

It was a warm, dry year and Lieutenant Pike, unaccustomed to the look of the October prairie, started the characterization of the region as a desert, although he crossed the heart of the ranges that fed the greatest of the buffalo herds, the Republican, estimated at around twelve, fourteen million head. He went on west to name but not to climb Pikes Peak. If a swift mountain blizzard hadn't driven him back he might have gone to the top and stood with his shoulders hard against the winter-white backbone of the continent to look down on the handsome red rock outcroppings that ran in a bright band all along the foothills of the Rockies. Beyond he would have seen the rolling plains that stretched eastward in a browning, dappled sea for almost a thousand miles.

Against the advice of the Pawnees, Pike pushed on into the Southwest. He landed in jail at Santa Fe but was treated well, perhaps because his wife's father, and certainly Wilkinson, had worked so long with Spain. Although he was permitted to see much of the region and its defenses, nothing came of this. The War of 1812 stopped any plans Governor Wilkinson might have had for expansion against, or with, Spanish America. His favorite son, James Biddle, was killed in the war. Pike too was lost to him, dead from a falling rock when the British, retreating, blew up a powder magazine.

By now the riverman, Lisa, was coming to the fore. The only Spaniard of prominence in all the Missouri trade, he was also the first white man known to have settled in the Nebraska region. He had appeared in St. Louis back around 1790, little more than a youth. By 1800 Lisa had displaced Pierre Chouteau in the Osage trade, and held to it for almost twenty years despite the fact that the Chouteau name was, and would continue to be, a power in the fur trade of the West.

In 1807, convinced that the United States planned to penetrate the entire upper Missouri, the swarthy, dark-browed, determined Lisa had set out for the Yellowstone and its tributary, the Big Horn, with a large outfit. He made several temporary camps on his way north, laying plans to glean the beaver pelts from all the streams on his way back. One story puts a Lisa camp at the later settlement of Bellevue, Nebraska, and credits him with the name, from his exclamation at the handsome prospect overlooking the wide river valley.

During the next twelve years Lisa made many journeys of varying length with his boats, taking the hardship and the danger of the frontier by the side of his men, white, breed and Indian. He helped pull the towline when necessary, slept on the ground, was hungry and wet and frozen with them—over an estimated total of 25,000 miles. But as the name of Manuel Lisa grew he made enemies, some among other trade outfits, who accused him of trickery, claiming he brought trouble and bloodshed upon them. He aroused animosity among his own partners in the St. Louis Missouri Fur Company, organized in 1809, and including, it was said, that complicated man of political intrigue, Governor Wilkinson. Even with some of the best known traders, like the Chouteaus, the company was not very successful. Their first great shipment of merchandise upriver, with 172 men and considerable whisky, ran into a regular blizzard of bad luck, desertions and finally a powerful attack by the Blackfeet, with the loss of goods and furs and some of the men. In addition to the hostile Indians and the increasingly arrogant British, Lisa had Astor's American Fur Company, with its newly organized and very determined western department, to fight. In 1811 he got involved in a desperate keelboat race to overtake Hunt and his American Fur party headed for Astoria on the mouth of the Columbia. Lisa had only about twenty men, too few to risk the Sioux country without Hunt's big party. He was late in starting, about one hundred and fifty miles behind, and managed to make it up in a race that was the talk of the river for years.

The next winter Manuel Lisa gained more power in the company's reorganization, but the war of 1812, with the British and their In-

dian allies powerful and ready for war upriver, made operations there
very dangerous. He improved his camp near Council Bluff, about
ten miles above the present Omaha. Soon this Fort Lisa, the first
white settlement in Nebraska, became the most important post on
the entire river, with Lisa the most important man.

British agents were stirring up the northern Indians with reports
of slaughter in the Ohio country and the revenge there—the scalps,
prisoners and rich booty taken. A visiting Shawnee and a Santee
Sioux carried these stories in sign talk all the way from the upper
Missouri past Fort Lisa and the Platte. Obviously the British planned
to inflame the whole frontier, perhaps take even St. Louis, suddenly
very vulnerable. The government needed a representative with influence among the river tribes and needed him immediately. Lisa,
through his Omaha wife, had become very powerful, so powerful
that he was made subagent to all the Indians above the mouth of
the Kansas River. With typical energy he plunged in, organized war
parties against the Indian allies of the British, secured pledges of
friendship from most of the tribes up to the Yellowstone, including
the Mandans and the Crows, and escorted nearly fifty headmen to
St. Louis where they touched the quill to treaties of friendship and
peace with the Americans. In the winters he returned to Fort Lisa,
his trade, and his handsome Omaha wife.

As soon as the war was over Manuel Lisa turned his dark and
calculating eyes full upon business again. He became the first white
farmer in Nebraska and of the upper Missouri. Before long he had
around a hundred employees at his posts, each provided with a small
farm—horses, cattle, hogs and poultry. He furnished potatoes for
planting and spring seeds: turnips, lima beans and the great golden
squash that the Nebraska Indians have been growing ever since.
Some of these, Lisa reported, reached 160 pounds. They were always
a favorite baked in the ashes or dried in strips for midwinter, and
later in the pies that the missionary wives taught the Indian women
to make.

In 1817 Lisa resigned as Indian subagent and concentrated on his
fur posts. Sometimes the Indian wives of traders went to them, and

remained only out of duty to their people, for the power and presents the trader husband brought to the family. Sometimes they
stayed through fear of the trader and sometimes of the Indians too,
who might have become enslaved to the husband's whisky and would
be infuriated if it were cut off. Manuel Lisa was more fortunate.
Apparently he had the undying affection of his Indian wife, Mitain,
and out of this the romancers made a dozen stories. Some tell of her
on a high point overlooking the river, shielding the light from her
eyes with her slim brown hand as she watched for his return from
the day he left.

Lisa, like most of the French fathers of Indian children, wanted
them to have the same opportunities he could give his white family.
When Mitain's daughter was two, he carried the child to St. Louis to
grow up with his family there, receive the education and culture
necessary to the position of her wealthy father. Accounts tell of the
wild grief of the Indian mother when the little Rosalie was taken
from her arms and the boat disappeared around the bend. She gashed
her skin to bleeding, tore her clothing, and threw ashes into her hair
as in mourning for the dead.

That fall the Mrs. Lisa in St. Louis died. One of the varying stories
of her background said she was an Indian captive ransomed by
General Harrison in the Ohio country and that Lisa, moved to pity
by her pathetic condition, had married her. She left one child that
lived and Lisa soon married again, this time a widow from a prominent family, one befitting the spouse of the most important man in
the fur trade that was to make St. Louis rich and powerful, as an
eastern visitor recalled years later. It was a happy marriage, despite
the language difficulties between the Spaniard and his American wife,
who soon became Aunt Manuel to everyone. She was a charming
woman and Lisa refused to be separated from her by his usual trips
north. He sent word ahead to Fort Lisa ordering that presents be
given to his Indian wife and instructions that she must keep away
from the post. For a while Mitain obeyed, but the sight of her husband from far off was too much. She slipped back in the evening
shadows and, with her infant son on her back, squatted against the

wall of the fort, her face hidden in her shawl. The situation was apparently managed with dignity, the first triangle involving a white woman living on Nebraska soil.

Later, while the Lisas were away at St. Louis, the Sioux attacked, catching some of the Omaha women, including Mitain, in their gardens. They started to flee, Mitain with the rest until she remembered her small son sleeping in the shade, and ran back, grabbed him up and got clear to the fort. There she managed to throw the child over the wall just as the Sioux cut her down. She was rescued and lived, but with a lifelong scar across her face.

When Lisa returned he was very disturbed by the attack. He gave Mitain and her son a pack horse loaded with presents to lead home to their village. But the next year, when the boy was old enough to be taken to St. Louis, he sent for Mitain and the son. It seems she didn't come, and Lisa went to get her. Sensing danger, she ran for the river with the boy and rowed him across to the east bank. But in the morning she was back and placed the son in his father's arms. She knew it was best for him, but she begged to be taken along, be permitted to live in some corner or hut, just to be near her children. Lisa refused, promising her many presents, but the woman still wept. What was to become of her? Now that she had been the wife of a white man she could never expect to marry among her own people.

There is a story that Lisa planned to take the boy away on the next boat, but the anger among the Omahas at this deprivation of a mother of both her children, children who, by their custom, belonged to her people, and the gathering sullenness of the Indians against all white men brought interference by the army officers nearby. The trader was compelled to return the son to the mother. Lisa died soon afterward, before he could return to the Nebraska region, but he left proper provision for the education of both his Indian children.

Evidently Mitain lived for many years. Prince Maximilian reported seeing her on the Missouri in 1832-33, although this may have been the other Omaha wife Lisa was rumored to have taken. In nomadic or seminomadic societies like the Omahas, with the high casualties of war and the hunt among the young men, there was always a surplus of women without hunters, so they doubled up. Besides the more important men had many visiting dignitaries and needed extra help with the cooking and the guest presents, such as moccasins, pipe bags and gifts to take home to their women. Without servants or slaves an extra wife or two was handy to have, and a sign of prominence.

The possibilities of the story of Mitain, who was a relative of that other romantic figure, Blackbird, were obvious to both the sentimental visitors to the region and to Lisa's enemies who were happy to stress his unfeeling cruelty. New versions of the Mitain story cropped up for years. In one she threw herself into the roaring spring flood that carried the boat of Lisa and her son away. In another she plunged from a high Missouri bluff with her son in her arms, the bluff becoming one of many Lovers' Leaps scattered along the river and westward to the Rockies. Usually these were named for some legendary maiden whose beloved warrior had fallen on a far battleground, but perhaps no more beloved than the white trader.

Basically the story of Mitain come to huddle outside the Lisa fort with her blanket over her head is true, but it seems no one made up a song to be called "Her Spanish Love."

III Elysian Fields

Even back before Lisa's death the Plains were taking on a complexity beyond anything since the age of the great beasts there—the dinosaurs or the mammoths and their kind whose bones were scattered around in such careless disarray—creatures that were proved ridiculously incongruous by changing space and time. The era of the white man was bringing not only its own complexities but extravagant absurdities as well. November 13, 1818, the *Missouri Gazette* of St. Louis quoted from a letter that was going the rounds, announcing that a U.S. military expedition was fitting out for the Rocky Mountains and the northwest coast:

> A steam boat [*Western Engineer*] is now building at Pittsburg for this expedition, and which it is expected will be able to proceed up the Missouri to its source. It is ascertained that *there is a passage through the Rocky Mountains, and at the distance of about five miles after you pass the mountains, a branch of the Columbia commences running, to the Pacific Ocean!!!* It is intended to take the

steam boat to pieces at the mountains, and rebuild her in this river. The expedition is to traverse the continent by water, and to be absent about two years.—It will pass the winter on this side of the Rocky Mountains!!!!

Apparently these fantastic statements were not to be amended or questioned or publicly dismissed. So far as the public knew, no one in Washington paid any attention to the reports of Lewis and Clark's arduous journey or what hundreds of men had seen for themselves, men who had taken several routes over the continental divide and could tell stories of the harsh experiences of many others, Indian and white, in those granite heights. Not much was said about the Astorians, led by Astor's partner Hunt, the large outfit Lisa had worked so hard to overtake for protection past the Sioux in 1811, or Stuart's more southern route from Astoria toward St. Louis the next year, over far unwatered stretches from the Snake River to the bend of the North Platte and down it, worn and half-starved, dodging Indians for months.

The stories of such men were knowable and should have stopped the talk of a short portage, any possible portage over the northern mountains to the Pacific waters, but apparently there was no one to challenge the absurdities credited to the military, including the grandiose plans published for Colonel Henry Atkinson's so-called Yellowstone Expedition. Then, the spring of 1819, the *Missouri Gazette* told its readers: "The time is fast approaching, when a journey to the Pacific will become as familiar, and indeed more so, than it was fifteen or twenty years ago to Kentucky or Ohio." May 26 the paper offered a detailed description of the scientific vessel, Major Stephen H. Long's *Western Engineer*, that was to accompany the military expedition as far as the Yellowstone and then undertake practically unlimited exploration beyond. Long's party was to gather a thorough knowledge of the country—the history and description of the inhabitants; the soil, minerals, vegetation and curiosities—and to survey the mountain region intersected by the Canadian boundary— all this carried out by qualified scientists and two artist-ornithologists: Samuel Seymour and Titian Peale. The seventy-five-foot scientific boat had only a nineteen-inch draft for the shallows; the paddle wheels were at the stern to avoid catching snags and sawyers. The vessel would display a flag painted by Peale, showing a white man and an Indian holding a pipe of peace and a sword, and shaking hands.

The *Western Engineer* and its cargo of equipment and presents for the Indians were protected by three brass field pieces, the artillerymen under Major John Biddle, a brother of Commodore James Biddle, recently sent to Oregon in the ten-year joint possession agreement with Britain; of Nicholas, director of the Bank of the United States, and of Thomas, who would build Jefferson Barracks near St. Louis and marry the daughter of one of the town's wealthy men. Although Ann Biddle's husband, Wilkinson, was discredited in the public eye, and in Mexico most of the time now, the Biddle family was sinking its roots deep into the financial West, tapping the riches to be drained from the Plains.

Major Long and his party seemed eager to plunge into the unlimited exploration that was to remedy the defects in the plan made for Lewis and Clark fifteen years ago, and to fill the gaps in their journal. This implied, but public, criticism of the two men would not trouble many now. Lewis, former governor of Missouri, had been dead for years, if not by suicide, at least no murderer was ever apprehended. Clark, now the governor and the Superintendent of Indian Affairs for all the Missouri country, controlled everyone who went in and out of the region except the British. He had complete power over all aspects of the Indian trade, including the whisky. This was the ultimate power. To deny a trader the right to take liquor into the Indian country was to destroy him. William Clark was a pleader for humane treatment of the Indian, a responsible man who tried to solve the financial tangles of his brother, George Rogers Clark, and made protégés of his two nephews, the sons of his sister Frances who had divorced their father, Dr. James O'Fallon, another of the conspirators with Wilkinson and Citizen Genêt. Yet Clark was deep in the Indian trade himself. He got one of his nephews, Benjamin O'Fallon, appointed Indian Agent under him, and sent him with Major Long. John, the other nephew, was going too, as sutler with Atkinson's force. Plainly William Clark could ignore a little criticism of that long-ago expedition, and concern himself more now with the problems of British penetration into the fur trade, and the benefits that the Yellowstone Expedition should bring to them all.

The winter and spring of 1819 brought anxiety, angry denunciation and failure, with some controlled amusement among the British, who were outlawed by the act of 1816 that forbade foreign commerce in the Missouri country. Finally Atkinson got his expedition of 1,126 men on the five steamboats built expressly to buck the Missouri current, but the engines blew pistons, the boats sprang leaks and caught on snags and bars. Two of the boats never got into the Missouri at all, and not one made it past the mouth of the Kansas River—the first concern of the Indians turning to whoops and laughter when the great fire monsters pounded and roared, helpless as crippled bugs on the water. June 30 the *Gazette* reported: "Last week Col. Henry Atkinson, on seeing the ferry boats worked by wheels, immediately conceived the idea of applying them to barges, bound up the Missouri with U. States troops, stores &c. In about three days he had one of the barges rigged with wheels and a trial made, in which she was run up the Missouri about two miles and back in 30 minutes."

It was a humiliation, after all the big talk of conquering the mighty Missouri with steam. There would be some delay in establishing that strong post on the Yellowstone that was to drive the British running home. Yet Long might still, the dreamers hoped, get the *Western Engineer* over that five-mile portage to the headwaters of the Columbia, to float majestically down the great stream and out upon the bosom of the Pacific.

Apparently Atkinson still hoped that the keelboats with their wheels turned by the troops would reach their destination, the Yellowstone, in season, although he had made such arrangements as he could if the wheel drives should fail. There was always that final degradation—the towpath of the lowliest rivermen along the bank— and while the American troops might learn the rhythm of the pull,

they could never sing the French-Canadian patois songs that eased
the miles for the *voyageurs*.

The *Western Engineer* started later than the troops and made slow
but steady progress past them, in spite of her deceptively fancy design
and ornamentation that the St. Louis *Enquirer* described:

> The bow of the vessel exhibits the form of a huge serpent, black
> and scaly, rising out of the water from under the boat, his head high
> as the deck, darting forward, his mouth open, vomiting smoke, and
> apparently carrying the boat on his back. From under the boat at
> its stern, issues a stream of foaming water, dashing violently along.
> All the machinery is hid. . . . Neither wind nor human hands are
> seen to help her; and to the eye of ignorance, the illusion is complete
> that a monster of the deep carries her on his back. . . .

As anticipated, the boat's appearance brought alarm to the Indians
along the banks, but the few who had been to the wharves of the
Mississippi recognized the pounding of the paddlewheel, the puff of
engine and the smoke rising along the trees from far off. They
whipped down on their ponies to welcome the new boat and explain this fire-breathing serpent that swam the Missouri to the rest.
Farther on many of the Indians would have fled or fallen down in
terror if the boat hadn't moved in such slow pain, as wavering and
uncertain as a dung beetle going up hill, stopping, backing with
angry roar and complaint, turning, taking another ponderous lunge
at the obstructions, perhaps helped over at the last panting, shaking
moment by the angry shouts and sweat of the polemen. Sometimes
torn by perhaps a great submerged jag of stump, the boat paddled
desperately to reach a shallows before it went down. And regularly
Long tied up to this or that bank for a sturdy ringing of axes to
replenish the great rick of wood carried for the firebox.

Several times parties set out overland afoot to inspect the growth
and the wild life or merely for relief from the painful advance on
the river, but wilderness walking was difficult too, and the Indians
not always friendly to men so plainly strangers to the country.
Finally the boat reached Fort Lisa and was received by a great gath-

ering of Indians and some river whites. The salute from the swivel guns boomed over the valley, followed by a congratulatory welcome from the post. True, they were still practically eight hundred miles from the Yellowstone and infinitely farther from that five-mile portage to the waters flowing to the Pacific. Unfortunately this was September 17, and soon fingers of ice would come reaching down the river margins as the nights chilled, to spread and thicken until it was strong enough to bear great buffalo herds, and certainly not to be bucked by a panting little serpent-headed steamboat.

Long decided to winter half a mile above Fort Lisa. He set his force to their axes for log huts and then headed toward Washington, the current sweeping his pirogue past many spots made familiar by long and arduous days on the way up the river, past Atkinson's keelboats too, and the places where the army steamboats had broken down, one by one.

This was 1819, Lisa's last winter at his post, and the relationship of the scientists and artists with him and the other Missouri Fur Company men was a pleasant one, the winter enlivened by Mrs. Lisa and one of her friends from St. Louis she brought up for company. Atkinson's keelboats dragged in slowly. By November all except one were anchored under Council Bluff where Lewis and Clark had met the Indians in 1804. The lagging keeler was the *Johnson*, named for the inept and grafting contractor of the Yellowstone Expedition, the first extensive public graft to touch the upper Missouri region, and for years the largest. Johnson's wood-burning hen coops, as they were called, met bitter denunciation, particularly where the fantastic stories of a steamboat portage over the Rockies had been swallowed slick as a skinned fox grape going down.

Secretary of War Calhoun's enemies roared that he had no business risking the expedition to the untried propulsion—steam—on the wild Missouri. To his protestations that he had obtained the advice and approval of Colonel Atkinson, the quartermaster general and President Monroe, it was pointed out that Monroe had a personal stake in the West. He had studied law under Jefferson, and, violently anti-Washington and anti-Federalist, he had been happy to help purchase Louisiana for Jefferson. In addition he was a friend of William Clark and his relatives and connections. This gave the anti-Clark faction around St. Louis an opportunity to complain that Monroe ordered larger advances to Johnson than Calhoun had anticipated. And still the steamboats were useless.

Atkinson laid out winter quarters on the Missouri up beyond Council Bluff. He struck the fine fall weather for which the Plains were to become famous, until the sudden white knife of the first blizzard cuts it off. The handsome Missouri valley lay golden under the bluing haze, the rocky line of bluffs that stood back from the river pushing their grayish faces out of the russet and yellow brush that bearded their lower reaches, with stray patches of darkening sumac still standing along the brows. Clouds of migrating ducks, geese, cranes and swans darkened the sweeping curves of the river. In the evenings long strings of Indians, the pack horses meat-laden, trailed in across the tawny western prairie, back from the fall hunts far out on the buffalo plains. If Long mentioned any notion then that the region out under the brilliant sunset was a great American desert, no record was made of it.

In less than a month most of the barracks for Atkinson's Sixth Infantry were ready to be roofed. To keep his communications open when the river froze over, the colonel ordered a road cut from his Camp Missouri overland to the nearest town, down near the Mississippi. In the meantime his camp on the river bottoms was proving uncomfortable, good firewood was scarce, the diet so bad that half the troops were sick and many died that winter—some accounts say almost a hundred, others put the number higher. It was a bad start for a state whose small towns a hundred and forty, fifty years later were to offer the longest male life span in the nation.

Before spring the exaggerated plans, scandals and mammoth expense of the expedition, and the insignificance of its accomplishment, started a congressional investigation. Appropriations were cut and for the time, at least, no swift passage to the Pacific would be found, no Yellowstone fort established against the British, no attempt made even to reach the site. Instead, the little post near Council Bluff, the government's first military establishment west of the river, remained the only one for many years.

By now there was criticism of the Missouri River too, as though that were another failure of the administration in power. Much of this, however, was in a bragging tone. The stream was difficult and some fondly agreed that a boat must have "uncommon power to be propelled up a river every pint of whose water is equal in weight to a quart of Ohio water, and moved with a velocity hardly credible."

"Too thick for soup and too thin to plow," was a repeated comment, in one form or another. Yet plainly it was not a proper marching route of the U.S. army; not quite solid under foot.

Major Long's appropriation was cut too, cut very close, considering his serious purpose and that of his scientists, who lost most of a whole winter. Long had called some of the Indian tribes together in the fall for counciling and investigation, and the scientists had pushed out on short exploratory trips during warm spells. Samuel Seymour, apparently the first white artist to portray the local terrain and people, produced many sketches and paintings, several of them large canvases, the first a picture of Long's council with the Otoes. As art Seymour's work is disappointing, but historically his paintings would be of tremendous value. Unfortunately, except for a few reproductions, they are lost,* although the entire roll of his western canvases was said to be thick as a whisky barrel.

Long's appropriation would scarcely have financed a string of rowboats to the Yellowstone, certainly not the *Western Engineer*. He was permitted to take out about twenty men, including a few of the scientists, the artists Peale and Seymour, and seven soldiers. For this whole outfit he was limited to six horses and mules from government funds, and a mean little stock of goods to trade with the Indians for necessities and to make an occasional shabby little present. The expedition would not try for the upper regions and a crossing of the mountains, but seek out the source of the Platte

---

* Most recent reports, about 1850, seem to place the paintings at the American Philosophical Society, Philadelphia.

River and then swing around through the Arkansas and Red River valleys, not very far off Pike's route.

"It's always easier to bait the Spaniards a little than to confront the perfidious Albion," one of Long's men wrote home. It was also more romantic, with the dream of silver and gold, of handsome haciendas, and señoritas with roses behind their ears, and a good loafing climate. Besides, the West was angry about the treaty of 1819 that gave up all claim to Texas, and now revolution was boiling among the Mexicans, and disunion.

Long visited the Pawnees on the Loup River, fewer than the 6,223 that Pike reported fourteen years earlier, but they seemed vigorous and prospering, with arms and trade goods mostly from the British and Spaniards. They had between six and eight thousand horses grazing the prairie, to be corralled each night against their enemies, particularly the raiding Sioux.

From this affluence they scorned Long's party, their mounting and their equipment. In spite of the stony aloofness, Long managed to pick up two French guides at the village, followed the north side of the Platte to the forks and up the South Platte to the mountains. He had gone through one of the great buffalo pastures, saw the vast horse herds of the Pawnees at their permanent earthen village in the Loup country, where others found the grass belly deep and deeper, and still he wrote *Great American Desert* across all the map of this.

Perhaps it was the aridity of his own mind, the frustrations of his plans, his dream become barren and sere under the burning sun of reality, and the exigencies of an election year that brought investigations and promises of lower taxes.

Out on the Missouri Atkinson's Fighting Sixth Infantry and his Rifles, with no place to go, prepared to improve their stay. They started early hotbeds of radish, lettuce and seed onions against the scurvy of the winter, planted sod corn on the bottoms to utilize the gristmill ordered with the sawmill for spring. Long before this, the Missouri ice had broken up with its customary thunder and rose to grind into great dirty floes and piles, the troops amazed at the broadening anger of the river, submerging all trace of the obstacles of last summer, spreading ten, twelve miles wide in places, the current far too powerful to face with Johnson's smoking hencoops if they had them now. This was the tall-tale Missouri of Mike Fink, the hellroarer of the boatmen, the "Ole Big Muddy" of the song:

> Eatin' land an' droppin' it flat
> Drowin' steamboat an' river cat.

In June a second and swifter rise from the mountain snows swept away most of Atkinson's cantonment, the men hurrying to tote and drag the supplies and goods to higher ground as the buildings crumbled or were lifted on the rolling gray-brown flood. The receding waters left mudflats and stagnant pools to stink, to buzz with mosquitoes. Soon fever and ague took up where the scurvy had barely retreated, and the commander realized that the permanent post must be on higher ground, west of the river, as the Indians recommended, pointing out their own village locations. West, wind-purified, where no mosquitoes came to annoy, up on Clark's "Hansom Prarie."

While agricultural squads tended the plantings and guarded them from hoof, wing and moccasin, the rest swung axes and bent their backs to building a new post up on what was now called Council Bluff or Bluffs overlooking the many miles of river. Logs were dragged up, brick burned for foundation and chimney as rapidly as possible, with the lieutenant in charge of stores complaining that he had $15,000 to $20,000 worth of clothing and goods exposed to every "beating rain that falls." But housing for the sick was given priority and the complaining lieutenant was relieved of his duty with the stores.

Atkinson's force of around 1,100 troops were rather typical peacetime soldiers: some war veterans, many aliens and unemployed, some with criminal records, and many escapees from mother, wife or the sheriff. Many were illiterate and the general physical fitness was low. The discipline was harsh, with few rewards except the regular whisky ration, which was often increased for special exposure or hardship. Even the laundresses received the whisky ration and drank it or turned it into money in the way of laundresses at frontier posts.

But the remoteness, the bounty on the head of the deserter—paid to Indian or white man—and the drastic punishment discouraged running away. A sergeant, two corporals and twenty privates stood ready to chase the fleeing deserters at the sound of the ordnance officer's signaling gun. Deserters were to be brought back alive if practicable, but the pursuers were expected to do their duty. Once seven men were followed clear to Santa Fe, perhaps seeking those señoritas with roses behind their ears. The bounty was thirty dollars a man, paid in hard cash to a white captor; in strouding, scalp knives, hawk bells, vermilion and so on to the Indians.

The real disciplinarian, the real order keeper was that ancient tonic for humors of the disposition and the heart—hard work. Quarrels were to be settled by matched fisticuffs, but the most serious troubles between officers ended in a couple of duels, illegal but staged in full formality, with a Lieutenant Clark dead—perhaps the first such death in what was to become the spreading Nebraska territory.

By October 1820 the troops, cut to around 850 men, were moved into the post on the bluff that rose sheer out of the river, standing as the first permanent symbol of organized law in the upper Missouri country, and guardian of the 1,000 or more men employed in the American fur trade. For those who had no interest in knocked-down steamboats to be dragged over the mountains or in continuing British infiltration of American soil, there was the argument of economy for Camp Missouri. With all the wild meat available and the gardens and fields that the troops could tend, it was cheaper to keep the Sixth and the Rifles out at Council Bluffs, if not on the Yellowstone, than loafing around some eastern barracks, where every mouthful had to come out of taxes, and the unruly men were in trouble every day.

The first crop surpassed even the most optimistic hope of Atkinson, the yield over 10,000 bushels, mostly corn, which was left out until late October because only the original Indian variety was really ripe, hard. But every kind of creature from deer to rabbit and wolf, swarms of ducks and geese, flocks of gobbling turkeys, and sneaking Indians had to be fought off night and day. Then the moon suddenly turned watery pale, forecasting the fall rains, the old Omahas said, enough to turn the fields to mud until the snows came to lay on. Atkinson ordered the troops to drop everything and get the corn in, utilizing teams of every description, storehouses to be thrown up later, as possible. The corn was husked out fast and piled at the edge of the bluff in a long rick, open to all the winds and where it could be covered with the old field tents when it rained. Even so, the rick heated, and a trooper from an Ohio farm wrote home that field corn would surely never ripen west of the Missouri in this latitude. He would have marveled to see corn ears practically as long as his forearm ripen flint-hard as far out as the mountains and deep into Montana, and to hear the region of his post called the Cornhusker State. But perhaps the man was back-weary from scooping the souring corn back and forth to let the air in, and stopping to throw the riper ears aside for spring planting, very early next time, early enough to get the crop well out of milk before frost.

Colonel Atkinson reported his disappointment in the potatoes, only about 4,000 bushels, and only 5,000 of turnips. Grasshoppers had stripped both crops to stubs in August and cut the yield in half. But the colonel, whose origins were kept obscured, was certainly a country squire at heart. He worked to make the post self-sufficient at least in agricultural supplies, putting this ahead of military drill and training. Sometimes by sunrise he was walking the top of the bluffs, seeming very tall in the first rays glinting off the epaulets, perhaps, and the scabbard of his sword. More often the sun found no gold but only the colonel's fatigues that he wore to wade the snow or the deep tangle of summer meadow on the bottoms, the grass rustling and squeaking against his boots much as the frozen snow did under their winter soles. He was building up a dairy and getting together a drove of perhaps a hundred grown hogs, with a sergeant to oversee the farrowing—an ideal way to run a country stead.

The colonel had a beef herd started too, the first in the region, although the walking commissaries of the Spaniards must have included meat animals. The post herd was a sort of prophecy for the Plains and their supremacy in cattle production a hundred and forty, fifty years later, with Omaha, the great beef-packing center, to grow up not more than a good bull's holler down the river. But Atkinson's domestic stock had to be watched day and night against enemies—poultry from skunks, weasels and coyotes, his cattle from the wolves, bears, mountain lions and Indians—and the natural perversity of the cow brute.

Finally the harvest was in, even the corn-shuck mattresses all filled, the post battened down for the winter, and needing it, up on the wind-swept heights at twenty below zero that drove the last Indian from the watching row usually around the parade ground. The whitewashed buildings were a sort of wintry protection for each other, the barracks, magazine, mess halls, hospital and commissary stores all facing inward, joined or connected with gates permitting entrance to the large enclosed rectangle. There were high bastions at diagonal corners overlooking the prairie and the river for many miles, the flag alive in the gray sky. About fifty paces outside the buildings, the fort proper, stood the stockade, and the barns and stables. Between the fort and the bluff that shouldered over the river were the icehouses and more stores, the blacksmith shop, quarters for the laundresses, John O'Fallon's sutler store and the private dwellings of some of the officers. The brick kilns, the bakehouse and dairy had been set off some distance, the band house too, so the practicing would disturb no one, although Indians crept up to lay an ear to the chinks, and on moonlit nights the wolves and coyotes seemed drawn close to howl.

There was the usual reveille at daybreak, with the morning chores and a couple of roll calls before "Molly Put the Kettle On" for the eight o'clock breakfast, then more roll calls and some drilling, but subordinated to the agricultural activities, the day ending on taps and the fifth roll. "The post will serve as a fine check against the encroachment of our neighbors, the gentlemen of the N.W. Company," the little handwritten weekly journal of the troops promised.

The second year farm work became so urgent that drilling was suspended from June practically to December. Camp Missouri was not only one of the largest garrisons of the nation and Colonel Atkinson's command and country stead, it was also a town of many civilians, including the families of most of the officers and some of the privates too, which helped make it attractive to the ranks, although a few of their wives brought contention, fights and trouble. There were crews of hired workmen, such as carpenters, masons, tailors, and shoemakers; several flourishing traders off the military reservation; the Indian Agent Benjamin O'Fallon and his employees; and the constant stream of river fur traders, trappers, *voyageurs*, and eastern or foreign visitors coming up the bluffs. The laundresses were civilians too, those who did no noticeable laundering as well as those who did, and the former perhaps needing the whisky ration even more, for their task was to help keep the desertions down. These extras brought deep red-lipped laughter to the bearded faces of the trappers coming in from years spent upriver, and aroused much curiosity among the Indians, who knew nothing of such women—the first of their kind in the region. But they were not the last, by any means.

Fall, with its big-game hunting was the glory of the Rifles, the nation's one regiment of sharpshooters, trained for rapid fire at fifty to one hundred and twenty yards without rests. Their uniforms set them off smartly anywhere—gray, well-cut, the design so attractive that it was permanently adapted for West Point cadets. The Rifles made a particularly gallant show in the chase of buffalo, elk, and deer, or running antelope and wolves with the dog packs of the officers. Sometimes they caught a ride on a fast upriver craft for a try at the few bighorn sheep left near the mouth of the Niobrara and perhaps brought home a head with the great snail-coiled horns, half the post suddenly burning to start up into the mountains of the Yellowstone country, where, some said, those creatures ran in bunches and bounced on those big horns in their leaps from high crags. So successful were the Rifles and the rest of the troops, with practically all the target ammunition going into the hunts, that the

Omaha chiefs came in formal array to protest the wanton destruction of their herds, their livestock, from quail to buffalo, the meat for their hungry. They were given a hearing, some presents, with a bottle of whisky secreted in a roll of blue flannel, and for a while their complaint was forgotten.

This second winter offered more time for play. Horse racing had to be stopped when the ground froze hard as stone, but hunting, skating, billiards, whist and other cards (with betting by privates forbidden if caught) and debates filled in. The little library was growing, adding more books and magazines bought from a small percentage of the sutler's assessment, and from fines and other sources. One year $500 was spent, including subscriptions to literary periodicals, American and English. But it was the St. Louis papers that were always worn to tatters before the next mail.

Then there was always whisky, the daily ration from the post's stores which varied up to 8,000 gallons, that available from the sutler, the nearby traders and from the laundresses who bootlegged their rations to those disciplined by losing their purchase permits. Extra purchase allowances were issued as reward. The sergeant who taught the post school was allowed to buy an extra two gallons of whisky a month for his trouble.

In the summer the regimental band gave concerts in the evenings, the lowering sun shining on the brasses. In the winter they moved to the mess halls and elsewhere, mainly to the big new Indian council house, often for dances there, to which the ordinary soldiers, the laundresses and laborers, as well as the officers, were invited. Sections of the band furnished music for the amateur shows and theatricals and for the special events. The Christmas celebration included everybody, even the slaves of the southern officers, who sent them down to the big dance at Cabanne's American Fur Company house in wagons in the evening. The post's Christmas ball was the formal event of the year, with the handsome Rifles and the usual gold braid and clatter of swords the background for the satins and brocades of the ladies. There was always a scarcity of young women, particularly for the ranks, who welcomed the handsome breed girls swinging from arm to arm, their wide skirts flying out, some of them teaching the American soldiers the dances their fathers had carried from Cahokia, or New Orleans or even France.

There was always drunkenness at the balls and along the areaways. Once, of the 136 men court-martialed after a delayed payday, 38 were for drunkenness. Punishment for post infringements varied— solitary confinement, wearing a ball and chain, fines, reduction in rank, police duty, loss of the whisky ration and so on. Some rode the wooden horse before the guardhouse, endured an iron collar with projecting points or stood on the public block wearing a placard: "I stand for theft" or "I stand for slander." A deserter was usually drummed out of camp with his buttons cut off, his coat on backward and a straw collar around his neck. Colonel Chambers was suspended from rank for a month because he had the ears of two deserters cut off without convening a court-martial. A private who fired his gun directly into the body of a sergeant was sentenced to be hanged. All men able to bear arms were ordered to witness the execution, carried out on a windy April day in 1821, probably the first legal execution on Nebraska soil by Americans, and certainly the first such triumph witnessed by the gathering Indians.

The new Congress cut the appropriations for the military expedition even more drastically, reducing Atkinson's force to 548, less than half the original, the early plans apparently all forgotten. But the post was named for the builder and formally acknowledged as the best location to control and protect the settlements spreading westward, and worth its cost. Working from this suggestion of permanence, Atkinson increased the installations as much as possible with his material and men. He had regimental, company and private gardens laid out on the bottoms, and ordered books and periodicals on agriculture for the library. General Gaines, inspecting the Sixth, reported enthusiastically that the troops at Atkinson were quite equal to any other corps not less occupied with cultivation of the soil, and added that "habits of useful industry are known to create moral sentiments and strengthen virtue in every grade of mankind. . . ." His phrase "useful industry" was to become a sort of watchword for

Nebraska, portrayed for all time on the Great Seal of the state.

Not everyone was to look upon the accomplishments at Fort Atkinson with the benevolent eye of General Gaines, but for the present the post commander rode the reaches of his little domain with some pride. His patrol kept out every varmint and pest except the grasshoppers that might suddenly darken the sky for thirty, forty miles, and destroy every vegetable, strip the blades and tassels from the corn, perhaps already curling with drouth.

Atkinson took pride in the health of the troops, excellent, so good that the post doctors had time to record the daily wind and weather, and such events as the passage of sandhill cranes, the ice breakup, and the first appearance of wild onions in the spring. A good fall gleaning of those onions could have helped prevent some of the appalling scurvy of the first winter. Simple observation of Indian practices would have saved many lives. In the midst of winter the Omahas chopped into the muskrat houses for the store of tuberous roots, dug for young sproutings in the swampy brakes where piles of decaying cane and rushes warmed the earth; they chewed the sweetish flesh from the glossy, purple-brown hackberries that clung to the rounded, straight-standing trees along the bluffs all winter. That first fall soldiers who later died of scurvy hooted and mocked the Indians for eating every visceral part of the buffalo and deer and perhaps taking a hearty drink of paunch water now and then from a freshly killed ruminant during the winter. Some retched to see the slant-eyed little Indian children munch squares of small intestines barely emptied of the contents, usually with a droplet of gall from the tip of the knife, perhaps sucking these bits as white children would sugar sweets.

In the fall Atkinson, now a brigadier general, was made head of the Western Wing, Western Military Department. Colonel Leavenworth, who replaced him, brought his gay and energetic lady, who went with him happily to any post, whether desert in name or in fact. By now the wonders of the wild Missouri country were discussed all over the literate world, the fantastic scenery and wild life of the American West, actual or like the one-horned creature of the Rockies, still to be discovered, and particularly the Indian, clearly the unspoiled Rousseauan natural man recently so fashionable among the sophisticated. Visitors from far off began to hire passage on the keelboats, helping with the pushpoles or the cordelling when necessary. They always climbed up to Fort Atkinson, its whitewashed walls gleaming in the sun from far off, the flag a tiny blur of color. One of these, Prince Paul of Württemberg, entertained at the post, wrote that the military establishment must be looked upon as a great industrial center. He diagnosed what he called a typhus epidemic there, meaning perhaps the typhoid that often followed the white man into the wilderness. True typhus,* jail fever, seems unlikely at Atkinson, with all the open air and the emphasis on cleanliness. Even the Indian women, who blamed body vermin on the white man who had brought so many diseases, kept pungent prairie wormwood and silver sage scattered all through the bed robes. Once a moon these were spread over anthills, to be cleaned of the white man's lice and nits by the voracious ants. Winters the bedding was hung on the meat racks outside over a thick smudge of burning sageweed and sweetgrass.

By now the Indians up near the mountains that stood with their backs to the waters of the Columbia were growing angrier. They had watched the white man come up the streams like oar bugs or like fall ants marching across the prairie; they saw their fur animals, their game left in bleaching bones. Back in 1822 the thousand men working in the American fur trade were probably matched by as many from the British companies, these taking an estimated million dollars across the line a year. The Indian unrest was growing down the river too, the anger open and plain in the very shadow of Fort Atkinson, with growing intertribal conflict over the shrinking hunt-

---

* Dr. William W. Gerhard of Philadelphia was apparently one of the first to differentiate between typhoid and typhus fevers, and published his observations in *The American Journal of the Medical Sciences* in 1837.

ing grounds, heightened perhaps by British agitation but caused mainly by hungry mouths.

Suddenly Atkinson, the peace fort, seemed to shake like a Missouri sandbar in a rising flood. The Sioux raided the Omahas, killing two of Chief Big Elk's brothers and bringing loud demands for revenge, for help from the troops they were tolerating here among them. An entire Oto war party against the Osages never returned. The Sauks whipped the Sioux in a pitched battle and although they certainly did not kill the ninety or a hundred they claimed, enough died to arouse the proud Sioux dangerously. Then the Iowas lost their chief in a Sioux raid.

So Agent O'Fallon called the headmen of the tribes to Atkinson to a feast and to listen to his peace talk. Some treaties were signed, but the unrest was general, most of it blamed on the traders, who resorted to any tactic to obtain furs, chiefly by whisky, and by placing prominence and power into the hands of compliant men. In this the traders followed the example of the government, both deliberately undermining the influence and authority of leaders set up by the Indians, themselves, chiefs with the good of the people in their hearts. Some, like Big Elk, were being turned into pathetic drunks.

Finally Congress, by enactment, ordered that every trader's outfit into the Indian country must be searched for whisky, all alcoholic stock confiscated and the trader's license revoked. No one was to pass Fort Atkinson without inspection. But there was no way to enforce this, not with the entire Missouri country, Indian administration, trade and inspection all in the hands of one family: William Clark, Superintendent of Indian Affairs and an important partner in the fur company; his nephew, Major Benjamin O'Fallon, Indian Agent, quartered near Atkinson, the inspection largely his responsibility; and John O'Fallon, Indian trader too, and now sutler at the post. All of these, with several other relatives and in-laws, had money in the company that was running the whisky up the Missouri—the whole family a tightly interlaced economic unit, a little like a floating island. This one family was in absolute command of what must have been the largest piece of earth ever in such private control, and without one soldier of its own. No wonder those eager to break into the fur trade complained to Washington that the watchers and the watched were the same men.

There are no figures on the money made from whisky sold at Fort Atkinson, but in 1823 John O'Fallon wrote his mother, William Clark's sister, that he was clearing a thousand dollars a month profit as sutler at the post. That was with only 447 men from the beginning of the year, most of these on a private's poor pay. It seems unlikely that this profit came from the troops or even the officers' wives, who did besiege the sutler at every shipment for pretty dishes, a hank of yarn, a dress pattern in silk or mull, a yard of lace or ribbon. John O'Fallon wrote that he was putting his money into real estate. He already had a good start toward the wealthy philanthropist he was to become. In 1823 he was succeeded by James Kennerly, his former partner and also a member of the family. Kennerly was a cousin of William Clark's first wife and a brother of his second and thereby uncle to the O'Fallons. As a man at Cabanne's trading post was heard to remark when Kennerly brought his family and slaves up the river: "Looks like he'll do all right too."

The summer of 1823 was an important one on the upper river. William H. Ashley, with Andrew Henry of the earlier Missouri Fur outfit, organized the Rocky Mountain Fur Company and changed the entire face and procedure of the trade. Ashley was a tall, lithe, blue-eyed Virginian long in Missouri. He had manufactured gunpowder at a nice profit during the War of 1812, helped develop the Missouri militia, became the commanding general of it and went into politics. Then his wife died and suddenly he needed elbowroom, as many had before him, men who had lost a woman, or could not.

Ashley started up the Missouri with a party of one hundred men, including the tall-tale Mike Fink and several others who would become even less probable than Mike. There was Hugh Glass, who would be left for dead after a grizzly mauling and, regaining consciousness alone beside his open grave, would crawl many, many miles to confound the gravediggers who had left him to die but at least unburied. Young Jim Bridger, apparently one of the grave-diggers, was to become the father, legitimately and by courtesy, of more windy western stories than any other man.

General Atkinson, honored by an agricultural society at St. Louis for his work at the Missouri post, his old country stead, had been promoted away from the river just in time. The last of May the Blackfeet killed six of a Missouri Company party heading down the Yellowstone and took their furs and equipment. They attacked Henry, Ashley's partner, got four of his men and drove him back down to the mouth of the Yellowstone. Then, June 18, word reached Fort Atkinson that the Arikaras, the Rees, had struck Ashley's big outfit, killing thirteen men and wounding ten more, largely with the British-traded London fusils that the Indians handled with long ex-pertness.

Even without Ashley's frantic call for help it was plain that the troops from Fort Atkinson had to move now, show their purpose, if the upper river was to be held at all. Leavenworth's entire force was little over four hundred men against the thousands of Indians and the British traders. The colonel realized he must punish the Rees with speed and ruthlessness if this new arrogance was not to spread through the tribes like a smallpox scourge; all the trade, perhaps the whole Missouri country, be lost. He selected 220 men, all he dared spare from the post, with so many women and children huddled inside the little white walls that were suddenly very weak against the rising anger of the Indians everywhere.

Leavenworth ordered his men into gray jackets, white pantaloons and forage caps, with as many knapsacks as possible, and hoped to lend a military appearance by the swivel guns mounted on the keel-boats. Toward embarkation time, Indians, many painted as for war, with bows or guns across their horses, came riding in from every direction to watch the nation's first military expedition really head out toward the Yellowstone, but with no bright hope for a portage to the Pacific waters this time. It was a hot, oppressive summer day and the colonel's lady came to the landing in a pale dress with a ruffled parasol to appear gently gay for the women around her, all of them realizing the danger of the expedition, perhaps to be ambushed and overwhelmed almost before they got out of sight. There were moments when Mrs. Leavenworth touched her handkerchief to her temples and glanced covertly back at the wall of mounted Indians behind them, the men motionless on their horses but surely seeing how few soldiers were being left here.

Off to the side, standing a little away from the white women, silent, without the need to chatter, were the Indian wives of some of the soldiers, their faces quiet and distant even when an old Omaha woman came to sing a strong-heart song for her soldier son-in-law. No one cried openly, not even the white women, when a towheaded little boy broke for the embarking soldiers, the mother running to catch him by the seat, his father standing erect at the prow, not turning his face.

Then the polemen pushed the boats out into the shallow summer current and Agent O'Fallon, although a sick man, hastened to make a little feast of hardtack and molasses for the warriors, to help them forget how few remained to hold the fort here, how very few not shaking with the ague from work along the bottoms. He was anxious to hold the Pawnees, relatives of the Rees who were to be punished, and aware that many other tribes might accept the pipe of war if it carried the hope of looting all but the British fur posts along the river, and all the trade boats on the way.

Now there was a strangeness among the Indians at the traders, an aloofness, and even the children remained close to the post, the smaller vaguely afraid in the night, many of the older aware what failure of the keelboats might bring, with gun-armed Indians always watching along the bluffs now, the fort itself empty as a blown white egg on a shelf, and as easy to crush.

When even Mrs. Leavenworth could scarcely keep a smiling face, a lean, brown-skinned runner finally came in with news flashed by mirror from the north. Leavenworth's force had indeed been weak, even with Ashley's eighty men and the forty gathered up by

Pilcher, Indian subagent and head of the Missouri Company plundered by the Blackfeet. A large force of Sioux had also joined the colonel, happy to strike their enemies with the white man's cannon to help. Leavenworth bombarded the Ree village and killed the chief. The Sioux raided the cornfields and, wanting only plunder, they slipped away before the dangerous fighting. The traders urged that the Rees be annihilated, cleared out of their way forever, and were furious when the Indians sued for peace and got it, Ashley particularly. The Indians had returned only part of the goods they took from him in the earlier fight, and now he demanded an immediate attack on the fortified village for the rest. But Leavenworth knew he was too weak. Besides he could not risk uniting all the western Indians, enemy and friend, against the whites by destroying the Arikaras, even if he had the power.

By August the colonel was back at Fort Atkinson with nobody satisfied except perhaps the wives, including the Indian women and the small boy who had run for his father at the embarkation. The expedition's failure stirred the anti-British everywhere, particularly at St. Louis, which existed on the fur trade. General Atkinson hurriedly reinforced his old post against any concerted attack by sending six companies of the First Infantry and a hundred recruits to the Sixth. Winter finally weakened the prairie-fed ponies of the Indians, the river closed in on all the traffic, the wood haulers sanded a road over the ice to the timber on the east bank, and the new troops were reassigned.

Long before this, many complained that Leavenworth had run away from an unfinished fight up at the Ree village as surely as the Sioux. In October the *Missouri Republican* published a long denunciatory letter from Joshua Pilcher to Colonel Leavenworth and another to Agent O'Fallon about the Ree affair. The Louisville paper jumped in to ask: "How came an Indian *trader*—the acting partner of the Missouri Fur Company, to be appointed *sub-agent of Indian Affairs?* If Col. Leavenworth was censurable for anything during the expedition it was perhaps for failing to arrest Mr. Pilcher, and to have him tried by a court martial for mutinous conduct."

There was complaint too that Pilcher, paid to guard Indian welfare, had set fire to the Arikara village, but few in any position of power concerned themselves with the ambiguous position of the men in charge of western Indian affairs, even at this tardy day. The Britishers were the troublemakers, the enemy, and war talk ran strong all the way west from the Alleghenies, the farther west the stronger —open talk of an attack on Canada, but this time without the romantic dreams of five years ago when at least one boat of the Yellowstone Expedition was to reach the Pacific, wrest that region from England.

At Fort Atkinson there was a pleasant increase in sociabilities when winter brought some security. The colonel's wife spread her spirit and gaiety through the wilderness post. The new sutler, James Kennerly, and his family were settling too, their ornate music box set up in a makeshift parlor until their two-story house overlooking the river was completed. Mrs. Kennerly was the daughter of the French doctor and botanist, Antoine Saugrain, friend and brother-in-law of Dr. Guillotin, who had suggested reviving machine decapitation during the French Revolution. Dr. Saugrain was an old friend of the Clarks and had furnished some of the instruments for the Lewis and Clark expedition and apparently brought the first good classical library to St. Louis and with it a real appreciation of the arts. Unfortunately his two sons loafed around the Kennerlys at Atkinson, sometimes in the storage shed sleeping off their intemperance—their conduct graciously ignored as any connection of George Rogers Clark knew how to do. But in Clark there had been greatness.

The dashing, dueling Captain George Hancock Kennerly, brother of the sutler got transferred to Atkinson and put money into the store. He was married to the daughter of Lieutenant Governor Menard of Illinois, long important in the fur trade. The Kennerly wives and the other post ladies, led by Mrs. Leavenworth, with their military and commercial connections all closely tied into St. Louis society, treated the winter in the wilderness as a spirited lark. There were early fall drives along the river, with the servants and slaves and an escort of Rifles, to gather the rosy-sweet wild plums and the wild grapes that hung in dark ragged canopies from thickets and great trees. Later these were boiled into marmalades and jellies in the big mess kettles and put down in eight- and ten-gallon crocks and kegs covered with sacking dipped in tallow. The ladies started the help walnutting too, the nuts gathered by the wagonload and scooped into a long rick, to be hulled, dried and cracked for taffy and cakes. Tubs of the meats were pounded with sorghum sugar and pressed into pans for a winter sweetmeat. Later this was cut and stacked in brownish bars, as the soapmakers cut and stacked their much larger slabs made of wood lye and buffalo tallow.

Evenings there was music, reading and an increased interest in the post's weekly handlettered journal that reported the debates, theatricals, and other goings on and sometimes discussed literary subjects. Later someone shipped in a box of type, the blacksmith made a little flat press and copies of the first issue of the printed journal were distributed free, even to the traders coming through. The post library flourished, with Brackenridge's *View of Louisiana*, Gibbon's *Rome*, Scott's poems, and such magazines as *Edinburgh Review*, *New London Review*, *North American Review*, some agricultural publications, ladies' fashion periodicals, and, of course, *Gentleman's Magazine* —establishing a literary standard difficult to match on the Plains for over 150 years.

The winter wasn't all culture and social maneuvering and balls. Several times the late and brittle night hours were shattered by explosions inside the fort or up in the bastions, the effect horrifying, with the possibility of a British-Indian attack always alive in the darkness. But it was the work of practical jokers, both officers and men, and always brought out the towering rage in the colonel.

The time passed pleasantly, even on the coldest winter days, when the glaring white drifts reached in from the far prairies and, sweeping unbroken down over the bluffs, lay deep as the treetops there. Everybody could go sleighing, tobogganing and hunting. There was a magnificent snow fort for the children, the snow balls stacked like cannon ammunition. The frozen Missouri brought skating parties, with great bonfires of driftwood that sometimes burned late into the cold white starlight. There was iceboating above the section where the sawyers worked to fill the icehouses, and hole fishing and many Indian games of snow snake and ice ball. Then before Christmas John Dougherty, interpreter and subagent under both Lisa and O'Fallon, brought his St. Louis bride in overland. The post ladies welcomed the pretty newcomer, sizing her up for the poise she would need in a woman-scarce society, admitting to her that this was no St. Louis and that the sunrise gun might disturb her at first. But as James Kennerly said, it was an excellent location for an ambitious man, the women looking toward her husband as he said it, and perhaps toward their own.

There was hard winter work for the troops, butchering, wood-cutting, the care of stock and personnel, shoveling snow in subzero weather, and some drunkenness and violence too, particularly until the spring work opened. After that the men were out in the fields and gardens, out of mischief, everyone thought, until the burning detail at the lime quarry beat their corporal so he died.

All the next year the frontier was stirring, with frequent murders by the Indians, and some supposedly by Indians but perhaps by fur outfits, eliminating the lone hunters to whom they owed plew money, the men found dead face down along the trap lines. With new companies moving in, there was real war between them. Cabanne, at Astor's American Fur Company post below Atkinson, urged the subagent to restrict other outfits in his territory, unconcerned beyond that. Nationally the British were an increasing threat, and the demand for a real Yellowstone campaign this summer was loud in Washington.

Before any troops moved, Clyman, one of Ashley's men, staggered in to Fort Atkinson, a tattered skeleton. Almost three months ago Indians cut him off from his party out beyond the North Platte. He had made it afoot with nothing but his gun and very little ammunition. Ten days later three more of the party stumbled in, in worse shape, the flag over the white walls of Atkinson the most welcome sight of their lives. But they brought word of a good route to rich new beaver grounds in the Green River country. Late as it was, Ashley hurried up the Platte and the South Fork with fifty loaded pack horses and a wagon, the first where so many thousands would fellow.

To make a show of vigilance against hostile Indians and the British, a new expedition was planned, with more silly stories in the newspapers. It was estimated that $30,000 would put 200 soldiers from Fort Atkinson to the mouth of the Columbia River, including the ten boats to carry them to the headwaters of the Missouri, 200 horses to cross the divide and the material for boats on the Columbia side of the mountains.

The spring of 1825 General Atkinson was ready. He sent a captain with forty mounted men ahead overland to scout and hunt. Eight keelboats with the man-powered paddlewheels were loaded with 432 men instead of the original 200 planned. Like sluggish ducks, the boats swung out into the river, one after another, and turned uncertainly into the face of the rolling gray flood. Young Indians rode wildly back and forth along the bank, showing off, and a couple of small boys, bare to breechclout and moccasin, sprinted up the tow path to show how much faster they were than the boats, disappearing around the far wooded bend ahead of them all.

Three months later the expedition returned, the men adding their cheers to the trumpet's blow as the whitewashed walls of America's outpost came into sight. They hadn't seen the Columbia, but treaties had been made with seventeen tribes, from Atkinson to beyond the mouth of the Yellowstone.

The newspapers gave little space to Atkinson's return. He hadn't really been anywhere and his old post had lost its romance, was deteriorating and shabby, the men in worn uniforms, their pay many months in arrears. The civilians were deteriorating too. In October several women, diseased and troublemakers, were put on a down-river boat, one carried there bodily and screaming. Nothing really was good there any more except the health of the troops, even the desertions of the whole year practically nothing. The next summer a flood washed away much of the lower gardens and left stagnant water, mosquitoes, buffalo gnats and deer flies thick as the musty vapors that crept over the night patrol and sickened the field soldiers. Congressional favor turned from Atkinson to a proposed string of posts farther up the river as the most effective move against the British. Besides, the fur trade was taking a new route. Ashley's men had gathered on the Green River, out beyond the upper Platte, starting the frontier's lustiest institution, the annual trapper rendezvous, far from the Rees and most of the Blackfeet. The route there turned west from the Missouri far below Atkinson, now suddenly the Old Fort. The St. Louis papers reported that Ashley had brought in 125 packs of beaver, valued at fifty to sixty thousand dollars, the most valuable harvest ever brought in by one party. Clearly a new era in fur trading had begun, and a great new highway, along the Platte.

October 1826, Inspector General George Croghan denounced the agricultural practices of Fort Atkinson. He was a nephew of William Clark too, his mother one of the four Clark sisters who had married Washington's officers, and so related to the O'Fallons, Kennerlys and the rest. Inspector Croghan's stinging report started rumors swarming like buffalo gnats in August. What was the Clark family to make out of this condemnation, one way or another, and how?

Many were uneasy about Croghan's frankness in reporting that Atkinson was the weakest fort with the most helpless and untrained garrison he had ever seen. No officer seemed to know his place in an alarm or where to find shells to fit the bore. To argue that there was no danger was to argue the army was not needed. Military spirit was destroyed and officers were turned into base overseers of a troop of awkward plowmen: "Let the soldier be one. Look at Ft. Atkinson and you will see barnyards that would not disgrace a Pennsylvania farmer, herds of cattle that would do credit to a Potomac grazier; yet where is the gain in this, either to the soldier or to the Government. Why all the corn and hay? To feed the cattle. Why the cattle? to eat the corn and hay."

That was the end. Council Bluffs, to become Fort Atkinson, had been started by a Clark in 1804 and was ended by another one of the blood twenty-three years later. June 6, 1827, the troops, their women and children, watched the flag come down for the last time and then boarded the boats that would take them away, leaving a little group standing aloof, mostly young Indian women with children on their backs and perhaps beside them, their smooth brown faces strong, the children lighter-skinned but as still-faced as the mothers. It was said that the quietness had spread to the boats as they were pushed out into the river and turned down stream, a quietness over them all except the drunken private who had tried to drown himself before they left and, arrested, was sobbing softly in his irons.

Almost at once the post on old Council Bluffs took on the look of long desertion. Mice, gophers and cottontails moved in, followed by rattlesnakes and owls. Swallows gathered by the hundreds, dipping and skimming down toward the river that also moved away, to the far side of the valley. But the men of the regiment remained attached to the post with a long nostalgia until the white walls on the bluff with the color fluttering against the windy sky became a sort of mirage of memory. In 1831 Lieutenant Philip St. George Cooke wrote a friend: "I took a trip to Council Bluffs the other day—the 6th's Elysian Fields."

IV   The Golden Floods

The closing of Fort Atkinson on the river bluffs ended a halcyon
period on the Missouri and all the Plains, a sort of high point, with
a long, long wait for another such time and place of orderliness,
haphazard, true, and not sufficiently military, but more orderly than
any but an isolated community could ever hope to be, and never for
long. To the Indians around Atkinson it had seemed that somehow
even the proper man's horse always won in the races, that is, until
some Pawnees from down on the Republican brought in a lean-
flanked bay that had lost most of his tailbone somewhere. But he
could run, and by holding him back to a bare winning in the first,
the scrub race, they cleaned out the bettors for one day at least.

Perhaps the Plains would never see such concentrated sociability
again—nothing like Mrs. Leavenworth and her friends when there
were almost no common people to dilute them—ladies with their
carriages, servants and house slaves, their literary evenings, their

music in the wilderness, the little square piano, a harp and a music box. There were the dress parades for some inspecting officer, the farm-horny hands of the privates hanging awkwardly against their worn white pantaloons, everything scrubbed and polished as well as possible on short notice, the ladies adding a diverting little show with their flowered bonnets, their ruffled parasols, and in the evenings their elegant tissues and satins among so much blue-gray.

Some of the stories told the longest were based on the curious and carefree ways of the white women of Atkinson, stories of their pleasant morning trips on the deck of some downriver keelboat to Cabanne's post. They returned in Agent Dougherty's carriages, with Indians watching to see the excitement at the washouts in the worn road, or from a sudden flash of deer or smell of bobcat that scared the spirited horses, the ladies courageous in the danger; and if a topheavy vehicle overturned, quickly rearranged their skirts, perhaps passing the little bottle of smelling salts as they repaired the damages to hat or veil or to less conspicuous garments while the escort righted the carriage. When sickness came or a boat foundered on a submerged obstacle and lives were threatened, or when there was the danger that the Pawnees around them might join the Rees in a general attack on the river whites, the women did not cry to go down to St. Louis. While such courage was not to be uncommon in the region later, the elegance of these women was, and remained unequaled for many years and never among so small a company.

Nor would a comparable region ever see the concentrated nepotism of those years again, with practically every public position in the region in the hands of a relative, the whole area up from St. Louis cross-twined by blood and marriage, like the floating hyacinth of the bayous, lovely in flowering blue on top, underneath tough and impenetrable.

The extraordinary success of the military agriculture was remembered, too, as a sort of tall tale, sometimes considered a whisky-fostered story, particularly as the country from the Missouri to the mountains slid under the shadow of the alcohol that darkened so much of the beaver country. Not only the Indian but the trader, too, was caught by the seductive tin cup of golden brown firewater.

Almost imperceptibly the old region around Atkinson had been dominated by Astor's American Fur Company. It started very gradually, back in the days when Crooks' and McLellan's little post near the present Omaha joined Hunt, back in 1811. Later it centered around Cabanne's post. The company encouraged a certain standard, a certain tone, in their post keepers. At his private quarters, John Cabanne's life was as gracious as the cultured Frenchman could manage in a raw wilderness. He had an excellently trained Negro chef, and kept a well-stocked *garde-manger*, containing choice young buffalo hump and tongue, venison and bear all well-iced in warm weather, with fresh small game: goose, turkey, swan, duck, grouse, plover, quail, rock rabbit, trout, and sweet water clam and the *écrevisse*, the crayfish from the river bank for the delicate flavor in the bouillabaisse seasoned with prairie garlic. While there was the raw liquor of the company for the trade, for his frequent guests, whether from Fort Atkinson while it lasted, but mostly up from St. Louis and beyond, he kept a secret little cellar of wines and liquors fitting the palate of the man whose father, according to family stories, was Count Jean Cabanne. John had come to St. Louis as a youth to see the world, and had fallen in love with Julie, daughter of the urbane Swiss, Charles Gratiot, and his wife, a Chouteau, the two finest lines that the city afforded.

Cabanne's chief clerk was Peter Sarpy, a cousin of the Chouteaus, who came up to the post when he was eighteen. Although short and compact, Sarpy was volatile too, alert and intelligent, with good manners and school polish when it seemed advantageous. He fitted very well into the life, was able to drive the necessary bargains with proper ruthlessness and to work his helpers hard and long, so in 1824, at nineteen, he was made manager of the post under Cabanne, who moved farther up the river.

As Fort Atkinson declined the center of the region had shifted to Lisa's *la belle vue*, with traders on that site, on and off, so far back as the oldest Indian could recall even when Lisa came. In 1831 the government bought the old Missouri Fur Company buildings there for the expanding Indian agency, leaving Sarpy, Astor's man, at Bellevue in control of the gateway to the upper Missouri and the Yellowstone trade, as well as most of the Platte country and beyond. There were small traders along practically all the streams now, even out in the sandhills not far from where Mackay crossed thirty-five years before—a century in movement. Laboue's place on the Snake River in 1830 was an Astor post; the furs were pack-horsed overland or rafted down to the swift, deep-canyoned Running Water, as the Indians called the Niobrara.

By now Sarpy, already related to that first tight little group of relatives that built up the St. Louis and Missouri fur trade, had married a Gratiot daughter. But he had his Indian connections too, as did Cabanne, the Chouteaus and most of the rest. This tie held Peter Sarpy to the day of his death. Nicomi, Voice of the Waters, was a very beautiful Omaha-Iowa Indian girl, with fine large eyes, a warm, swift intelligence and a deep loyalty to her people and her river. At seventeen she had married Dr. John Gale, physician and surgeon with the Sixth Infantry at Atkinson. When the troops were ordered away she was among the women who stood back from the landing with her two children, the small one on her back, and watched her man go.

Later Dr. Gale returned to take Mary, the elder, away to be educated, but he found Nicomi in the tatters and ashes of mourning for the baby. Unable in his heart to give her more grief, the grief he had seen in the wife of Lisa because her child was taken from her, he left. But the doctor became very ill, and, knowing he would die, he made one more desperate and harrowing trip upriver for the little girl, to place her with relatives for the education and advantages his daughter should have. Knowing that the mother would not consent, he bribed an Indian to bring the child to the landing just as the boat was ready to leave. The Indian, sympathetic and full of pity for Nicomi, told her the plan. She fled to the woods with the small girl and remained hidden until the boat was gone. Dr. Gale barely reached St. Louis before he died.

Apparently the doctor had once saved Peter Sarpy's life, and on that last meeting he asked a great favor of the trader: to look after Nicomi's comfort and see that she and the child were cared for; that as a white man's castoff she would not be in need. Young Sarpy had promised, and after the proper four years of mourning for her husband, Nicomi married him. Peter Sarpy had his enemies as his power grew, but not even the most bitter could have charged him with neglecting the Indian wife or his stepdaughter. He saw that Mary got the education her father wished, and married her to Joseph LaFlesche, a Sarpy partner. Their seven children would have made Dr. Gale proud, particularly Yosette, Bright Eyes, who became the wife of Thomas Henry Tibbles, Populist candidate for vice-president in 1904, and Susan—Dr. Susan Picotte, who was a long-time practicing physician in the region that had become Nebraska.

Once Peter Sarpy had managed to toll Nicomi from her people and her river to live in St. Louis, near the young Mary, promising the woman she could return to visit her tribe at least once a year. But Nicomi was so homesick, huddled silent under her handsome shawl, that he took her back up the river. In later years, it seems, she lived in a comfortable house near Sarpy's post, pointed out as his Indian wife of whom he was very fond and proud, and who had saved him several times from angry Indians. In the meantime his white wife, apparently a second one, lived across the river at St. Mary, Iowa, about four miles from the post.

But Peter Sarpy's life was not limited to the narrow confines of his fur post and his families. He received the appellation of "colonel" in the customary frontier manner—from some strictly nonmilitary and perhaps illegal action. He embroiled Cabanne and the American Fur Company and John Jacob Astor in a nationwide high-court uproar.

When Sarpy took over the post at Bellevue, Astor had already become the first of the great western robber barons, his company hated by both its competitors and its employees. Small traders stood no chance whatever against it, and many an employee who finished his term of labor or trapping and started for St. Louis with a letter of credit never reached there and was reported killed by Indians. Astor and his willing underlings brought into the West the techniques that would work so well for mine, railroad, packing, finance, oil and other magnates in the future: crush all opposition; failing that, buy it out, even admit the opposition to an interest in the company if there was no better way; or in final desperation, divide the field until the opportune moment for the crushing. Because the Indian trade required a license, controlled by the Clark family, revocation was a constant threat although often amenable to favors, but always there, even with the increasing power of the American Fur Company in Washington.

The first real opposition to Astor, the Columbia Fur Company, soon sold out, but it was followed by the French Fur Company, the eight partners including such old-timers as Papin, the two Cerres, Delaurier, and Picotte, with an investment of $16,000 and the effrontery to do what they could to "debauch all our clerks," as Chouteau wrote to Kenneth McKenzie. McKenzie was called the King of the Missouri from his long service with the North West Company before he helped form the Columbia and made it indestructible except by purchase, which included a powerful position with Astor for himself. The French Fur outfit lasted two years against the combination of McKenzie and Astor. When they sold out, Papin, Picotte and one of the Cerres became Company men and properly so, for they were related to the Chouteaus and others now powerful in Astor's company.

The year 1831 finally opened the era of steam on the upper Missouri, twelve years after the romantic dream of a portage over the northern Rockies. The American Fur Company's side-wheeler, the *Yellowstone*, described as a cracker box with two tall smokestacks set on a platter, made the first serious attempt to conquer the river. The news of the steamer's coming flew on the south wind. Indians gathered to stand on the spring bluffs looking under shading palms for the first twist of smoke rising into the clear air. Runners hurried from village to village with the news, others dropping in beside them for a distance to become part of this new thing. Young children were told of that wondrous and frightening time when another fireboat, the *Western Engineer*, came up years ago, belching smoke and flame from the mouth of the great snake that was the figurehead.

This boat was larger, with more noise and fire and sparks flying, but the regular June rise from the mountain snows was late, the voyage slow and difficult over the baring bones of the river, even with the waters of the Niobrara twisting clear as molten glass through the muddy drag that was the Missouri. Above the Niobrara the Missouri was so low that the *Yellowstone* was trapped in the shallows, her wheels thrashing mud and air.

Pierre Chouteau ordered the engine shut down and went ashore every day to climb the high bluff where the bighorn sheep were sometimes seen. He stood there, a small dark figure against the windy sky, watching for the rise, a gray roll of waters born in the sun-struck snows of the mountains, or even a rain cloud. He sent a fast pirogue up to the company post for lighters to pull the *Yellowstone* past the fanning spread of bars just ahead. The men came, they sweated and swore, but they got the steamboat into floating water again and worked her slowly ahead to the site of the later Fort Pierre. In a few weeks she was back at Bellevue, loaded with furs and with Indian-tanned buffalo robes and ten thousand pounds of smoked buffalo tongue to make up for the shrinking beaver yield.

On the 1832 trip the steamboat started earlier. George Catlin, the painter and columnist, was aboard and took advantage of stops along the shore to sketch some of the Indians. This year the *Yellowstone* made it past the mouth of her name river. But there was bad news too, another threat to the company's business, not from any powerful trader combine but from a nobody, a former upriver employee. Perhaps it was the insolence of this that brought the ruthless and illegal attempt to stop him. Anyway, Narcisse Leclerc was efficient, knew the business and had a good following. With his small savings and a little from others like him, he was so successful in 1831 that it was plain he must be stopped before he reached the upper country in 1832, and that without endangering the Company's license. Apparently the problem was turned over to Cabanne, with rumors that he was empowered to offer Leclerc a cash payment if he would not take his outfit as far as the Sioux country. Perhaps Leclerc viewed such an offer as weakness, perhaps it was too unlikely a concession to come from Cabanne, with his interest in the lower reaches.

Although Washington put a more stringent ban on liquor into the Indian country in the summer of 1832, the inspection the responsibility of the army at Fort Leavenworth, Leclerc was authorized by William Clark, still Superintendent of Indian Affairs, to take 250 gallons of alcohol up the river. Chouteau protested this, but Clark would not revoke the license, claiming, it seems, that he had no official notice of the new enactment. Perhaps he was pleased by the loophole for various reasons, including the fact that much of his fortune and the great wealth accumulated by his nephews, his brother-in-law and further relatives came largely from the liquor in the trade.

When the *Yellowstone* returned from the early 1832 trip, the captain was warned at Leavenworth that no more whisky would be permitted to pass there. Clark did, finally, give Chouteau authority to send 1,400 gallons of liquor out on the next Company trip. But this would probably be next spring, while Leclerc would reach the trade grounds by fall and skim off the winter's richest yield. Chouteau decided not to wait for spring. Two hundred gallons of raw alcohol turned into frontier whisky by diluting* could, with

---

* The recipes varied, actually and in the tall tales. A reported Montana "blend" required:

1 qt. alcohol	1 handful red pepper
1 lb. rank black chewing tobacco	1 quart molasses, black
1 bottle Jamaica ginger	Missouri water as required

The pepper and tobacco were boiled together and, when nearly cool, the other ingredients were added and stirred with a willow stick, the alcohol added last. As the Indians became drunker, more water was added.

An upper Platte River recipe called for:

Leclerc's monopoly, make him a fortune in one season and win over the more influential of the alcoholic river chiefs for years.

The steamboat was headed up the river immediately, the second time that summer, but at Leavenworth all the liquor was confiscated, as the captain had been warned. Leclerc, either by favor or subterfuge, had slipped his smaller store past and was safely on his way, out of reach of military and law. Now only Cabanne's ingenuity could save the trade. He had left St. Louis after Leclerc, but he traveled light and fast to reach Bellevue first.

Opportunely three of Cabanne's men who deserted in one of the Company's skiffs met Leclerc on their way downriver and hired out to him. Cabanne, some distance below Bellevue with annuities for the Indians, ran into the trader and, with his typical southern attitude toward employees, demanded the deserters as his property. Leclerc refused to release the men, and without the force to take them Cabanne had to wait. When the trader's outfit arrived opposite Bellevue, Cabanne and his men seized the deserters, put them into irons and got testimony from them proving what Cabanne already knew: that there was liquor in Leclerc's cargo. With this pretext Cabanne decided to stop the expedition, although law enforcement even up the river was the business of the proper officials, Cabanne's duty only to report the infringement. Instead he sent Peter Sarpy with an armed party and a small cannon ahead to a point commanding the river where the channel swung in close. When the boats came along, Sarpy ordered Leclerc to surrender or be blown out of the

---

1 gal. alcohol	1 handful red Spanish peppers
1 lb. plug tobacco or black twist	10 gal. river water (in flood)
1 lb. black sugar or black molasses	2 rattlesnake heads per barrel

These ingredients were dumped into a keg or barrel, stirred with any old stick and set aside to season in a cool place. Some varied the flavor. Sometimes the old Frenchmen threw in a "brush" of what they called *vermout,* the soft, velvety wormwood of the Plains, which made the whisky a remedy for Rocky Mountain spotted fever, although it was considered better to cook a bunch of the wormwood fresh in an iron kettle until the liquid was very concentrated and practically black. (An old friend of my father's liked a musk gland of the beaver in his private two-gallon jug of whisky. It gave off a musky, almost perfumish odor. M. S.)

water. The angry trader hove to and was escorted back to Bellevue, where all his goods, including the alcohol, were put into the American Fur Company warehouse in spite of the furious threats from Leclerc's men and the winter-cold announcement from the trader himself that he was suing.

It was said later that Cabanne did offer to restore the goods, improbable unless he realized that his arbitrary treatment would make trouble. Leclerc hurried off to St. Louis, sued the Company and instituted criminal proceedings against Cabanne. The matter went to Washington, brought much publicity and a great outcry against the arrogant, law-beating John Jacob Astor, with demands that he and his whole outfit be expelled from the Indian trade. All the ingenuity and resources of the Company were required to avert disaster, to preserve the trade license. W. B. Astor, son of old John, wrote to Chouteau that it seemed to him "in case of defeat I would appeal the case to the Supreme Court of the United States." To Cabanne it looked like financial ruin for him and perhaps worse.

A compromise was finally reached and Leclerc was paid $9,200, charged to the account of the Upper Missouri outfit of the American Fur Company. Apparently it ended Cabanne's power to give any such orders and entrenched "Colonel" Peter Sarpy for his efficient and effective dispatch of orders that should not have been given.

This was the last of the fur competitions that had much effect on the Missouri below the Rees, although a more formidable struggle with Sublette and Campbell started in late 1832, just when the Company was under criticism for the Leclerc incident. William Sublette had been with Ashley in the Arikara fight. Robert Campbell, a young Irishman, had gone out with a later Ashley party, after a prostrating hemorrhage of the lungs. It was cure or die. He was cured, to become one of the outstanding fur traders, president of two banks, hotel owner and finally to die in 1879, at seventy-five.

Plainly Astor's new competitors were men of experience, of highest business and credit standing, and with the friendship and backing of Ashley, who had gone to Congress after he established the Platte route and the trapper rendezvous. Sublette and his partner used the popular Platte trail but established competition posts on the upper Missouri too. McKenzie, Astor's manager up there, ordered his men to buy the fur at any price in money or whisky, to put a real forty-below freeze-out on the upstarts.

At the Mandan post beaver went as high as twelve dollars a hide, a bonanza for trapper and Indian, but it wiped out all the year's profit. McKenzie, trained in the North West Company, was certain this would drive the new men out of business, and he helped all he could by bringing confusion and bad luck upon them whenever possible. Then the St. Louis office, probably for reasons of family and business connections, came to terms with Sublette and Campbell for one year. Angry, McKenzie tried to plan for the future, when the agreement expired. He found that running liquor past the inspection was too uncertain and far too expensive. He went to Washington to get the prohibition eased and, failing, had his supply confiscated the spring of 1833. The Company guest, Prince Maximilian, had trouble getting barely enough alcohol past the officers at Leavenworth to preserve the specimens of natural history he planned to collect. Fortunately Maximilian's aritist, Bodmer, who immortalized the snags of the Missouri, like whitened bones sticking out of the carcass of some ancient serpent, needed no alcohol worth mentioning.

But McKenzie had anticipated the confiscation and took a distillery along to make his own alcohol from Indian corn up the river. He started men planting fields at the mouth of the Iowa River and, some said, loaded up all the grain he could buy around Bellevue. At Fort Union the still was set up, and although the Mandan supply of corn was small, it made a fine sweet liquor, which fed no hungry women and children that winter but brought profits for Astor's company. McKenzie, fond of display, extended himself for the fine rush of important travelers coming up the Missouri these years: Catlin, Maximilian, Audubon and a dozen others, as well as the company officials. He entertained these dignitaries as he had seen it done by the North West Company and couldn't resist showing off his post and his special pride, the distillery.

There were protests, particularly from other traders, usually to Chouteau, who pretended ignorance of the still and talked vaguely of some more or less scientific experiments—testing the wild pears and berries for wine, which he understood was not forbidden, as though unaware that wine distilled is not wine, or that the vats contained corn.

McKenzie tried to save himself and the Company by pretending the distillery was for a friend up in the Red River colony. He had merely carried it as far as Fort Union for the man, and in the meantime was experimenting a bit with the fruits native to the country. But news of his activities reached Washington and the enemies of Astor. This, on top of the Leclerc and other instances of lawlessness, endangered the trading license. Senator Benton of Missouri interceded to save the company, but McKenzie, the King of the River, had to be fired. He came down to St. Louis like any poleman out of a job in 1834, and went to Europe. Astor, off in Switzerland, got out of the company. The beaver trade was failing anyway. In 1833 Astor had seen the styles of Paris change. "It appears that they make hats of silk in place of the Beaver," he wrote.

Ramsay Crooks bought the Northwest Department of the American Fur Company and retained the name, while Pratte, Chouteau and Company took the Western Department under their own name. It was the end of an era, the end of a great American tall tale, with the beaver barely escaping extinction. True, there were still traders and traps. Peter Sarpy was still a power in the region, although more and more of the trade took to the great trails, particularly the Platte route, its sod already worn, the furrows multiplying to spread in corduroy ruts miles wide in places across the Plains, with trading posts and military forts pushing up along the way like mushrooms along any well-manured road.

Now that his power was gone, the frontier was full of stories of this John Jacob Astor who had become so powerful in a trade started long before he was born—tall tales repeated to the farthest outposts. Running through them all was a thread that told of a man born in

Germany, poor, irked by poverty and the social layerings of his society, layerings as clear as those of the red stone band running along the Rockies that his traders were to know so well. Disgusted, young Astor had gone to his flute-making uncle in England, surely a freer country, but there too he found that money and station counted for everything, so he came to the new nation in America, built on freedom and equality. New York proved even more tightly closed against a penniless vagabond. He took some of his flutes upstate to trade to the Indians and discovered that he got a better price if he had a jug along.

Sometimes the story tellers wondered what he used in place of whisky in the China trade, but those who had tried to stand against him anywhere insisted that he stopped at nothing, nothing short of failure of the supply or changing fashion. Now he had the most imposing house on the main street of the New York City that had snubbed the poor young German with his flutes; now he was going all around those foreign countries that had high-toned him, high-nosing them.

So the great tall tale burgeoned as the great riches of the beaver disappeared, literally drained down the river. All that was left were piles of rusting beaver traps and quiet, glassy ponds where the beaver houses were now torn and moldering; the slap of the broad tail (so tasty served on a cottonwood plank with a garnish of watercress) was seldom heard any more, or the fall of the cottonwood and aspen in the axless wilderness. Nothing remained of the rich passing except a few shabby little outposts and a debauched people.

St. Louis, seen by some as the future Rome of the Western world, owed little to Astor but a great deal to the men who had hired out to him, or sold out to him, serving him as the invader is served. The city was the gateway to the Plains, built by men who grew into stature in the fur trade that they developed if not discovered, handling the greasy, stinking, beautiful golden furs themselves, even setting the traps with their rock or sandbag to drown the captive swiftly. The culture of the city grew from the combination of increasing wealth and from the freedom from fixed patterns, grew from an uncaked, fluid society in thought as well as in action. The time was coming when St. Louis would be called the philosophical center of the world, based upon a golden flow of fur that shone in the sun a while and then was gone.

V   Tall-Tale Country

The year 1834 was a sort of dividing line over all the upper Plains—
the end of the dominating American Fur Company and the reign
of the beaver. While the harvest of the plews had covered over 150
years in the region, the richest period was since 1807, when William
Clark was appointed Superintendent of Indian Affairs for all the
Missouri country under Jefferson. The years had been profitable
but not without growing criticism. August 18, 1835, the *Missouri
Republican* quoted an unnamed man who had been around the
Indians for fifteen, twenty years. He said that they

> derive very little benefit from the furs and skins they are enabled to
> take; and when the Government pays out an annuity to them, the
> traders, and particularly the whiskey smugglers soon get it, giving
> little or nothing in exchange. The whiskey vendors immediately on
> the frontier, produce nearly all the misery which exists among the
> Indians, and are *the cause* of the bloodshed which so frequently
> assails the ear. It is no unusual thing, just after an annuity has been

paid, to find the guns, blankets, powder, horses, in short everything necessary to the comfort of the Indians, transferred to the hands of the whiskey trader; and the wretched savages rioting in bestial intoxication.

Those who opposed this rising criticism of William Clark's administration of the Indians' country based it on the plea that the "veteran," now sixty-five, must not be turned out. But nothing could really quiet the loud and open demand for an end to Clark's thirty years of power over the Indian trade, not with the profits about gone.

The stories of the Indians that drifted out of the West for years had drawn adventurers and the curious, but now finally they fired the missionary spirit, always strong in a self-satisfied people, a people convinced they have a special monopoly on revealed truth, at least of such truth as they are prepared to recognize. The Indian was not a citizen, and even if he had been, he would not have known that the Constitution guaranteed him religious freedom, including, presumably, freedom from religious pressures and importunities.

While the Catholic missionaries were the first in much of the Mississippi valley, on the upper Missouri the Baptists were the pioneers. By 1833, after hearing the stories of the eastern and foreign visitors to the Indian country, the Reverend Moses P. Merrill came to Bellevue to establish a mission, Mrs. Merrill to teach the school. The Indians, whose religion permeated every act, every puffing at their sweet-scented pipes, welcomed the white holy people with curiosity and some paint-and-breechclout dancing, as was due such honored guests, although the guests seemed most pleased to protest the nakedness. The Indians overcame their surprise and listened to the Big Stories of the holy people with open ears for a while, particularly those of the First Man, the Big Rains and the Splitting of the Waters. In return their orators recited their own Big Stories, as seemed only courteous, but were told that their accounts of the First Woman, the Big Flood and the Corn Woman were superstition, to be thrown away, but that the stories these whites brought must be believed. The Indians had sat with still face at this unreasonableness, treating it as from badly reared children. Yet the holy couple had good hearts, to come so far to them, and one does not quarrel over beliefs.

Later the Reverend Merrill was appointed government teacher, and although the pay was a pittance it augmented the slender funds provided by the Mission Union. He worked hard, learned something of the languages as fast as he could and wrote spellers, readers and collections of hymns and prayers in the native tongues, but with waning enthusiasm. In 1840 he became ill while on hunt with the Pawnees and died, certain that he was a failure, a failure due to the whisky and influence of the whites—of the traders, particularly Peter Sarpy.

By this time Bellevue, center for Indian agencies and trade, had drawn other missionaries, including a pair of energetic young Presbyterians, Allis and Dunbar, who met the Pawnees there and, at the urgent appeal of the Indians, reluctantly separated and went out to the two main tribal divisions in the Loup River country. Here the buffalo had once passed in great herds that darkened the horizon, their hoofs shaking the earth as they came. But the long boom of the guns had scared them far to the westward years ago. Now, this fall, the herds returned—suddenly coming in a vast dark blanket that rumbled over the ground, headed for the Platte near the Pawnees, closer than in twenty years.

The scouts who brought this news were feasted and sung around the villages, the missionaries brought out and looked upon in awe, for it was plainly their powerful medicine that brought the buffalo back. With this sudden good will, they established a mission on the Loup for the Pawnees. It didn't succeed, perhaps because the missionaries disagreed about both their duties and the tenets of their belief. The men spent more time working against each other, the chiefs decided, than in converting the Indians, the heathen, as the missionaries called them. Eventually the whole work was abandoned, the buffalo gone too, and only bleaching bones were left within a day's ride on good horses.

Perhaps a wandering people is naturally difficult to convert. The Pawnees and their relatives, the Arikaras, were outsiders on the

Plains, apparently from the far Southwest, with beliefs and rites very different from those around them. Like any people without a written creed and no organized priesthood, there was considerable flexibility in the religious beliefs of the Indians, but apparently less among the Pawnees than their neighbors. Every people carries something of its religious sites and symbols in its migrations. The Pawnees didn't toy with half-measures; they brought their center of the earth with them and settled it at Pahuk Point, overlooking the Platte River. Here, as old Pawnees used to tell the story at evening fires, all living things originated:

Once, long ago, all things were waiting in a deep place far underground. There were the great herds of buffaloes and all the people, and the antelope too, and wolves, deer and rabbits—everything, even the little bird that sings the *tear-tear* song. Everything waited as in sleep.

Then the one called Buffalo Woman awoke, stretched her arms, rose and began to walk. She walked among all the creatures, past the little *tear-tear* bird, the rabbits and all the rest, and through the people too, and the buffaloes. Everywhere as she passed there was an awakening, and a slow moving, as when the eyes were making ready for some fine new thing to be seen. Buffalo Woman walked on in the good way, past even the farthest buffaloes, the young cows with their sleeping yellow calves. She went on to a dark round place that seemed like a hole and she stood there awhile, looking. Then she bowed her head a little, as one does to pass under the lodge flap, and stepped out. Suddenly the people could see there was a great shining light all about her, a shining and brightness that seemed blinding as she was gone.

And now a young cow arose and followed the woman, and then another buffalo and another, until a great string of them was following, each one for a moment in the shining light of the hole before he was gone, and the light fell upon the one behind. When the last of the buffaloes was up and moving, the people began to rise too, one after another, and fell into a row, each one close upon the heels of the moccasins ahead. All the people, young and old and weak and strong went so, out through the hole that was on Pahuk, out upon the shining, warm and grassy place that was the earth, with a wide river, the Platte, flowing below, and over everything a blueness, with the *tear-tear* bird flying toward the sun, the warming sun.

The buffaloes were already scattering over the prairie, feeding, spreading in every direction toward the circle that was the horizon. The people looked all around and knew this was their place, the place upon which they would live forever, they and the buffalo together.*

Although the Pawnees apparently agreed on the center of their earth, there were differences in their ceremonials. Only the Skidi retained the practice found among no other Indians of the central and northern Plains—human sacrifice, at the summer solstice, much as Prescott reported it in Mexico. The accounts of the Skidi sacrificial ceremonial, almost invariably second or third hand, are told with the natural zest for horror that was not actually witnessed by the narrator. These rites were usually carried out in the privacy of the special group, often away from the village and never before outsiders. When induced to talk about past sacrifices, the Indians, polite in the Oriental way, apparently accommodated the visitor's hunger for shock, particularly if gifts were involved, for the Indians or the interpreter. According to Prince Paul of Württemberg, the Loup Pawnee medicine man told him back in 1823 that the victim was selected from their prisoners, kept in the house of the priest, well cared for and trained until the day the morning star shone the longest. Then the victim was tied to a post, killed with arrows, and finally burned with special ceremonies. In the ashes the priest read the future, for the Pawnees believed in pyromancy.

Perhaps there is as much Teutonic lore as Pawnee in Prince Paul's account.

There were less lurid stories of attempted sacrifices. In 1817 a Padouca girl was rescued by the Pawnee, Petalesharu, for which he was awarded a silver medal by the young ladies of a fashionable female seminary in the East. In 1818 a Spanish boy, intended for the rites, was "sold" under duress to Papin and taken to St. Louis by Lisa. In 1827 Agent Dougherty, Captain George Kennerly, Papin and some others purchased a Padouca woman intended for the sacrifice, but she was killed as they attempted to carry her away.

* Mari Sandoz, *The Buffalo Hunters.*

De Smet, the good Jesuit Father with the keen nose for horror stories from the heathen, wrote of the Pawnee sacrifice of a Sioux girl in 1837, from hearsay, and with the same gusto and romantic fondness for lurid detail as in the death of Blackbird:

> This young girl was only aged fifteen; after having been well treated and fed for six months, under pretense that a feast would be prepared for her at the opening of the summer season, felt rejoiced when she saw the last days of winter roll by. . . . But as soon as she had reached the place of sacrifice, where nothing was to be seen but fires, torches, and instruments of torture, the delusion began to vanish and her eyes were opened to the fate that awaited her. . . . She burst into tears, she raised loud cries to heaven—she begged, entreated, conjured her executioners to have pity on her youth, her innocence, her parents. . . . She was tied with ropes to the trunk and branches of two trees and the most sensitive parts of her body were burnt with torches. . . . When her sufferings lasted long enough to weary the fanatical fury of her ferocious tormentors, the great chief shot an arrow into her heart, and in an instant this arrow was followed by a thousand others, which, after having been violently turned and twisted in the wounds, were torn from them in such a manner that her whole body presented but one shapeless mass of mangled flesh. . . . When the blood had ceased to flow the greater sacrificator tore out her heart with his own hands and . . . devoured the bleeding flesh. . . . The mangled remains were left there to be preyed upon by wild beasts, and when the blood had been sprinkled on the seed to render it fertile, all retired to their cabins, cheered with the hope of obtaining a copious harvest.*

Father De Smet mixes horror details from the accounts of ancient European rituals with those of the Pawnees, and his time is off. The summer solstice is far too late to sprinkle seeds. Pawnee crops were up a moon's time before this. One wonders, too, what the powerful Sioux were doing that winter and spring that they failed to rescue the maiden. Usually the stories are of captives from small, defenseless tribes.

Just as gaudy in some ways are the accounts of the Presbyterian Dunbar and Allis about the captive of 1833, and that by John

* *Letters and Sketches, with a Narrative of a Year's Residence among the Indian Tribes of the Rocky Mountains*, 1843.

Treat Irving (nephew of Washington Irving). Their stories are based on Agent Dougherty's version and are tinged with the usual romantic and righteous outrage without the check of actual observation. The agent said he heard that a Cheyenne woman prisoner was to be sacrificed. With five companions he hurried to the Loup Pawnee village, to discover that the news of his coming had preceded him. The tops of the domed earth houses were dark with women and children, and a crowd of painted, angry-faced warriors jammed the space before the head chief's dwelling. Realizing the agent's purpose, they refused to lose the tribal benefits from the sacrifice, benefits sorely needed with the buffalo so scarce and the village full of sickness and death from the white man's diseases.

The agent and his men forced their way through the sullen and dark-faced Indians and, stooping through the low entrance of the house, met the first friendly face. The chief harangued the crowd pushing in and ordered that the woman be delivered to the agent and dared any men to offer her injury. The Cheyenne woman was passive through all this, making no appeal or gesture, as though without hope, as though every sense and feeling had been paralyzed by the horror of her fate, the stories say. Perhaps this was really the result of hypnotics or hypnotism, in which the Pawnees, like other Plains Indians, were sometimes expert.

The next morning the chief led the young woman out, forcing the angry gun- and bow-armed crowd back before his commands while he put her on a horse between two white men and urged them ahead. But the mass of roaring warriors hemmed them in and only fell back, one after another, before the thrust of the horses against their painted bodies. At the edge of the village the agent had to pass the earth lodge of the war chief. A bow twanged in the dark doorway and an arrow buried itself to the feathers in the side of the captive. She screamed, threw up her arms and fell forward over the neck of the horse. A high, thin yell of approval rose from the Indians, and two of them grabbed the bridle, jerking her horse away.

A whooping behind the agent made him turn. The head chief was gripping the throat of the war leader, the two in a furious death struggle. The agent knew, whichever won, he and his companions would be killed to avenge Pawnee blood shed in the village. Leaping from his horse, he managed with the aid of several other chiefs to drag the men apart. By then the crowd had swept the captive out upon the prairie. Dougherty spurred after her, but too late. The woman had been torn to pieces, the frenzied Indians smearing themselves with her blood and whirling her head and her severed limbs around high above them.

It is true that Pawnees have tamer versions of such incidents, and not even their worst enemies give the stories the horror these early white narrators brought to them. Accounts of perhaps the last of the Pawnee sacrifice attempts, on Birdwood Creek about the 1860's, come from the Sioux and carry a different connotation. Because there were white settlers all around the Pawnee reservation by that time, they moved the solstice rites to the wild and isolated spot in Sioux country while those Indians were off on their summer buffalo hunts. But some of the scouts had spied out the Pawnee gathering. A big party of Sioux warriors fell upon the preoccupied ceremonial camp. Afterward, when the warriors went over the battle ground to gather up guns and trophies, they discovered a naked youth, apparently a Pawnee, stretched in the center of the camp, his hands and feet bound to stakes, but very lightly. When he was rescued he wept in frustration and defeat, cheated, it seems, from the dedicated sacrificial end he had long anticipated. He fought his release and would not come out of his silence afterward. The Sioux believed he had been put into a dream, a trance, by the ceremonial medicine man. There is apparently no reliable account of what finally became of this youth who had known the exaltation of impending sacrifice for his people and then was rescued and condemned to the long and mundane existence of ordinary men.

The practice of human sacrifice was plainly deep-rooted in the Skidi, the Loup Pawnees, to persist after two hundred and more years with Frenchmen married into the tribe and all their years around the trading posts, around the river travelers and the army. By the 1860's Christian missionaries had been among them for most of thirty years, preaching hard. But even before the missionaries came, someone had told the Pawnees that there was human sacrifice in the white man's Holy Book. Besides, with the American Indian's deep understanding of symbolism, they called the white man's communion in the missions "eating Christ."

The impact of the Indian on the writings of nineteenth-century England, on the literature of the Romantics, was considerable. Wordsworth, who apparently read little except travel accounts by this time, soaked himself in the work of the naturalist Bartram, and of Hearne and Carver. Coleridge, Byron, Southey and the essayists Lamb and Hazlitt were deeply attracted. Their vision of this un-civilized, this natural man, added to the eighteenth-century dream of an ideal society, became a kind of enchantment for the romantic young man of means. James Fenimore Cooper heightened this with his romances and his visit to Europe, where he attracted such ad-venturers as the Oxford scholar, Charles Augustus Murray, grandson of the Earl of Murray, the last colonial governor of Virginia. Cooper fired the young sportsman's imagination, and with his American background and the Murray family property in Virginia that might be looked into, young Charles set sail for America and after great difficulties headed out toward the Plains in 1835, with his valet and a couple of American companions he picked up, all horseback, with three pack animals carrying their baggage, camp equipment and some trade goods. At Fort Leavenworth he missed Colonel Dodge's expedition out to the Rockies, but with an interpreter he joined Agent Dougherty and about 150 Pawnees returning home. They went up the Great Nemaha and the Blue, finding the headwater regions apparently very desolate, with no game. According to Murray they returned southwestward to the Republican River and joined the hunting village of the Grand Pawnees, numbering at least five thousand, their horse herds darkening the prairie to the horizon.

Apparently young Murray brought more discernment than most of the visitors. "Where the buffalo is exterminated, the Indians of the prairies must perish," he wrote.

But he had lesser concerns too. He complained repeatedly of the trouble keeping his horses, the American horses which were so greatly admired by the Pawnees that he lost them all and had to buy Indian ponies. There were further exasperations too. "I never met with liars so determined, universal and audacious."

Others had been reporting similar opinions of the Pawnees for years, although occasional old Indians, somehow untouched by whisky and the white man's ways—resisting both firmly—still spoke with a straight tongue and the stringent honesty demanded by a society without locks. Murray found the old chief in whose lodge he stayed such a man, a gentleman, made so by nature and remaining so in spite of the corrupting examples all around him. The drunken, sodden Indians of the camp convinced the visiting Englishman that he must not contribute to the intoxication. The occasional hospitable cup of brandy he passed out was well watered.

The quarreling between the Grand and the Republican divisions of the Pawnees disgusted Murray particularly. But when the ceremonial move out to the meat-making was finally begun, he found it impressive and formal as a marching army, with a discipline that somehow survived all the destructive forces of the white man, even though most of the trappings were from him—even the fine cream-colored horse the hunt chief rode, his Mexican peak saddle, the Spanish gilt spurs at his heels, the heavy Spanish bridle adorned with gilt stars, chains and buckles.

The Missouri and the Platte River country had been practically overrun by white men just passing through: explorers, soldiers, missionaries, adventurous travelers and the artists who set up their easels anywhere or propped a sketchboard on a whisky cask or the knee. Alfred Jacob Miller, for instance, sketched anywhere, picturing the Indians, the trappers and mountain men with a wonderful sense of movement, swift movement that was light as the clear thin air of Wyoming, the feathers and fringes, the beards and hair like tatters predicting their own impermanence, their own passing.

One visitor who, like Murray, stayed some time in the Nebraska region was the twenty-one-year-old John Treat Irving who helped spread the lurid accounts of the Pawnee sacrifices. Like Murray, he found desolation south of the Platte, particularly along the Salt Creek slopes, and told his version of the many legends common of salt basins everywhere. In this Irving managed to make a sort of Byronic hero of a war chief of an unidentified tribe, a man he pictured as so fierce that not an enemy people within hundreds of miles could evade his deadly arm, the creeks running red with the blood. He led his warriors from village to village, spreading death and destruction, but often he went out alone to "bathe his hands in blood," and while his tribe gloried in these exploits they dreaded the man, and no friend lifted the lodge flap to see how it was with him, and no one walked through the village at his side. There was only one to love him—the daughter of the head chief, a beautiful maiden, graceful as the fawn of her prairies. Against all advice she married the terrifying warrior and softened his heart. But she died and her husband buried her without one tear or a wail of sorrow. The next dawn he emerged, once more painted for war, the old angry fire burning in his eyes. At the grave of his wife he "plucked a wild flower from among the grass and cast it upon the upturned sod. Then turning on his heel, he strode across the prairie."

In a month he returned laden with scalps of men, women and children, but the next time he brought back only a large lump of white salt. He had traveled many weary miles into an isolated region and was awakened from his sleep by a low wailing. In the moonlight, he saw an old hag brandishing a tomahawk over the head of a young woman kneeling, imploring mercy. Denied this, she grabbed for the tomahawk but was overpowered, her head twisted around by the hair for the death stroke, her face revealed. It was the face of the war chief's dead wife. He sprang up, buried his tomahawk in the skull of the old woman, but before he could grasp his beloved, both women sank into the earth, and a tall rock of white salt rose there, in the region that became a glistening salt basin. It was a piece of that tall rock that the man had brought back to the tribe.

The story was in the typical romantic, white-man pattern, but the salt basin was certainly an ancient region of conflict for both animals and men. Every tribe from as far as the Canadian River and up to the Yellowstone told stories of this lick. Game collected there, hunters came and war parties of various tribes set upon their enemies. Stories were told of lone hunters trampled in stampedes started by warriors in battle, or by lightning. A small party of Sioux was annihilated by the Pawnees at the licks, who paid for it in years of reprisal. Then suddenly, in the 1820's, all this was stopped by an appalling pestilence, a whistling death of the animals. So complete was the dying that far into the 1830's there were reports of a dead ground, a dead region, with no game, particularly none of the cloven hoof, from the headwaters of the Blues across the salt basin toward the Platte.

The Brule Sioux told earlier stories of finding the region dark with stinking carcasses—buffalo, deer and elk, the stench and silence so frightening that with all the carrion around there was not a wolf or coyote, not even a magpie. Some of the dead animals were scattered far from the salt flats, particularly along the buffalo trails toward the sweet water of the Little Blue, the hand-wide trails suddenly easy to trace half a mile away by the dark bodies along them. During this time a party of seven Sioux on a foray against the Missouri tribes were discovered, and, pursued, they cut through between the salt basin and a small creek running into the Blue. Not daring to move during the day, to hunt at all, they had found no game and were starving when they ran into many buffalo scattered like a sleeping herd in the moonlight, but dead and silent, with a horrible stench like a cloud over them. Only one still lived, his nostrils vast and dark as a rotting old tree stump, his black tongue protruding and swollen too, so swollen that the breath whistled. But the men were desperately hungry. They killed the buffalo and died, all except the one who couldn't bring himself to taste the meat.

This incident of Indians poisoned by their gift animal, their brother creature, the buffalo, was so conspicuous and strange in Plains history that it appears in six or seven of the more common Sioux winter counts. For example, Lone Dog, the Brule, offers:

> 1827 Winter When Six Lakotas [Sioux] Died of eating a diseased
> buffalo on the Little Blue.* One man who did not eat of the
> meat lived.

Among the upper Missouri Indians, the Flame, of the Two Kettle
Sioux, puts this incident in 1826-27, but without locale, as does the
Minneconjou named Swan. Another Minneconjou Sioux lists the
incident as:

> 1825 The Whistlers Die after They Come Home. A hungry war
> party killed a sick buffalo and ate its flesh. The buffalo was
> afflicted with the disease known as "whistlers."

The salt region of Nebraska, unpromising for crops, was settled
much later than the surrounding prairies. In the 1840's a bull trail
of sorts crossed west of the present Lincoln, with a night stop in
the low sandy hills beyond old Capitol Beach, away from the
scrubby, inedible salt grass of the basin. Here a man had a log shack
and a forge to repair wagons, set the drought-loosened iron tires,
and shoe the footsore oxen.

There was talk even then of loading trains of freight wagons with
salt, free for the scooping in dry weather. But somehow there
always seemed better payloads from farther west—usually furs and
tanned robes waiting to reach St. Louis, or even smoked buffalo
tongues and flint hides—these bull trains, like all the others, draining
the wealth of the Plains eastward.

The nation's suspicion of the British and their hold on the Oregon
country was publicized and sentimentalized by the Nez Perce request
in 1832 for missionaries. The resulting plan was not so much the
conversion of the Indians as the settling of Oregon, and not by the
unhappy route of Lewis and Clark but over the old, old Indian trail
up the Platte, with its gradual ascent toward the continental divide,
the route characterized by Robert Stuart in 1813 as the world's best
natural roadbed for wheels.

Ashley had taken a wagon up the South Platte, but it was 1830

* Apparently this was not the Little Blue of the white man but a small,
partly dry creek emptying into the Blue near Milford, Nebraska.

before the first wheels crushed the grass of what was to become the Oregon Trail beyond there. That year Smith, Jackson and Sublette started out with ten wagons drawn by five mules each and two Dearborns—curtain-sided carriages drawn by one mule apiece, which seems pretty foolish business for men so familiar with the vast distances and stiff pulls. The party angled northwest to the Blue, up the Platte and the North Fork as far as the head of Wind River, but they reported that wheels could certainly have crossed the Rockies at what they called Southern Pass. Six years later, Whitman and Spalding, headed for the Nez Perce, got a two-wheeled cart to Fort Boise and two years after that one made it to Oregon—by land wheels, not the steam-driven paddlewheels of the almost forgotten Yellowstone Expedition, and not up the Missouri.

By now visitors usually took the Platte route for a sight of the wilder, the less spoiled, natural man, and to take part in the great hunts of the Plains. Then, too, there were the fabulous mountains which these braggard American blowhards had invested with springs boiling hot, and within fishpole distance of cool mountain streams, so a man could swing his trout around and drop it, still on the line, to cook in the boiling waters. They also claimed a place with bubbling paint pots of red and yellow and green, and with geysers that shot to the clouds at regular intervals like the spouting of some giant whale held captive underground. Then there were the brawling, drunken excesses of the trapper rendezvous.

The years that Maximilian, Audubon, and a dozen others were up the Missouri, a dashing Scottish sportsman, William Drummond Stewart, was spending much of his time with the Oglala Sioux in the North Platte country. The gaunt-nosed man, with black hair and mustache, came up the Platte trail in time for the 1833 rendezvous, and stayed much of the next ten years, getting out even as far as Scotland, but returning. In 1837 he brought in the artist Alfred Jacob Miller, who made handsome and spirited water colors from the Missouri to the mountains—paintings of such landmarks as Chimney Rock, Scotts Bluff and Independence Rock; of travelers and caravans on the trail; of Indians in camp, in ceremonials and on the hunts; and many pictures of the trapper rendezvous. Selections from the whole group were to be enlarged in oil for the walls of Stewart's castle in Scotland.

Stories about the Scotsman drifted back to the high country for years. It was said that Stewart, Sir William by then, was "so coarsened" by his wilderness experiences that he wouldn't sleep in a bed but spread his buffalo robes on the castle floor, much to the annoyance of the women of his household. Years later, when a young brownish-haired Oglala Sioux called Crazy Horse outmaneuvered Crook at the Rosebud and cut off the retreat of Custer on the Little Big Horn, there were stories about his origins. Certainly no Indian could outsmart a couple of West Point generals like that; it must be true that he was half white, perhaps the son of Sir William Drummond Stewart. But no one who understood the old Sioux could believe that a man known to be half white or even a quarter could have become the war leader Crazy Horse was—not in a society where war leadership depends upon voluntary following. Furthermore, lightish hair and a pale brown skin were characteristic of several members of the Crazy Horse family, and apparently ran far back, at least two hundred years, long before Sir William crept into the buffalo robes in the Oglala camps.

The Indian Intercourse Act of 1834 forbade all whites without government licenses to trespass on Indian lands, on any portion of the Indian country, but it was a scrap of paper even before the signing. Not only visitors but more and more white men with permanent intention encroached on the forbidden region, particularly when articles, pamphlets and handbills were distributed all over the states urging the nation to act on her right to Oregon. Sermons from practically every pulpit and brush arbor called for action, usually through missionaries to the heathen Indians, but the real impetus to the movement came from the unemployment and dispossession that followed the panic of 1837. In May 1841 about eighty settlers and a few missionaries set out under the guidance of the veteran mountain man, Thomas Fitzpatrick. They went up the trader's trail to South

Pass and down the western slope, the first true emigrants to Oregon. Next year the missionary, Dr. Elijah White, in Washington to urge action against the British and to mend his own Northwest prospects, headed back as subagent to the Indians of Oregon. He led more than a hundred men, women and children, the Indians of the Platte coming to stare, many seeing for the first time that the whites were not only male but also female, and with young ones, some with hair white as milkweed down. Fitzpatrick guided this party too, but only as far as Fort Hall, the Hudson's Bay post.

That summer Frémont took his exploring expedition up the Platte to South Pass and was called the Great Pathfinder, over a road already wheel-rutted and washed to gullies. His account, written by his wife, the daughter of Senator Benton of Missouri, did stimulate interest in Oregon and the Platte route. The next year the full tide was on—more than 1,000 people, with perhaps 120 heavy canvas-bowed wagons drawn by six pairs of oxen each, and several thousand loose horses and cattle plodding in the dust behind. Now the Oregon Trail up the Platte was well started. True, everybody hurried across the vast and easy stretches of the Flat Water, the Nebraska, country as fast as possible, aware of the mountains far beyond that must be crossed before the snows. Few except those who found shallow graves along the route stayed even one extra night. Some never reached the trail at all. The steamboat *Edna* burst her boiler in the mouth of the Missouri early July 1842, scalding more than sixty emigrants, none of them cabin passengers. Within a week forty-four of them were dead.

By now the emigrant trail was well laid out across the corner of Kansas to hit the Platte near the head of what the trappers called Grand Island, up the broad, watered valley to the South Fork and along it to a good crossing. From there they swung back toward the North Platte by way of Ash Hollow and Windlass Hill, which was so steep that the oxen, even horses and mules, couldn't hold back the great wagons and had to be unhitched, the wagons let down by ropes wound around what served as a windlass. Some reported this as the butt of an old tree soundly rooted on the hilltop, with an actual windlass roped to it for awhile. Others said that a large cottonwood trunk had been set like a piling deep into the crest and was used like a snubbing post in a horsebreaker's corral. With the ropes tied to the front axle and tongue, the men eased out slack very cautiously from the dallies around the creaking post, inching the wagons backward down the steep decline, while others, men and often women too, in blowing calico skirts that caught under their feet, pushed at both sides of the awkward, topheavy covered wagons with all their might to keep them from tipping one way or the other.

There was always the problem of starting west early enough to get across those western mountains before winter and yet not too early for grass to forage the oxen and horses on the stretches through Nebraska, with its retarded spring. Besides, there were the floods of the Platte to consider, boiling in sullen gray snow water, the shifting bottom treacherous with quicksand. Later the stream bed might be practically or completely dry, the trailers compelled to dig holes into the sandbars for water. Even the rawest greenhorn knew it was there after he saw thirsty buffalo herds stampede in from the sun-burnt prairie to mill around on the dry sand of the river bed until the surface shook and water began to boil up around their hoofs in what the old trappers called buffalo springs. But the holes the emigrants dug back from the caving, sliding sandy river bed were open to every contamination, particularly typhoid and the appalling cholera that had ravaged the Ohio country and St. Louis, and now was spreading so many unmarked graves westward to the swift-water regions far up in Wyoming.

With these thousands on the road—all kinds of people, good and bad, responsible, wild and unsane, and moving through a region with no law, with nothing to prevent even the extreme of murder, or to punish it—there was bound to be bulldozing, fighting, thievery and bloodshed. The only law was the Indian's, for his own people. From the first there were complaints about the thieving Pawnees, too long accustomed to the white man and grown contemptuous and covetous. The young Indians had to see so much that they desired pass through their country, the hunters killing their game, making it very wild for the bow, leaving the people hungry and the grass so eaten down, so worn out, that in the fall, when the trail was empty again, no creature returned, even though it was most urgent to make enough meat for the frozen months.

Not that the Indians wanted the oxen of the travelers; they preferred the sweeter, juicier meat of fat young buffalo cow to the stringy, stinking cattle, but there were very many good horses going by every day and the mules that were so tough in the hunt and the battles. The Indians turned their hungriest eyes toward the good guns they saw in the emigrant parties, very many good guns, and powder and lead, and whisky too, or the things that could be traded for whisky. Besides there were fineries and gaudies that some of the foppish young Indians saw on the eastern stretches of the trail— a feathered hat, perhaps, or a gay shawl, sometimes a length of fluttering veil hopefully employed against the burning sun. There might even be a ruffled parasol until it was turned inside out by the wind or carried bouncing across the prairie, some lucky Indian riding it down. And who could guess what other hidden and wonderful things were in the darkness of the covered wagon that no Indian was ever permitted to see.

Inevitably fantastic tales sprouted along the great migration trail, with the inevitable atrocity stories, sometimes told to entertain and shock, sometimes by those who feared that settlement would kill what was left of the fur trade, or those who wanted the Indian destroyed to free the land, as had happened all the way from Plymouth Rock to the West. Out of these tales came such names as Rawhide Creek, which was on maps, at one time or another, all the way from the Alleghenies to the Pacific mountains.

There were several versions of the Nebraska rawhide story spread over perhaps fifteen years of time, all with the inconsistencies and anachronisms that betrayed alien origins. The general locale of several of these was the north bend of the Platte River, one near the present Rawhide Creek, not far from Pahuk Point. Simplified, these stories tell of a party of perhaps a hundred Iowans who struck straight westward "through the Great Desert of Nebraska." The party included a reckless young man of around twenty-two who claimed that one of his relatives—the stories differ on the degree of relationship—was killed by some eastern Indians. Now that he was going out into the wilderness, he swore he would avenge his relative by killing the first Indian he saw. One day while the party was crossing a little stream they passed an Indian woman and a girl of about twelve sitting on a log weaving rush baskets. The man drew his pistol and, before anyone could stop him, fired at the woman. She fell, and the girl fled silently into the brush. There was anger and concern over such recklessness. Scouts were sent along the strung-out party to warn them of a threatened attack, but hours passed and nothing happened. That night the camp of the overlanders was suddenly surrounded by Pawnee warriors threatening a general massacre if the murderer was not delivered to them at once. Far outnumbered and surrounded, with the dark empty wilderness all around, the party decided to let the Indian girl and three or four braves come to the campfires to pick out the man. The girl pointed to the young braggart, and although he cried to be saved, he was dragged away to the bank of the stream, stripped of clothing and bound to a tree. Then, while the rest of the party had to see this done, listen to his screams, the Indians skinned him alive, taking off pieces here and there, but carefully at first, so he wouldn't die too fast; at last growing impatient, they cut loose bigger strips and ripped them off, until the man was only bare quivering flesh. Then they scalped him.

According to one story, the young man's relatives received no letters, heard no news of him, for years. Finally they inquired of a member of the party and were told of the skinning with much detail that couldn't possibly have been seen in the night. There was no mention of a burial spot because it seems the party hadn't even rescued the body. One version of this rawhide story has a warrior killed instead of a woman. Another says a man named Rhines, a silversmith from Wisconsin, headed west in the gold rush, and shot a young Pawnee woman out of a group of morning visitors. He was tied to a wagon wheel and skinned alive.

Altogether these stories, in any form, were proper ones to tell the timid stay-at-homes.

But there were raids on horse herds, and thieving by the wilder of the young Indians, particularly the Pawnees. To bring a little law to the Platte region, the government planned some military posts along the trail that was the temporary home to so many thousands during the summers. The first post was started by Colonel Stephen Watts Kearny, married to the stepdaughter of William Clark, and with early familiarity around old Fort Atkinson himself. He laid out his little post at the river too, but below the mouth of the Platte, for the trail, not the Missouri trade. Leaving a small force to throw up the blockhouse and shelter huts, Kearny hurried on to the Mexican War, with the government promise that as soon as possible there would be a permanent post farther out on the Platte, out where its influence and striking power would reach up and down the river, like two strong protecting, and avenging, arms.

Little Fort Kearny could not protect the foolish from their folly any more than the whole string of larger ones built some years later would, for the fool will be fooled, and most frequently, perhaps, by the ambitious. It was inevitable that other men besides Clark and his relatives and the other profit-seeking fur traders, or men like Wilkinson and Frémont, would be stirred to ambition by the new West, the West of the homeseeker, of real estate booms, and of politicians.

One of the newly ambitious was Lansford Hastings, a young Ohio lawyer who had started with Dr. White's Oregon caravan back in the spring of 1842. As far as Fort Laramie they had moved without escort or guide or even fur-brigade fellow travelers. From the start Hastings stirred up so much dissension that the party would have been in serious trouble if there had been Indian danger or other emergency, perhaps a cloudburst, a prairie fire, a buffalo stampede or an epidemic. At Laramie they wisely took in Fitzpatrick, who let Hastings know who was captain of the outfit. From Oregon Hastings went down the coast to California, and, returning east, published his emigrant guide to the two regions, lauding particularly the beauty and fruitfulness of California. On his way back west in a party of ten men, all horseback, he cut straight through the empty, trackless waste of the Humboldt River country, getting over the Sierras barely ahead of the great snows. The next spring he prepared to boost his Hastings Cut-Off to California, stressing that it shortened the route by three hundred miles, hoping to settle the region so he could make himself president of a new nation there, or at least governor of a new state. With Clyman, already familiar with the West when he stumbled into Fort Atkinson twenty years ago, Hastings headed east on his cut-off, horseback, starting before the scorching heat of summer, and even so they suffered crossing the desert.

Hastings camped near South Pass to coax travelers on the Oregon Trail to California with the sweet promises of his shorter route. By firelight he wrote hundreds of letters advocating his cut-off and sent them east to be handed out to emigrants, particularly to those on the long, weary stretches of the Platte and anxious to reach lush green country quickly. Some were attracted to Hastings' route, notably the Donner party. They had started very late and were further delayed by quarreling and disorganization. Even so, they took the cut-off, against the urgent advice of Clyman, who spoke frankly of his suffering even on a strong, fast horse, and before the watercourses were all dried up. Some of the party smiled a little. They had just come through the Great American Desert marked all over the Platte country on their maps, and without any real trouble.

There were eighty-one in the party that took the cut-off, half of them under twenty. With slow, ox-drawn wagons, the burning desert of late summer proved an appalling experience, aggravated by accidents, sickness of beasts and man, by dissension and even madness and murder. Far too late, and wretched as they were, they could still have taken a long route around the mountains, but, as though driven to self-destruction, they attacked the towering Sierras and were caught in the snows long after every sensible creature that a hunter might have pursued had gone below. Death by freezing, violence and starvation struck them down. In the end some of the thirty-three who survived to plod the western slopes of California had been saved by cannibalism, perhaps even carried human remains along for the road. Thousands of parties, large and small, crossed on the Overland Trail, through cholera and Indian raids and all the lesser vicissitudes, but the most tragic was the Donner party, their sad end directly due to the exaggerations, the self-serving tall tale, of an ambitious Ohio lawyer.

Within a few years California was booming beyond all Hastings' dreams, but the world-wide notoriety of the Donner tragedy killed his political chances, at least for awhile. During the Civil War he tried again, offering to seize the Arizona region for Jefferson Davis and to lay out a thoroughfare from the Confederacy to California and take that over too. But Davis was not that easily beguiled by a tall dream.

The thin high song of gold on the wind had drawn the first white men up the Plains back in 1541, its ghost voice always just ahead of Coronado's advance, enticing him deeper and deeper into the wilderness. Now, three hundred years later, the song rose again, but from a definite location this time, from a stream called the American River, the call of it loud and lusty enough to toll the gold-hungry from all the world. For many the news was accentuated by the adventurous writings of travelers to the western country, writings that spread the scenic grandeur and the magnificence and prolificacy of its wild game before the reader, and, in wondrous addition, the nobility, the curious and intriguing freedoms, of its red-skinned savage.

The news of gold discovered at Sutter's Fort in California swept down the trail like a fevered windstorm. Suddenly every party, every encampment, was infected, drunken on the news. Back East, an entirely new type of trailer set his face westward. Instead of the homeseekers, with a scattering of adventurers, and missionaries and refugees from the law, the Plains earth resounded to the impatient tramp of the gold-hungry, including the foolish, the greedy and those disciplined in avarice. They came by the ten, the hundred thousand, mostly over the Platte route. The spring of 1849 the tardy start of the grass along the trail was holding up 20,000 impatient gold-seekers and hangers-on fretting at Independence, Missouri, the usual jumping-off place, and up along the Iowa coast too. All were waiting for the first tinges of color to run like a greening fire along the sun-warmed slopes—grass for the stock of the wagons, the swift carriages, the hurrying horsebackers pursuing the hope of gold. This year the emigrants included some of real wealth and station, going out to finance the mining, the banks, the emporiums, and the palaces for gambling gentlemen, leaving lesser dens for gentlemen gamblers. But most of the trailers were common people, and common riffraff, card sharps, pickpockets, thieves, prostitutes and common murderers.

Many too poor for even an ox team or a mule tried to walk to California, loaded down with pick and shovel and gold pan. One man with a long rifle over his shoulder, his baggage a small bundle no bigger than his hat, and a savage-looking bulldog at his heels, had walked all the way from Maine and was going strong as he passed Fort Kearny. Bets were placed that he would make it, and then the bettors scattered before anyone had to pay.

This year there was even more dumping of goods as the emigrants struck the long trail across Nebraska, and a growing realization of the hardships ahead. Some tried to sell the extra loading, others just gave it away or dropped it, even if it was a young sow and her pigs from the leather belly hung under the wagon and now scraping the ground at every high center of the corduroyed trail. Some burned what they couldn't carry, or contaminated the foodstuffs by dumping turpentine into the sugar, sand into the flour or human ordure into anything. Many started with too little, as if California lay just beyond the next sundown, and were already begging at Fort Kearny. Often they could have gone no farther, perhaps even starved, without government help. The first tender grass of the Platte valley was eaten out of the ground, the prairie bald and blowing in great dust clouds where fourteen years ago Dodge and his dragoons slogged mud most of the way to the forks of the Platte, with buffalo herds days in passing. Now there was only dust, the hunters for the emigrant parties ranging out ten, fifteen miles and more, lucky to come back with even a deer.

Once more cholera struck, all the way from the congested eastern cities westward, the victim often dead within twenty-four hours, the disease dogging the trails on both sides of the Platte, one out of every five emigrants dead by the time the trains passed Scotts Bluff. The Indians fled in alarm when their people began to die at the river camps, and fell like bundles of rags and old hides all along the running trail, until everybody contaminated at the water holes of the drying Platte was gone or strengthening in the cleaner country. Among a band of Oglala Sioux a young chief named Red Cloud fasted for a dream to stop this most fatal of the white man's diseases. Afterward he had a pile of cedar boughs brought to him, and helped the women strip green twigs and bark into big boiling kettles to make a dark brown medicine that all must drink. From that day not one of all the camp along the swift, clear-bottomed White River was found by the sickness.

But runners from down along the Arkansas River brought very bad news from Red Cloud's uncle, married into the Cheyennes. Those people had gathered for a great dancing with the Kiowas, some Osages and other tribes, and when one after another began to fall from this sickness of the white man, the Cheyennes ran too, horseback or afoot, leaving their tipis and their goods, fanning out over the prairie, the sick and dying falling everywhere. When it was over at least half of the Southern Cheyennes had died, and many relatives there visiting from the north. It was one more count stick against the white man, added to all the others, the earlier diseases, the whisky, the Platte trail that was a knife cutting the great herds of the fine buffalo ranges in two, and driving away all the other game so the people were starved. There were many count sticks against the white man now, so many that two Indian hands could scarcely hold them.

Another story, less credible than most of those told in the land of the Flat Water, was being enacted there. For some years a new religious group, the Latter-day Saints, the Mormons, had been having difficulties with their neighbors in one community after another, from York State to Missouri. It was not that they were chicken thieves or dog poisoners or murderers but that their religion was different. Although safely Christian and fundamentalist, it espoused polygamy, open polygamy. Worse, the communal organization of the Mormons enabled them to outstrip the surrounding communities in economic progress. Mobs and even officials used burning, imprisonment and murder to drive them out of one place after another. Finally they were expelled from their own Nauvoo, which they had built, and which overshadowed all the other cities of Illinois. This time the leaders decided they must move where there was not one Gentile, one non-Mormon. This time they would go beyond the farthest boundaries of the United States.

Early in 1846 the newspapers reported that the Mormons were on the road again, traveling toward the Missouri River, but under the watching eye of militiamen so they would not settle anywhere short of Indian country. They claimed to be heading for California, in Mexico, with war already declared. In June the advance division of 1,000 wagons actually had reached the east bank of the Missouri and was building boats to cross, the later parties spaced out for grass and game, as was necessary with around 12,000 men, women and children moving. The first group had planted something like 2,000 acres of corn on the Grand River, on land leased from the Indians, the next party to cultivate the fields, the last to harvest the crop, carry it all along.

The government needed troops for the Mexican War, and the Mormons were asked to furnish 500 men. Without much protest and almost no scorn for these Gentiles who had driven them out, Brigham Young made arrangements for 500 of his younger and able-bodied men to head toward Santa Fe. After some hesitation he was given permission to camp his people, temporarily, of course, on the Indian lands west of the Missouri. They selected an attractive spot above Bellevue and called it Winter Quarters, to be a sort of jumping-off place on the way out of the country, perhaps to the

Great Salt Lake region, well beyond the borders of both the Louisiana Purchase and the new Oregon Territory. Foresighted, early in the summer Young sent five Missouri Mormons under Gleason ahead to report on the region. They went by light rig, traveling fast, up the north side of the Platte to avoid the Gentile trailers. Gleason kept a faithful record of each day—the mileage, wood and grass available, the buffalo and smaller game sighted, as well as the location and description of the Indians, with whom the Mormons made friends, calling them the Lost Tribe of Israel. Gleason noted the problems that crossing the swift and deep Elkhorn and Loup Rivers presented, and the long arid stretch from the Loup to the welcomed North Platte valley, with its handsome scenery laid out across the river: Chimney Rock, Scotts Bluff and the Wild Cat Hills, usually called the Nebraska Mountains by the Easterners until they saw the Rockies.

Up at Fort Laramie, established by Sublette and his partners on the North Platte, Gleason hired a couple of very experienced guides: the mulatto Jim Beckwourth, said by some to be the son of Pierre Chouteau, Sr., and O. P. Wiggins,* a Canadian who had helped nurse Frémont over the 1842 route. At Salt Lake the guides went on to the Mexican War, and by that fall, 1846, Gleason was back at Winter Quarters and working to get his little emigrant guide into print for the various parties going west next spring and summer.

Life at Winter Quarters was very different from what it had been at the height of Fort Atkinson, just up the river. Only the valiant resolution of the Mormons to sing a little, dance a little, and pray got them through that first winter west of the Missouri, but it gave the Plains a term for that first desperate cold season that always seemed to hit the new settlers after a pleasant Indian summer— Mormon winter.

Many of Brigham Young's emigrants had been stripped of all their belongings by the repeated attacks on them, and their many flights.

* Coutant, *History of Wyoming*; O. P. Wiggins' list of six Mormons to Salt Lake, 1846, Denver *Times*, December 22, 1920; O. P. Wiggins letter to Coutant, January 8, 1898, in Colorado Historical Society.

Some of the latest party came in through a snowstorm that swept around them as they huddled on the ferry rafting them over the surly river. The best shelters at the Quarters were the few log huts hastily thrown up, but most of the people had to live in holes dug into banks and hillsides, or even in the blizzard-swept wagons. The poor housing during this hardest winter that most of the Mormons had ever faced, and on very thin rations, added to the aftereffects of malaria, and now the colds, pnuemonia, galloping consumption, scurvy and starvation, struck the people down. Over six hundred died there that winter; some place the number much higher, the dead buried in the iron-hard earth by the weakened survivors.

Brigham Young was impatient for spring, for grass, so he could start with a small picked band for Salt Lake, led, some liked to say years later, by an angel with a fiery sword pointing the way through trackless wilderness to the chosen land of Deseret. Unfortunately many remembered the old and deep-rutted trail of the early fur traders heading west from Atkinson and Bellevue, up along the north side of the Platte, a ready-made trail welcoming the wheels of Young and his party as it had Gleason's the year before. Perhaps the angel with the flaming sword carried Gleason's *Guide*, reported published the winter of 1846-47, but successfully lost since 1850.

So, the spring of 1847, Young's Pioneer Band of about 150, including three women and two small children, started west with perhaps seventy wagons, many horses, mules and oxen, also some cows, dogs and chickens. They were a small party compared to most of those moving along the Oregon Trail on the south side of the river, so many parties over there now that it seemed there was not one spot, from the Missouri to the western mountains, where an Indian could sit on his horse at the trail and be out of sight of white men traveling through his country, wearing out his grass, killing his game, splitting the buffalo herds that were the food, clothing, shelter and fuel of his family. Now there was nothing but the great rows of the white-man wagons hurrying, hurrying, from far off looking like strings of ants running fast before approaching winter.

Mormons were on the move from the Missouri all that summer.

Some had crossed farther north, near the Ponca village at the Niobrara, although most of these gave up their faith, it seems, and with it the necessity to flee. Others crossed the river even higher up, while some moved west through Texas. But not all went west. Mormon missionaries in twos and threes were sent all over the nation and to Europe, offering land, a place for a home free to those who joined the church. Because so many converts were unable to finance even part of the passage, the church created a perpetual travelers' aid fund. It was never large enough, with the hordes of impoverished Europeans anxious to escape to the land of hope—America. Sometimes it seemed there was scarcely one Protestant family among all the common people of Europe who did not have someone among the Mormon converts, the Mormon landowners.

With his people so very poor from their years of persecution, and most of the newcomers penniless, Brigham Young had to announce in 1855 that the church could no longer provide wagons to carry the emigrants across the Plains. Instead he would "make hand-carts and let the emigration foot it." The first company, of about five hundred, was three-fourths women, more than half of these single but certain to find husbands immediately at Salt Lake, or part of a husband, as the sour-mouthed said. The party started out in July, the two-wheeled carts generally drawn by a man and three women, although some had only women, with perhaps a strong girl to help over the long, long route.

The first group was largely Danish, with no knowledge of English and no experienced leader. The able hurried on as though Salt Lake were just beyond the coming sundown, the rest strung out in a long, pathetic line, the heavy handcarts, piled with goods and baggage, blistering their hands, galling their shoulders, as the ungreased wheels screeched their dry way westward. Behind these came the stragglers, the aged and sick, perhaps supported by a son or daughter, some crippled, lamed to crutches, now and then a mother with a little one in her arms and two, three hanging to her skirts, others heavy with child—all plodding along so slowly, so drearily, the distance to Salt Lake an incomprehensible farness to all these people from small places, from cramped localities, and with the winter not nearly as far away.

Now even the most callow young Plains warrior looked with pity upon these whites, so helpless, so poor.

Two of the five handcart expeditions of that year were caught in the snows far west of the Nebraska earth, which might have protected them as it did at Winter Quarters, as it did the rabbit, the badger and the prairie dog. One hundred and fifty of the last five hundred died from cold and hunger and heartache, a tragic occurrence exceeded only by the reckless Donner party ten years earlier.

Brigham Young never operated the handcart expeditions on so broad a scale again. Only two crossed to Deseret in 1857, one in 1859 and two in 1860. Perhaps something like three thousand people, men, women and children, walked the weary dusty miles to Salt Lake drawing the loaded handcarts with their narrow tracks. The trail to Fort Laramie was the easier stretch of the journey, the route well watered, the grade gradual, without stony climb and no alkali deserts to burn the eyes and parch the throat, no mountain snow winds, but it was this level stretch that wore the marchers down by its very monotony, and accounted for some of the joy that the first sight of the Nebraska Mountains mentioned in the emigrant guides always brought. After 1860 Young sent church teams to meet the emigrants at the railroad terminal, the trip shortening as the rails crept westward, up the broad highway of the Platte. Long before this the Mexican War was won and all of California became part of the nation that Brigham Young with his Salt Lake City and his Deseret had hoped to escape.

But the story of his people remained the heroic tale of determination and persistence, of raw and spiritual courage, the tallest tale of all.

VI   Friendly Earth for Hoof and Plow

Long before the old Missouri was tamed, even before she reached her greatest turbulence, with steamboats churning most of her waters, the Overland Trails were gathering settlements to themselves, particularly the Oregon route up the Little Blue and the Platte. Log shacks and sod buildings squatted beside the trail like flies come to feed along a streak of dusty sorghum. The first were saloons, blacksmith shops, and supply stores, often all in one long low building of sod or, out in the region of little rain, of sun-baked brick.

By 1848 the Oregon Battalion, theoretically to expel the British from Oregon, had located a new post out west of Grand Island on the south side of the Platte, to oversee the main trail. It was the second one named for Stephen Watts Kearny, the first, back at the Missouri, had been only a temporary camp where Nebraska City was to grow up later. Although Kearny had soldiered at Atkinson, the new post bore little resemblance to that first American community in the Missouri country. The new fort was not a place to live, to make a home, but a frontier barracks to keep peace between the tribes and to protect the emigrants, often from themselves.

Although the reports of the Donner party's entrapment by the mountain snows had reached very far, for years there were some who did not know the story, some of the many illiterates and some of the skeptics who refused to listen to any tall tale, or considered this one the work of men who wanted to keep Americans out of the far West, perhaps the Englishmen or even Mexicans. Usually some lip-smacking storyteller at an evening fire during the first weary stretch of trail shattered any complacency, any sense of security, with his Donner account, and although there were those along the trail who would obviously profit from anything discarded, once more the Overlanders would start throwing away. Usually the first to go were the heavier, the less sensible pieces of furniture, perhaps a cherry wedding bed and bureau, a square piano, or an inlaid wardrobe or music box, despite a woman's weeping or her frozen stoniness. A man must get his family through, even if he had to treat them as he did his team, drive them unmercifully too, with shouted curses and stern leather on the hard pulls, not let them waver or hesitate one second if they were to get over the western mountains ahead of those snows.

But in spite of these momentary alarms, there were growing signs of softening on the trails as the stations and the road ranches multiplied, and letters of safe arrival appeared in all the newspapers. Even the sickly Boston visitor, Francis Parkman, detected the softness, although there were aspects of the frontier he never understood. He never realized that the Loaf-about-the-Forts, the Indians who hung around the posts, were different from those of the wilderness, those who tried to keep their young people away from the white man and his whisky. Parkman did, however, note that there were rocking chairs in the emigrant wagons and that the trappers and mountain men who once worked the beaver and gathered at the lusty rendezvous were now guiding emigrants. It seemed the end of the rugged West was not far away.

Until about 1850 Nebraska was little more than a highway, a roadbed, water or earth, for white men going somewhere beyond. But hired help was required for the growing number of roadhouses, and for the freight and stagecoach stops established about twenty miles apart on the trail, men to maintain the stock for the station, have the team changes in condition and ready to hike to the tongue for the continuous night and day runs west and back. Most of these hands were youths, often living in dugouts and almost as transitory as the stagecoaches they serviced. Some were to attain reputations of various sorts, like the young William F. Cody and James Butler Hickok. Then there were hunters and cooks to feed the drivers and passengers and any others stopping—all three meals usually fried buffalo or venison, with black coffee, saleratus or sourdough bread and sorghum, and sometimes beans, all dished up in tin plate and cup. Generally there were guns and powder and lead for sale, perhaps flour, tea and coffee and the various eases and sundries: physics, cough lozenges, painkillers and arnica, quinine for the ager that reached as far north as Fort Hall, salves and bandages for the chafings and sunburn, and always that universal cure for all the diseases of man, particularly all those covered by the term *colic*—whisky.

Most of the stations were in pleasant spots along streams, particularly up the Little Blue. On these earlier stretches of the trail the softer, the less equipped emigrants began to drop off first, perhaps because a horse was overdriven, sweenied, lamed or stolen, a bull died, a woman sickened in body or heart, the man of the party very ill or crippled, although many went on with sickness and dying in the wagons. Many had to face the long trail without a man, a few with both parents lost, perhaps to cholera or during the Indian uprisings, leaving only the children to go on because there was nothing else to do, the eldest perhaps twelve, or only ten, or eight—children who became men and women in a week, a day, an hour. Many of the journeys were completed by that sheer raw courage and ingenuity that has kept man's line alive when dinosaur and saber-toothed tiger died, died there in the very region where puny man now walked over their great bones, surviving without tooth or claw, his vulnerable back unprotected by wool or scale or shell.

More and more came up the trails without any dream of gold or at least without the heart and the pocketbook to try for California or the more sedate Oregon. These and hundreds of others sought homes no farther west than necessary, looking for the first likely quarter section of the public domain, all practically free during the early years of residence. At first, land along the trails was open only to squatters' rights, to be defended against claim jumpers by gun or combination of guns in the claim clubs, but after the surveyors came and the land offices were set up, the entries were legalized.

The first of the settlers kept close to the Overland Trails of the Platte for protection, even with nothing more than an occasional detachment of troops riding by all the winter months. Sometimes several landseekers came together, perhaps in one wagon, or even afoot, to select a site, step off their 160-acre plots, squinting at the sun for the approximate directions if there was no compass. They drove the temporary corner stakes, sank a dugout into some hillside or bank until logs could be raised, or, farther out on the prairie, sod laid up for a house, perhaps for the woman who would come later, or would not.

Often the landseeker brought his family along, usually in a covered wagon, the man walking beside his ox team, his gaunt face weather-beaten, his clothing sun-bleached. On the wagon seat a worn young woman might be holding a baby on her lap, and a dog might be trotting under the wagon, tongue lolling in the heat. If the man was foresighted, there was a water barrel tied to the side of the wagon bed, if a little more prosperous, a milk cow plodded at the end gate and the handles of an iron-pointed plow stuck out somewhere.

Such a homeseeker would be walking with his face lifted, his eyes squinting into the distant horizon, to where the grass must be un-worn by trail hoofs, grass dense and deep now that the buffalo had retreated, excellent forage for livestock and for prairie fires. Such a man turned firmly from the trail at some high ridge to look over

the country, farther and farther west as the settlements spread, and
north and south of the trail too, anywhere from the Arkansas to the
Niobrara and farther as the Indians were dispossessed. The man beside his oxen would step firmly, giving little notice to the weariness
of his animals, perhaps not even to the pleading face of his young
wife, for he was determined upon the best—a man going out to make
a place for himself and his family.

So the boomer traveled the higher ground looking for earlier
settlers, for water perhaps, and a little timber, a little wood, but
mainly for a likely plot of farm land, corn land, wheat land. This
was true from the 1840's over the next seventy years, the landseeker
pushing westward and northward as the public domain decreased.
Sometimes the grass thinned and the earth broke into ragged bluffs
and canyons or actual bad lands.

The homeseeker's wagon rode the ridges as the gray wolf traveled
them, hunting both sides and ready to dodge out of sight either way
at any sign of danger, Indians perhaps, at least in the Easterner's
mind, and a few times an actual menace. But no Indian scare ever
really stopped the settlers coming. Generally the first real danger was
the boundless sea of unmarked prairie, with perhaps a buffalo stampede in the early days, or prairie fires or the blinding blizzards of
winter. Food was usually a problem from the first day, but less
pressing if the homeseeker had a gun, some marksmanship and the
patience to move upon his game, perhaps on his belly into the wind,
whether upon antelope, deer in a brush patch or smaller game—wild
turkey, grouse and prairie chicken, ducks and geese at the waterways or on spring buffalo wallows. If the settler was a good hunter
he walked with his gun across his forearm, ready for anything that
might flush from the deep grass whipping his knees.

Somewhere, some evening, the homeseeker would drop the wagon
tongue with finality, water and hobble his team while his wife bent
over the supper fire of dead wood or buffalo chips. Afterward they
might lean against a wagon wheel, the baby at the woman's breast,
and look out over the prairie gilded by a sky that blazed beyond
anything they ever saw in the country left behind them, almost any

country. The man might test the grass with his teeth, consider last year's sunflower stalks to gauge the earth's fertility, the height he could expect his corn to grow. Perhaps he dragged a spade from the wagon, struck it deep into the ground, shook out a sod to examine the root system, tried a ball of soil in his hand and nodded to himself.

This was the place.

Usually the settler's first problem was shelter, even for the lonesome bachelor. Those who came in covered wagons might live in them until the first freezing north wind struck them. Then it was time to build. At best it was a frame or log shack with cracks for blizzard snow. More often it was a ruder but warmer soddy or even a dugout into a bank, with a dirt floor and the possibility of wandering stock, or, in the early days, a buffalo stampede coming through the roof. Yet many fine Americans were born in such holes in the earth: senators, oil magnates, doctors, writers, stockmen and preachers—all kinds of people.

Even more urgent than food and shelter was water. The early homeseekers usually located along streams and at springs, but later comers might not find even a drying buffalo wallow within miles of free land. Now and then a settler had to haul every drop of water in a barrel from a creek or pond ten, twelve miles away, from snow to snow. If the settler had any getup at all he sank a well as soon as possible. The first well on the high tables became a sort of mirage, a romantic sort of magnet to the rider of the prairie, and out of this grew the old cowboy saying "Pretty as a gal a-pumpin' water in the wind."

A pump suggested a kind of affluence, although it could be made from old plank ends, the watering trough a hollowed out cottonwood trunk, or a hole; but the pipe, pump rod and cylinder must be bought or picked up somewhere, an unlikely prospect until the hard times drove many settlers out, leaving everything in their hurry to go. The deep-water regions needed a lot of pipe, and while the Plains are generally underlaid with excellent water tables, there are spots from Canada down through Texas where good water sand lies three to five hundred feet down. Such wells, if drawn, required a team, the bucket usually a keg or a long valve-bottomed cylinder big as a stovepipe on the end of the rope.

Bad-water regions attracted witches, dowsers, who grasped their peachtree or willow fork by the two thin ends, one in each hand, the stem held out before them, and plodded impressively over the ground until the stem dipped down. That was the place to dig. Occasionally dowsers made great reputations with their witching on the Plains, until it was discovered that a spade sunk practically anywhere would strike a good flow of water somewhere between ten and sixty feet down.

With thousands of poorly equipped novices, greenhorns, digging wells, accidents were inevitable. Every community has its stories of well cave-ins, planks slipping down the hole and perhaps hitting the digger on the head or a rope breaking, even through a practical joke. But the worst accidents came from open or badly covered wells. Perhaps a child slipped down the depths, with the entire community working in shifts to rescue at least the body; perhaps a horse-backer rode into one while chasing the *remuda*, or a milk cow blundered in, preferably on a pleasant Sunday afternoon.

One night in Custer County, Nebraska, a settler named Carlin, while driving across an empty and unfamiliar prairie, struck the shadowy walls of an old deserted soddy. As he turned his team aside, one of the horses lost his footing for an instant. The man got out to investigate, and stepped off into space, crashing down an old well, deep but fortunately with thick muck in the bottom. Stunned, the man managed to stand up, in mud and water to his armpits. Coughing, spitting, wiping his eyes, he felt around in the darkness. He was inside a curbing about three feet across, with one small star shining down from far, far off.

Chilling, in pain from a sprained ankle and a broken rib, the man ran his hand over the rotting, slimy old curbing. With his jackknife, tied to his wrist with a bandana because it must not be lost, not slip from his awkward hand, he managed to pry out a curling board and wedge it into cracks across a corner, and then another board and another, making a little platform. Carefully, painfully, he climbed up on it and crouched there, his good foot braced against the far wall to wait for dawn. He knew there was no one within miles to hear his loudest yells, and if his wife and baby were ever to see him again it was up to him and the jackknife.

The first light of day showed that he was down perhaps 150 feet, in a well that was tightly curbed most of the way, and with his rib painful, his ankle swollen to bursting, unable to bear any weight. Bracing himself as well as he could above the hole, he hacked pieces of board from the curbing and wedged them across the corners for steps until his hands were torn and bleeding, his back as painful as his ankle. But he made at least fifty feet before the light faded and he had to build a perch of crosspieces for the night. It wasn't safe enough for a man who might move in sleep, but the best he could do.

With the pain and the worry he managed to get through the second night without dozing. By the next afternoon he had worked himself up to the end of the curbing, but was still far from the top, the walls crumbling clay and very dangerous. Carefully he cut steps into the uncertain soil, bracing himself across the three-foot hole as he eased his weight cautiously from one toe- or kneehold to the next. Near the top he reached a four-foot piece of round curbing, half loose and small enough to slip down the hole if any weight was put upon it. Now at last it seemed impossible to get out, to save himself, skinned and bruised and worn as he was. But somehow he kept from looking down, made himself dig very carefully around behind the curbing, and finally pulled himself up and over the caving edge of the well, out into the open. Exhausted he crawled away, far away, clutching the weeds and sod with his bloody hands even when he finally let himself slip into the darkness of sleep.

In the late 1870's windmills came into use on the Plains, first the homemade ones that almost anyone could afford if pipe and pump rod for those deep wells could be managed somehow. Later the manufactured product was produced in several Nebraska communities. Soon many western cow towns looked like flower gardens with the daisy faces of the windmills turned busily into the wind. But there were still pretty girls pumping water.

Girls and women were scarce in the early West, particularly the footloose, the unmarried. Many a man hit for the frontier to escape some woman's hold, only to yearn for her or her counterpart in his lonely sod shanty. And perhaps the woman who came out to sit beside her man on the wagon seat found that he had become a stranger through his months in this far country. It was even more difficult if the young woman was from the Old Country—Ireland, Scotland, Germany or Sweden, say—one of those who promised to wait while her man went to find a home, perhaps singing jubilantly as he departed for America:

> The clover there grows nine feet tall,
> With buttered bread and cheese for all.*

But many girls never came, never waited, and the young bride on the settler's wagon seat might be a compromise, a young woman ignored in the home community, but now, out where there were no others, she would do. Perhaps she took advantage of her unexpected bargaining position and demanded the groom's allegiance to the new Victorianisms, such as the W.C.T.U., and to the woman suffrage that was to establish a hundred reforms. Many a groom who had avoided taking on any of the "vile wilderness habits," as some lady periodicals called them, nevertheless had to promise that after marriage he would never drink intoxicating liquor, chew tobacco, play cards or swear. Strong drink was often easily avoided, with towns, even saloons, far away and money mighty scarce, but parodies of the temperance songs reached as far as the winds:

> The man who drinks the red, red wine
> Will never be a beau of mine.
> The man who is a whisky sop
> Will never hear my corset pop.

* From "Amerika," an old Swiss immigrant song.

To give up chewing tobacco was more difficult, and an open confession to any neighbor that the new husband was being run by his woman. With his mouth dry from the dusty fields anyway, the desperate man might chew grass or bitter willow and cottonwood leaves, or even coffee to stave off the craving for nicotine, or he might send away for some advertised "sure cure for the vile weed." Perhaps he sneaked an occasional rough twist of tobacco or a plug of Battle Axe and faced the anger and the tears of betrayal.

"We married anything that got off the stagecoach or the railroad," old-timers used to say, and so the bride might be a mail-order woman obtained through one of the heart-and-hand papers passed on from settler to settler. In the pioneer regions most patrons of such papers actually sought marriage partners, naturally stretching the truth a little about age, physical appearance and wealth. Apparently in those days few tried to lure the lonely out of their pitiful little savings, perhaps even their lives. Sometimes the mail-order woman did turn the man's hopeful stagecoach or railroad ticket into money and never appeared, but most of them were happy to come, at least until they saw the wild country. Many such unions, bound by mutual need and dependence, founded solid and even excellent families.

Of course there was no way to compel a mail-order woman to marry the man when she saw him, or he her, or to make the new wife stay—except by the persuasion of long, unmarked distances to the stage route or the railroad tracks, with prairie walking not good for tender feet. There are stories of extreme measures used by some of the husbands, such as a tie rope, or locked leg hobbles, but the more common and efficacious expedient was early pregnancy.

It was not surprising that a bride from a settled region, often from a cultured, sheltered girlhood, was shocked by her new home and its community, if there was one. Whether the bride came by mail order, by compromise, as a boyhood sweetheart or a wife of some years, she might leave the government claim, with or without her husband. Usually only one in four original entrymen, first settlers on a piece of land, remained to patent it; in the more difficult regions and in hard times and panic, only one in ten or even fifteen stayed. The maladjusted, the misfits—economic, social or emotional, men and women—normally drifted to the frontier. Many of these were further unsettled by the hardship and isolation, to end in a mental or penal institution or a suicide's grave. Sometimes they stopped a bullet, but usually they moved on or fled back to the relatives or in-laws. If the young bride stayed she might, in the rare case, have to face Indian scares or actual Indian depredations and murder. Most certainly she would see drouth, perhaps grasshoppers and ten-cent corn, often followed by the banker's top buggy come to attach the mortgaged oxen, the horses, the children's only milk cow. The wife might go into the field beside her husband or, if he was struck by illness, injury or death, fill his place entirely. Some of the more determined women of the Plains turned to politics, to the Grangers or to the Populists, like Mary Elizabeth Lease, who advised Kansas farmers "to raise less corn and more hell." Many followed the angry suffragettes stumping the West, encouraged when Wyoming gave women the vote in 1869, and Colorado soon afterward, followed by other western states, four by the end of Cleveland's administration. But not Nebraska, not even when the state was practically surrounded by woman-suffrage territory. Yet even here the settler's wife worked for school, church, lyceum or Chautauqua and for better roads to town.

In the end the Plains woman might be as weatherbeaten and wrinkled as an old boot top but still standing firm beside her husband and children, grown strong together while overcoming the calamities that dog the vulnerable—the wiry old settler at her side deserving the ultimate accolade of the Plains as a good husband: "He never laid a hand on his wife."

The first year or so most of the settlers on the Plains lived off the country, with much of the required lore from the Indians, directly, or through old-timers, not only the ways of weather that might save lives but much knowledge of fruits and herbs and wild game. The newcomers heard the fantastic tales of the one-horned creature of the mountains, the tiger of the Loup country and down on the Smoky Hill River, the blazing-eyed serpents reported flying over the Missouri. Most important, they learned about the animals that yielded flesh and fur and skin.

The earliest settlers often tried to make a little cash money hunting buffalo for hides and the meat, at least for their own table if there was no market. They learned the Indian way of preserving it even in summer heat. Well dried, jerked, the meat kept for months and was good with a touch of prairie onion or garlic in the boiling kettle, or lifted out and marinated in spices and wild-grape vinegar for pot roasting. With vegetables the jerky made an excellent boiled dinner or pie. Sometimes the cooked meat was chopped into cornmeal for scrapple—until there was pork. Lambs quarter, wild everywhere, made a tasty spring dish, particularly when served with homemade vinegar from the wild fruits—currant, plum or grape— started with mother of vinegar probably carried west in a bottle. Often the early settlers had no fat except buffalo tallow for years, using it for fry cakes and doughnuts, for dipped candles and to make lye soap from wood ashes, to waterproof the cowhide boots and shoes, and to grease paper or flour sacking for the window holes until glass could be managed.

Long after the buffalo disappeared from the region there were occasional bighorn sheep in the Wild Cat Hills and the edges of the badlands, elk in the breaks, deer in the canyons and buckbrush stretches, and the elegant-throated antelope on the prairie. The wild turkey vanished early, man-shy, as were the great flocks of plovers, but grouse and prairie chickens were plentiful, the quail and cottontail rabbits very good hot from the frying pan, with soda biscuits and red gravy at breakfast time. Ducks nested around the prairie lakes and marshes, the mallards moving into the high ridges. October brought a clouding of migratory flocks: several varieties of geese lordly in their honking V's among the curious winding flight of the sandhill cranes and the swiftly veering ducks. With a gun, powder and shot, or a shot mold, a man could provide his family with meats to be envied by a king. And if the powder was too scarce in the hard times that perhaps had sent the homeseekers west in the first place, a clever man, a boy or even a lady homesteader could learn to snare or trap grouse and prairie chickens with string, and catch rabbits in deadfalls or twist them out of their holes with a doubled length of wire armed with a few hooks until the more practical barbed wire was invented.

Good hunters close to the trails, or later the railroads, often shipped frozen ducks and grouse by the barrel to jobbers in Omaha, Kansas City, and Chicago. Winters they could take wolf, coyote, skunk, badger, ermine (winter weasel) and perhaps fox for the hide. There were a few otter, some beaver and a quantity of mink along the streams, and always muskrats by the thousands in the lakes and marshes. Out west, Indians paid what they could for an occasional eagle to get the breath feathers, the delicate white-fluffed ones under the tail of the golden eagle, necessary for their war bonnets, their ceremonial regalia.

Even with the shrinking of the buffalo herds, the Overland Trails a wide dead path along the favorite river of the Sioux and the Cheyennes, they made singularly little trouble for the early home-seekers, perhaps because there were few real Indian-haters among them. The settlers along the usual travois and hunting trails often saw parties stop on a rise and look under their shading palms down upon these curious, restless palefaces who always seemed to be running somewhere, always with talk, talk in the mouth. Now another kind of whites was coming in, to stay, to turn the grass upside down.

Yet when the lonely new settler's wife suddenly saw an Indian peer in at her window, particularly at night, it wasn't surprising that she ran to stuff her small children under the bed and send a kettle of boiling water or a charge of buckshot into the man's face, and perhaps brought retaliation. Generally, however, the settlers soon discovered that to the Plains Indian it was an insult not to go lift the lodge flap of a newcomer. Good manners demanded that he look in on the new whites in the country, see how it was with them. The window was plainly the place to look in. If he had intended an attack or any mischief he would have come more stealthily. Sometimes the peering Indian was hungry and hoping to see the settler eating. In

Plains Indian society so long as anyone had food, everybody ate. In fact, from Plymouth Rock west, the red man shared with every hungry paleface who appeared at his lodge so long as there was anything in the kettle or on the coals.

All through the early settlement period there was the usual complaint against the Pawnees as thieves and beggars, meaning generally that they came hungry and ate up everything in sight, which seemed logical in the Indian eyes, since the land and the grass were theirs. Occasionally horses and mules were driven off along the trail and sometimes a man who interfered was shot. But there were lone settler shacks all over the eastern part of the state, unprotected and without locks, and seldom molested. Then in 1854 the government's special Sioux chief was killed by the cannon of an arrogant young West Pointer who had dragged his weapon into a peaceful camp of Indians waiting for their annuities, long delayed. Grattan's shot started a general Plains war that lasted thirty-six years and fostered the extermination policy toward the Indians. With two brief exceptions it disturbed few settlers but it cost the army several other swaggering young officers besides that first one.

The next year Harney came up the trail to punish the Sioux who killed Grattan. As usual, the Indians who could be caught were friendlies with no reason to flee. Harney found the peaceful Little Thunder camped on the Blue Water, a short canyoned creek flowing down into the North Platte. The colonel conferred with the chief and the headmen, making a smoke and a parley until his troops had sneaked into position. Then he started the shelling, the bursting cannon balls blowing the fleeing women and children out of the rocks and bluffs. The action earned Harney the eternal name of Squaw Killer, and the furious, burning anger in the Sioux and their Cheyenne allies. This brooded along with increasing small encounters, particularly with raw eastern recruits who sought Indian scalps as big-game hunters pursued their trophies. Added to this was the aggravation of the new gold rush to Pikes Peak, cutting new trails through the buffalo ranges left in Kansas and Colorado. The peaceful Christianized Minnesota Sioux were driven to an uprising, with

settlers killed and captured, many, many Indians shot and many good
men to be hanged by the neck, the newspapers and the Indian camps
of the Plains full of angry stories but not the same ones. Then there
was another gold strike, this time in Montana, with more men running through the north country, scaring the game there too.

But mostly the trouble came from the growing urge of the white
man to take all the Indian's land, clear him out, exterminate him as
one would a troublesome varmint. To accomplish this the noble red
man, the free and natural man that the travelers sought and praised
as late as 1850, suddenly became—in newspapers and magazines, on
public and congressional platforms—a bloodthirsty savage. Although
the Indian was hungry through the scarcening of the buffalo, the
growing wildness for the bow, an embargo was put on all trade of
arms and ammunition. The meat racks became barer than ever, the
capture of guns and powder more urgent, not only for the hunt but
against the soldiers marching thick into the country where no white
man was to step. Every day the wild young men were harder to control by the treaty chiefs, whom they called fools, the fools of the
white man.

During the spring and early summer of 1864 there were repeated
raids on the stock of the stage stations and road ranches of the trails
crossing the Plains, and for any guns and ammunition that could
be picked up, with occasional emigrants killed. A chief or two trying
to make peace was shot down by the troops. Early in August the
governor of Colorado advised citizens to hunt down the Indians as
they would any predator, kill every hostile they met, which put a
hot gun into the hands of every braggart, every uneasy, frightened
or covetous white man.

The answer was war. August 7 the southern Sioux and the
Cheyennes closed the Platte and the Smoky Hill trails so completely
that not a wheel turned. Even the eastern mail from Denver had to
be sent out around by California and across the jungle of the Pana-
manian isthmus. In Nebraska the Indians struck at practically the
same hour all along the Overland Trail. The newspapers reported
the stations and road ranches from Fort Kearny westward aflame,

many freight trains too, and fifty, sixty people killed, in addition to
all those caught in an even more appalling raid, that down the Little
Blue. After the first scare wore off it was plain that comparatively
few lives were lost along the Platte, because the Indians struck first
at Plum Creek, on the telegraph line that had put the short-lived,
ineffectual and over-romanticized Pony Express out of business. The
alarm from there was sent over all the route west, and east to Omaha,
but in the valley of the Little Blue, with no telegraph to warn the
settlers and the trail stations, the loss of life was considerable, and
the stories, without exaggerations, were enough to throw the Nebraska frontier into a flaming panic.

Fortunately it was too late in the season to catch emigrant parties
heading west, cutting down on the number of people killed, particularly women and children. But the settlers all along the border
fled eastward, leaving buildings, crops, stock, everything. A few did
hide out, hoping to save something, perhaps the milk cow or the corn
patch. At Grand Island the determined German settlers fortified the
O.K. Store and stayed. Otherwise, for the first time in almost forty
years, the entire Platte region was dead except around the small post
of Kearny and a few scattered troop movements farther on. Not
even a trader pack train moved on either side of the river.

Gradually stories of horror and heroism reached the outside world,
multiplied and grew. But some were as tall as the sky standing over
the Plains in their actuality. Along the telegraph route stripped and
painted Indians surprised freight outfits until the warning got out.
They ran the horses and mules off, cut the harness to pieces, pawed
through the wagons for guns and ammunition, and burned some of
the outfits. They killed the men they caught and perhaps beat the
sunflowers or nearby brush patches for any who might have escaped.
Then they hurried on, finding more and more places deserted, but
to be ransacked and perhaps left in flames.

Off southeast, where the trail left the telegraph line of the Platte,
it was different. Without warning of any attack some of the settlers
and station keepers watched the Indians come without uneasiness,
particularly if the men had no arms but their usual bows. Many

whites who might have escaped were left scalped and dead on the ground. Stories vary, but apparently six or seven of the Eubank family, newcomers to the Little Blue, were killed right around the place. The young wife of one of the sons, the small child in her arms, and a sixteen-year-old guest, Laura Roper, made it to the timber. The three were captured, perhaps through the child's crying, and swept away. According to one story, the crying annoyed the Indians so much that they killed the baby, but when Mrs. Eubank was brought into Fort Laramie the next spring she had a small child with her. She was brought in by a couple of friendly Cheyenne chiefs who had bought her from the captors to return her to her people. But the commander at Fort Laramie was a drunken man, and when the woman was turned over to him he had the two Cheyenne chiefs hanged in chains and left there for all to see until the bodies fell to pieces. There was a noticeable decline in good deeds by Indians around Laramie after that.

Laura Roper's return was quieter. Newspaper accounts said she was brought in to Fort Lyon, Colorado, the fall of 1864, apparently for a thousand-dollar ransom. She denied this. Sixty-five years later she returned to the scene of her capture to help mark the spot, by then in a well-mechanized farming region, the few artifacts left from the Indians of the 1860's ancient as from some prehistoric time.

But the story of the Indian war of 1864 that was retold most often and in many versions is the one of the two Martin boys. Apparently they were haying with their father in the Platte valley some distance southwest of Grand Island. As they were about to start home with their loads, the Indians attacked the father's rack. He dug himself into the hay, and with his repeating rifle wounded one Indian and hit the pony of another, who whipped off toward the two sons and their saddle mare some distance away. They turned their ox team loose and jumped on the old mare, both boys kicking hard to get her into a gallop and out of sight around a knoll. The Indians were still chasing the father and his rifle, his frightened horses tearing over the prairie, the hay rack bouncing to this side and that while he tried to take good aim on the warriors whooping alongside. One of them managed to put an arrow into the man's throat, down into the collar-bone. The team couldn't stop at the house, but the wounded man slid off as they tore past. Although the Indians were almost upon him, the daughter held them off with the shotgun while Mrs. Martin dragged her husband into the house.

Most of the Indians followed the runaway team and rack, but one swung out past the barn for the herding pony there, and saw the boys hidden about a quarter of a mile off. He whooped and several of the others turned back for the boys, who tried to whip the terri-fied mare off to some brush and timber, but she whirled and started homeward to her colt, the boys clinging on as well as they could, the Indians after them, not shooting at first, perhaps wanting to capture them. One warrior tried to turn the mare by flapping his blanket at her, and finally he drew his bow. One arrow struck Henry, the boy behind, in the elbow, the second hit him under the shoulder blade and went clear through his chest and into Robert's backbone, pinning the brothers together. Henry started to faint, wavered on the plunging mare, and slid off, taking Bob along. The Indians caught the mare and returned. Henry seemed dead, with the arrow clear through him, so they hit Bob on the head several times and rode back to the house to help themselves.

In the meantime the Martins, seeing the boys overtaken and cer-tainly killed, had fled, heading toward Fort Kearny. When the In-dians seemed done with plundering the place and night came, the boys managed to crawl to the barn and into the bed kept there for emigrants, the arrows still in them.

On the way to Kearny the Martins overtook a westbound freight outfit apparently unaware of the raids. The men would not return for the bodies of the boys that night, but promised to go in the morning. By then an eastbound train came through, moving fast to get out of the dangerous region. The Martins joined it and at their home found the boys, still hidden but alive. The arrows were jerked out, but with such difficulty that Henry lost consciousness. When the wounds were dressed the boys were loaded on a wagon filled with hay and headed over the 150 miles to find a doctor at Nebraska

City, on the Missouri. But the rough trail started new bleeding from Henry's chest, the pain so severe that he lost consciousness again and lay like dead for a long time. Frightened, the father decided to camp and then, although injured too, he made the dangerous ride to Fort Kearny, and was told that they had no one to help him; that the post was already stripped of troops, the surgeon working night and day with the wounded brought in from all around.

Hopeless, George Martin returned to his sons. The rest had strengthened the sturdy Henry, and—with the Nebraska City doctor certainly away by this time helping the wounded, even if the boy could live to get there—they started back home, driving very slowly, avoiding every bump and hollow, trying to believe that the Indians were far away by now.

Although it was almost a year before Henry could stand straight and do much work, he recovered and lived to be seventy-nine. Robert died first, in the late 1890's, never free of spinal trouble where the arrow had pinned his brother to his back.

It was a time of storytelling around the forts, where the bull-whackers loafed while trains were held up to add together until they were strong enough to break through the Indian blockade, perhaps with a borrowed fieldpiece or two. That seemed the most that the laggard government would do, instead of sending troops "to blow the Indians to hell," as many urged, forgetting that other war down south. The whackers spun out the atrocity stories and added a bit of wry humor here and there, including the favorite story told by the peaceful Indians around the squaw camps, the soldiers' women, at the posts. At the height of the August raids a much-bedraggled woman of around forty had come plodding in and got to a smooth-faced young eastern officer of the day. Shocked at her story, he went to the commander of the post, begging for action. The hard-bitten old campaigner plainly had other things on his mind.

"But sir, she has been ah—attacked," the blushing O.D. insisted, "attacked by twenty painted Cheyenne devils, violated!"

The roar of the commandant had echoed all over the empty parade ground. The woman was Salt Lake Kate, the toughest woman of the trails. She had been making one bullwhacker camp after another for years, her profession so plain that no Indian would have touched her, not even for her scalp, which was full of buffalo burrs anyway.

That fall Colonel Chivington struck the Cheyennes at Sand Creek in Colorado, once more catching peaceful elements instead of the depredators. Black Kettle had taken his people where their agent told them to go to keep out of the way of troops chasing the hostiles. The colonel knew just where the Indians were, and that they felt secure in the agent's promise. He had no trouble falling upon them out of a cold November dawn, killing many, mostly women and children. Some felt that the whites struck along the trails in the summer were avenged, except that most of the killing along the Little Blue was by the Sioux Indians, chiefly the Brule, who were avenging a few of all the women and children killed by Harney on the Blue Water nine years ago.

The Indian war continued some time longer out west of the settlements, to the annihilation of Fetterman far up in Wyoming in 1866. There was some raiding along the new railroad along the Platte in 1867, but even the news of this was practically lost in the postwar rush to the free-land regions, the land really free now through the Homestead Act, which offered 160 acres for the $14 filing fee and a five-year residence—Uncle Sam betting 160 acres against your $14 you couldn't live on the land five years, as some put it when the hot winds blew in out of Kansas.

The new settlers came from all over the world, but mostly from America—veterans, men who lost their jobs in war industry, and Southerners from devastated areas—all hoping for a new start, many for a new forgetting. The rainfall increased, "following the plow," the hopeful told each other, to the all-time high in 1869. This was very important for the new settler, whose first problem was to feed his family and his stock. The many who didn't own a team and plow tried to trade handwork for breaking, at least enough for a strip of sod corn and potatoes, both of these perhaps dropped in the furrow behind the plow. The corn was usually planted on the breaking by spade, the planter, man or woman, carrying the seed in an apron or bag hanging open. At every step—every other one for a gentle-walking woman—the spade was thrust down into the sod, worked sideways to widen the slit, two kernels dropped in, the spade swung out and the foot brought down on the cut to seal it. All day long, up and down the field, the rhythmic swing of step and thrust was sustained. Millions of acres were planted this way, sometimes with beans and pumpkin seeds mixed with the corn for a stretch.

Before the invention of barbed-wire fencing, or afterward if the pocketbook was too flat, wild animals and longhorned range cattle had to be kept away from the crops. Children proved excellent herders as well as running scarecrows against birds and deer. Even coyotes were as attracted to the fine sweet watermelons as they were to dominicker pullets. The best protection against varmints of all kinds was an alert mongrel shepherd dog or a twelve-year-old boy armed with the delight of his life, an old shotgun, even if it kicked as hard backward as forward.

The second year the sod was backset, fine for small grain, oats, rye and particularly the newer varieties of wheat, all perhaps broadcast from a bag slung under one arm (much like the figure of the Sower striding the tower of the Nebraska state capitol, sixty-five years later). The seed was covered by harrow or drag, or, lacking machinery, a heavily branched tree, a hackberry perhaps, might be drawn over the ground by patient oxen. Later mechanical seeders behind fast-paced horses or mules brought bonanza wheat farming to middle and western Nebraska as they did to the Dakotas, to Kansas and to Montana.

With the panic of 1873, and the usual drouth that follows ten-cent corn, came the grasshoppers. There had been rumors of hopper devastation in Colorado and Kansas. Nebraska had some too, enough so the settlers grinned a little at the softies across the state line who let a few nibblers alarm them like that. Then one afternoon a gray cloud appeared in Southern Nebraska, with a curious fluttering hum that seemed of the earth and the air, and a shimmering in the sun that came from millions of wings. Here and there the grasshoppers began to drop until every leaf, every twig, every small branch trembled and bent under their weight. Some of the settlers ran out to flail at them with hoes, with sacks; some tried smudges and fire; some lifted their faces into the dropping, crawling hail and cursed or prayed, according to their nature. Train wheels spun on the tracks as in grease from the hoppers. Milk cows stampeded; women cried when their flower gardens were gone. Some screamed, some sat in brooding silence that was not to be broken for days, in one case almost a year. And when the hoppers finally lifted, there was no leaf or gnawable branch left, only winter-bare brush and rows of holes where the carrots and turnips had been. Even the spade handles were chewed where palm grease had soaked the wood. Chickens, horses and cows wandered a while and were taken away or lay down to die. Now the trails were dark once more, with settlers heading east this time, leaving the country.

Those who stayed saw the rains return, great regions turn golden in improved strains of wheat. Corn, vastly improved from the varieties that heated at old Fort Atkinson, was flourishing over most of the Plains, the first crop of the new settlers.

Many homeseekers came to the plains in colonies: Germans, Swedes, Danes, Scots, Irishmen, English, Welsh, Czechs, Poles, Frenchmen, and Dutch. Colonies arrived by region too, perhaps from Kentucky, upper York State, Iowa, Massachusetts, Cincinnati or Philadelphia, and by sects, such as Mennonites, Hutterites, some Latter-day Saints who didn't go on to Utah, some Campbellites and many Catholics. Atheists seemed less inclined to bunch up, but most communities had at least one or two, perhaps at the crossroads blacksmith shop or at the nearest town livery barn.

From the first there were diversions, perhaps a house raising of log or sod; church, Sunday-school picnics and prayer meetings and play parties instead of dances if the feet were what the early settlers called "Methodist." Sorghum boilings, taffy pulls and walnutting came in the fall, after the berrying and the plum, chokecherry and grape gatherings were over. Winters there were pie and basket suppers, literaries with spelldowns and debates, shivarees for the newlyweds, and feather strippings where duck and goose ticks and pillows had to be eked out with chicken feathers, to be separated from their stiff and prickly quills by the young people at a party. When there were three settlers in a community, political gatherings started, later perhaps protest meetings, and meetings to organize schools, churches and counties. Mutual-protection committees were formed against this or that oppression, and these too offered some relief for the lonely, the isolated.

If anyone had a fiddle, a mouth harp or a squeeze box there could be dancing as soon as two, three or, better, four families located within a half day's wagon travel or a day's ride for the ranch cowboys. Every settlement had a little music or managed to get some now and then. Brass bands followed the plow perhaps more surely than the rain. What later became Holt County, Nebraska, had three settlements interested in music from the start. One family had four key bandsmen, which brought in more, including a man with an E-flat cornet. Another E-flat cornet man started a band practically without an experienced player. In one town a band of eighteen, twenty members was organized and led by the local barber, a Negro. Band contests were held after the fall crops were in and the hunter's moon was full. Communities somehow managed to get uniforms even if the seats of the everyday Levis were patched. This music was for the people, with a place in every event, including funerals.

Some distance out of O'Neill an old bachelor, called Daddy Cook, lived on his homestead all alone. He always wore a mother hubbard instead of the usual man's rig, and pinched every penny until he had enough to hire the O'Neill band to help him celebrate his sixtieth birthday. He also hired a carryall in town to haul the band out to a clump of spindly cottonwoods. There he started a parade, the band in bright blue uniforms, the brasses shining, with Daddy in the lead in his mother hubbard and sunbonnet. He marched them several hundred yards to the little railroad depot, and back to the carryall, where a keg of beer was tapped, and iced pop, baked ham, fried chicken and loaves of bread were set out for everybody. Afterward the band got back on the carryall, the whip was cracked, the horses started up, leaving Daddy Cook waving his sunbonnet in farewell, the sun shining on his glistening bald head.

Rainfall on the Plains varied greatly, not only in quantity but by season. Some years it all came in the spring, others in the winter, or in cloudbursts that washed out the Fourth of July picnics. Some years, the Overlanders didn't see the sun for days through dust so thick they could scarcely breathe—yellow dust that made them cough and fever. It was stirred up in the Southwest, old-timers claimed, by unusual ground winds, meaning winds that struck the earth at a downward angle and boiled up great moving walls of it, to ride the sky northward, the same wind tearing at the bare stretches of the Platte, too, adding gray to the yellow there.

Sometimes these strong winds drove prairie fires roaring over the Plains, particularly in long-grass country. The worst were usually in the fall, set by carelessness, or malice, or by late lightning. Often the night horizon was reddened most of the way around, the nearer fires sending streaks toward the zenith like northern lights, the smoke thick enough to choke the throat, burn the eye, and turn the sun of day to blood. Some falls scarcely a day passed without the pearling smoke of a prairie fire in the sky. Buffalo herds stampeded, but were sometimes caught by a swift change of wind. In the early days the fires burned unarrested except by rain, by wide streams, barren deserts, or shifting winds that turned the flames to feed upon their own ashes. Later sparks from railroad engines, or smolderings from empty bottles focusing the rays of the sun like a burning glass, might be fanned into leaping blazes by the high wind. Homes, stock, hay and range on areas larger than New England went up in smoke, sometimes people too, although from the first the Indians had told the white men, "When fire come run for naked ground—sand maybe, or gravel, or water. Go on some place with no grass and dig in if you can. Do not run, the fire is too fast."

The worst case of running from a prairie fire came when the white man was rather long in the region. In October 1873, in settled

Saline County, Nebraska, the wind swept the smoke of a great fire toward a country schoolhouse. One of the mothers hurried over and, against the teacher's most earnest objections, took her own children and some others related to her out and started home. As the fire came close they began to run like frightened quail in the smoke and flames. Some took shelter in a neighbor's stable and were driven out when the building went up in a blaze. By then the children fell, one after another, the mother trying to rip off their burning clothing, and dying too, there among them. Afterward they were all found, scattered over the blackened, smoldering prairie, some literally roasted. Seven were dead there; the rest died a few days later— ten children and the mother lost. At the school the teacher had taken the pupils who remained with her to a nearby piece of bare breaking and got them all through without even a scorched eyebrow or coat-tail. Ironically, the schoolhouse was missed by the fire, left untouched on the blackened prairie.

But even the worst fire of fall finally had to die under the snows that carried their own menace, a menace not completely dispelled by modern communication, or by cars and airplanes. The blizzard of the Plains was and is particularly dangerous for the tenderfoot, the newcomer, because it is often preceded by days and perhaps immediate hours of such benign calm, such deceptive warmth and sweetness of air. But even in January the thermometer can drop from a warm and pleasant seventy-five above to thirty below within a few hours, the golden sun gone in a freezing, stinging drive of snow that shuts out everything beyond arms' length, a roaring blizzard that no living creature faces very far and lives.

The first great blizzard that cost many lives on the Plains was the buffalo hunters' storm, the one early in 1872, right after the pleasant midwinter hunt of Duke Alexis of Russia down in the Medicine Creek country. He had scarcely drunk the last toast to the troops, the frontiersmen and Sioux Indians who had made a convincing spectacle for him, and taken the train for the mountains, when the blizzard struck. With the rising unemployment in the East and the hard times, the Plains were full of buffalo hunters, many of them greenhorns, lacking the sense to let their horses have their heads in the blinding storm. They were found dead all the way from the Platte country into the Texas Panhandle, and no telling how many were never discovered. In the meantime the surgeons at the army posts from Kearny and McPherson down to Fort Dodge were busy amputating frozen hands and feet, even legs, as they turned gangrenous, not only of the hunters but troopers too, some freighters and an occasional old-timer caught in bad luck.

The winters of 1885 and 1886 were the Big Die-Ups of the cattlemen, when so many lost practically all their stock running loose on the prairie. These were hard winters, the grass under snow so long that the cattle starved. But January 12, 1888, brought the blizzard still called the schoolchildren's storm because so many died in it. As could be expected, the new settlers of the free-land boom of the eighties were usually not prepared to believe the reports of the Dakota winters, meaning a hard blizzard winter anywhere on the upper plains. They laughed a little at the old-timers' warning, in the warm weather: "Nothing between us and the North Pole except bob-wire fence."

The newcomers didn't understand the unusualness of Arctic owls suddenly appearing like silent-winged ghosts in the fine Indian summer. There was almost no winter into January, the midday hours of the twelfth warm and curiously hushed, to turn into a roaring icy blast out of the north, blinding, impossible to face, and full of winter lightning and thunder. The storm seems to have reached most of the upper Plains about the same time, around three, four o'clock in the afternoon, when the schoolchildren were getting ready to start home, many afoot over miles of open prairie. Accounts of the lost ones came from everywhere. A pathetic story in Dodge County told of two sisters, thirteen and eight, who died on their way home. The elder of the girls had taken off her coat and fascinator to put around her sister. A song written about the two carried this refrain:

> Dying in the night and tempest,
> Dying in the cru-el snow.

Where the blizzard started earlier, before the children left for home, some of the teachers kept them at school. If there was a house nearby, some tried to get there, perhaps by tying the children together. An imaginative young teacher who had no rope drew the arm out of each child's left coatsleeve and tied the sleeve to the right arm of the one ahead. Then she took the lead, a strong boy bringing up the end. These and the children who stayed at the schoolhouses were the fortunate ones. Near Plainview a teacher tried to take three young pupils, two nine and one six, to her boarding place only about two hundred yards off, but north against the storm. They never got there. Lost, they were driven by the blizzard wind until they hit a haystack, but too late. Although the storm, mercifully short, had lifted long before morning, the children were dead. The teacher managed to get to a house a quarter of a mile off for help. She lost both feet above the ankles and the use of one hand. Another teacher, alone, got to a haystack and buried herself there for four days before she was rescued. Both legs were amputated, but she died anyway.

The most appalling story came from Running Water, just across the South Dakota line. Apparently the teacher left the schoolhouse with nine pupils. Not tied together, they were scattered almost at once by the furious drive of the storm and never found each other again. It was some time before the bodies were all located, some not until most of the snow was gone.

"Watch the buzzards," an old trapper in the community advised. He knew. He had lost a partner in a winter gun accident and didn't find him until the buzzards began to circle.

When the sun came out over the Plains it brought one of the prairie marvels, a winter mirage. Here a house, there a hill or a clump of winter trees, usually far below the horizon somewhere, suddenly stood tall and shimmering in the clear morning air that danced over the mountainous drifts. Gradually it was discovered from the Omaha, Denver and Chicago papers that over two hundred people had lost their lives in that short, swift storm—two hundred from a region still largely unsettled domain. It seemed that the local papers dwelt mainly on the blizzard's unusual brevity, not on the dead. Perhaps they were afraid of alarming next spring's emigrants, cutting down on the land boom, particularly out along the western railroads. But, as with any calamity, tall tales grew up. One told of snow a hundred feet deep on the level out west, the great cattle herds all dead and the people too, even those in the stone-walled penitentiaries. Railroads were rolling up all their tracks west of Chicago, turning the whole country over to the Arctic owls and the snow maggots. Only one creature escaped alive, the drummer who brought the story out.

But the blizzard-fertilized earth was unusually dark and mellow in the spring, rolling smoothly from the plow, and once more the trails leading west were dark with the wagons of the land-hungry, the seekers after homes.

VII Speculators—

"All the main streets in Nebraska lead east," a runner for a Boston investment firm wrote his lady friend back in Massachusetts in 1890. It was a provincial statement, an ironic half-truth of the Plains, the direction in which the wealth was drained, if not the one in which wheels still moved.

There had been a sort of overreaching in the trans-Missouri country during the early 1850's, as in all the nation—much like a boy plunging into some vast and impossible venture to act out his preposterous dreams. True, the short-lived schemes to navigate the Rockies and to attack Canada had been given up by then. Even the old, old infantile fantasy of owning another human being, body and soul—somebody to do your work, accept all your tantrums and tyrannies without protest, and your quixotic kindnesses as well—this too was playing out, although the South clung to it with blind tenacity.

But other dreams were beguiling the young nation, including the one of hurtling across unmeasured miles in what were called coffins on wheels or rolling parlors of red plush and gilt, but were more often boxcars, like those for animals, equipped with plank benches for emigrants—rude cars that need never be stopped to feed and water the weary occupants. The welfare of the emigrants was not the business of the railroad.

By 1850 the Plains had ceased to be a vague sort of border exile to which the government herded the expropriated tribes of the East. With the annexation of California and the addition of Washington and Oregon Territories, the Indian country had become an awkward sort of hole in the heart of the nation, a little like the hollow in what seemed a fine potato.

The proposed Kansas-Nebraska Act to establish two new territories threatened the whole Indian frontier so hopefully inaugurated by the romantics and evasionists less than a generation before. The Act fanned the hope of the extreme expansionists, a hope smoldering even before the Louisiana Purchase but sometimes no more than a firefly along the dark Missouri bottoms, and as heatless. Now, with the possibility of the new territories, and a railroad to the Pacific, the China trade and China itself was only another jump ahead.

The chief obstacle to a transcontinental railroad somewhere was the growing rivalry between the North and the South, the South offering a snow-free path and, since the annexation of Texas, one skirting most of the Indian country. It did lack water for the engines, particularly water free of the alkali that foamed up in the boilers. Farther north the deep ruts along the Platte valley testified to its ease of travel; the Indian treaties of 1851 legalized it as the Holy Road of the white man, and there was good engine water readily available most of the way, yet Secretary of War Jeff Davis, authorized to survey prospective routes to the Pacific, ignored the Platte route entirely.

"He knows what a survey along there would prove," the speculators of Chicago and the Middle West said sourly.

Railroad backers, settlers in the Indian country anxious to legalize their squatter claims, and land boomers all backed the Kansas-Nebraska bill. Mass meetings gathered in Iowa and Missouri, with a lot of pulling and hauling. Missouri wanted the dividing line between Kansas and Nebraska pushed up to the Platte River, with rumors that the American Fur Company, what remained of it, was behind this, and the Commissioner of Indian Affairs still on the Company's side, claiming that the Omahas would not sell their land. But they did, and all the other tribes of eastern Nebraska. It was sell or have it taken and the Indians knew it.

The abolitionists fought hard against repeal of the Missouri Compromise, which barred slavery in the Louisiana Purchase anywhere above the southern line of Missouri. Stephen A. Douglas, eager to develop Chicago, managed to find a way to hold the Democratic majority in Congress together by his popular-sovereignty formula, empowering the voters of the two proposed territories to decide whether they would be slave or free. There was a rush of proslavery and abolitionist forces into Kansas, ending in bloody conflict. In the meantime meetings against the bill had been gathering through the North. This oppositon solidified and grew into a new party called the Republican, so it is perhaps fitting that the once-hated territory called Nebraska should eventually become, for a time at least, a home of the Grand Old Party's most reactionary wing. In 1854 the Republicans denounced Douglas for selling freedom out to slavery, although actually he helped open all that remained of the Louisiana Purchase to settlement, helped open the region that was to make most of the great fortunes that buttressed the Republican party as the haven of the Robber Barons, and later the so-called economic royalists. In the meantime the new party did put Lincoln into the White House and hatched if not nurtured the great liberals of the early twentieth century, men like La Follette of Wisconsin and Norris of Nebraska, although some good members of the party that put Norris into the Senate later promised to stone him if he got off the train at Lincoln, and even hired a grocer of the same name to run against him, to throw the election.

Late in May 1854 Nebraska became a territory and open to land-seekers. The Iowa speculators were ready. There were some squatter cabins scattered along the west side of the Missouri, but the only real settlement was Bellevue, where perhaps fifty whites clustered around the Indian agencies, the mission and the trading post. Sarpy, who had been taking it easier and running his business by ferry from St. Mary on the Iowa side, was galvanized out of his ease and alcoholic comfort. He helped organize the Bellevue Town Company with something of the old excitement of a beaver strike, and planned that the great line of commerce certain to develop between the oceans would cross the river at his post. July 15 the *Nebraska Palladium*, the first newspaper of the territory, although printed in Iowa, set the tone for the speculators with a description of Bellevue: "Within the last month a large city upon a grand scale has been laid out, with a view of the location of the capital of Nebraska at this point, and with a view of making it the center of commerce, and the half-way house between the Atlantic and Pacific Oceans."

Others had similar ambitions for other sites. Promoters and land jobbers from west Iowa were pre-empting town sites and laying out cities all along the Nebraska coast, each proclaimed as the inevitable gateway to the West. The custodian of the government property left at old Fort Kearny on the Missouri joined some men from over at Sidney, Iowa, to lay out Nebraska City at his post; a Glenwood promoter operating a ferry below the Platte-Missouri junction boomed a site to be called Plattsmouth; and some from the new Council Bluffs, on the Iowa side, crossed over to pre-empt the old Winter Quarters for a town named Florence.

Of the seventeen town charters later granted by Nebraska's first legislature, the most successful was Omaha City, on a site well warmed by ancient habitation. Early white men in the region told of a curious tract of about two hundred acres practically covered with mounds of different height, shape and size, the larger near the river, and all of sand or sand and earth. Some thought this was an ancient Oto village before they withdrew to the protection of the powerful Pawnees. Others called it a great burial ground, while some thought this might be an ancient nesting place of a great bird some Indians called the Knife-Wing-Bird-That-Never-Lights. The great piles might be the remains of nests built up by the birds to catch and warm their eggs laid in flight.

Most of the founders of Omaha, from the new Council Bluffs, had been sitting on the fence waiting to jump over as soon as Nebraska opened. Some of these had started west as Overlanders, but abandoned the long journey at the river. W. D. Brown, for instance, always a little ahead of civilization, had joined the California gold rush, but saw that fording the spring Missouri on hurriedly built rafts or the haphazard ferry offered a business opening. In 1850 he started to run a flatboat with oars called the Lone Tree Ferry and staked out an illegal squatter's claim on the Nebraska side, his 160 acres taking in practically the whole handsome plateau of the later Omaha, which he boomed as a place for the future great city of the Missouri Valley. Early in 1853 he helped organize the Council Bluffs and Nebraska Ferry Company. In September a substantial steam ferry arrived and entered a regular schedule of crossings the next spring, postered and advertised in the papers as constantly ready for stock, teams and foot passengers, with steam up and crew on hand. "Come on, emigrants, this is the great central ferry! Hurrah for Nebraska!"

Back in November three men had crossed the river in a leaky scow borrowed from Brown. One man rowed, one steered, and the third bailed as fast as he could to keep the awkward craft afloat, the river ducks scarcely back-paddling out of the way. The men staked their claims, but the Indians, through their agent, ordered them out. Two left; Jones applied for a post office and with this justification was able to hang to his land, carrying the mail himself in his tall hat.

July 4, 1854, was celebrated by a picnic at the new Omaha City on what was later called Capitol Hill. The excursionists from the Bluffs included Brown and Jones, their wives and other women and children too, as well as many men. Postmaster Jones, as a federal officeholder, and a couple of others, were to make the proper orations. Because the white settlers were still excluded from permanent location on these Indian lands, the U.S. marshal was along, to see that none stayed behind.

It was a bright, hot day, with a smell of dew still on the grass and fish jumping as the ferry pushed out into the river. A brood of geese lifted in the spreading swell of water from the prow, unconcerned, so accustomed to the pounding of river engines that their heads were cocked at the shadow of a fish hawk poised high above them. There was a gasp of pretty admiration from the ladies, but it was for the blue of a kingfisher as he flashed down in the shallows, and another as he rose with a silver fish wriggling in his beak. At the Omaha landing a wagon waited to haul the dusters, the picnic baskets, wine coolers, napery and silver and two blacksmith anvils up the hill. The party scattered to run here and there for wild flowers until the postmaster called them to follow the new road because the grass on the bottoms was so high it was difficult for the ladies to walk, even with their skirts lifted to the ankle, and there were snakes. So they gathered to straggle up the rise to where a stack of new logs lay— the future queen city of the Missouri.

As the women spread themselves and their picnic fans in the shade, the men dragged the logs around with the team and lifted them into place, building the first log cabin in Omaha. They finished it up to the plate, leaving the roof to be put on later, and afterward the men rested in the shade too, wiping off the sweat and looking away over the bench and the river. Most of the talk was about the town platted a couple of weeks before, with lots priced at $25 each, but free to anyone who started building at once, meaning as soon as the Indian treaty relinquishing the land here was ratified.

After the picnic lunch, with wine for the ladies too, a light one, there was a toast: "To Nebraska—may her gentle zephyrs and rolling prairies invite pioneers from beyond the Muddy Missouri River to happy homes within her borders, and may her lands ever be dedicated to free soil, free labor and free men."

After a couple of preliminary speeches, the two blacksmith anvils were set up on a bare knoll, one with a fused bag of blasting powder laid in the worn little hollow, the other anvil upside down on top of it, and the fuse lighted to the mock alarm and squeals from the girls and some of the women as they stuffed their fingers into their ears. The men ran, the black fuse gave one last sputter, followed by a great bang as the anvils flew apart, one going high and dropping, end over end, and rolling, while a stinking cloud of blue smoke spread off over the bottoms. It wasn't a cannon, but as a makeshift it was really more fun.

After the echoes of the salute to Independence Day were gone, one of the men started the real spread-eagle oration of the day, but he hadn't gone very far when the report of the anvils along the river brought results—a lot of Indians running into sight along the bluffs, whooping and yelling at what seemed a cannon on their land. The white women hurried into a cluster, the baskets and anvils were piled into the wagon and the team thrust to the tongue. By then the women had gathered up their skirts and were racing down across the bottoms, getting tangled in the knee-deep grass, slipping, falling. One stepped on the yielding coils of a snake, probably with a charmed bird or mouse, but thrashing away. The woman fled, still screaming in her horror as she stumbled up the plank to the ferry, crying, "Hurry! Hurry!" to those behind.

Up on the picnic grounds the angry Omahas looked around for the cannon they had heard, and then off toward the retreating ferryboat.

It was fall before the new settlement began to grow, and by then the Indian title was safely extinguished. The *Omaha Arrow*, which appeared the July before, described itself as "a family newspaper devoted to the arts, sciences, general literature, agriculture and politics." Pattison, the editor, a lawyer and business agent, gave his residence as Omaha, but he actually lived in Council Bluffs, where the *Arrow* was printed. Various stories were told about him, one that he was married in a double wedding out in the Indian wilds of the Elkhorn country, under a large tree on the river bank. Some of the natural romance was taken out of the occasion by a driving rainstorm that soaked everybody to the skin.

The first of September the *Arrow* fired an early shot in a prolonged and bitter war by announcing that Omaha City would be,
and deserved to be, the capital of Nebraska—a war that was still as
fresh in some minds a hundred years later as the War Between the
States in the Rebel kepi-wearer's heart. The *Arrow* ran for twelve
issues, into November, although it skipped a week now and then,
when paper was hard to obtain. By then Omaha City, no longer a
paper town, had twenty houses scattered around, two of them, with
dirt floors, serving as combination hotel and saloon. There were
other saloons too, and stores, and the promise of "an excellent
brickyard," the *Arrow* announced. Jones, still carrying the mail in
his hat, finally built a hotel and nailed up an ax box divided into four
pigeonholes—the first regular post office in Omaha. Later a Mormon,
who, it was said, fled from Florence during an Indian scare, managed
the office and kept the mail in a bushel basket in the middle of the
floor, everybody free to dig in for his own letters, and to snoop
into other people's epistles in the meantime, if he could read the
letters held against the light.

The most telling weapon of the real estate speculator was his plat,
preferably the survey map, socalled. The first one of Omaha City,
dated September 1, 1854, lithographed in St. Louis, offered lots to
those who would improve them, adding that a "brick building suitable
for the territorial legislature is in process of construction and a steam
mill and brick hotel will be completed in a few weeks." There was
publicity on the name Omaha, too, which some said meant Above-
All-Others-upon-a-Stream, and in a way it was prophetic. More than
a hundred years later there was still nothing to compete with Omaha
upon the Missouri.

Perhaps through frontier taste for the picturesque, a record was
kept of the "first case of delirium tremens." It seems that a man named
Todd built the first frame house or shack in town and stocked it with
groceries, both dry and wet. Alcoholism carried him off and gave
him the honor of being the first dipso to die in the town. A pioneer
wag wrote his epitaph:

Poor old Todd—he
Loved too well his toddy;
'Twas the intoxicating cup
That made him turn his toes up.
'Tis sad to think
He died of drink
And was buried 'neath the sod;
Gone to meet his God.

In the meantime the old town of Bellevue grabbed off the territorial capital. A grand reception had been arranged at Omaha to welcome Territorial Governor Burt and Secretary Cuming. On his way from South Carolina, Burt became ill at St. Louis. The river was so low the fall of 1854 that boats didn't get beyond St. Joseph. The governor hired a hack to old Fort Kearny and a wagon from there, but he was so weak when he reached Bellevue that he went to bed in Hamilton's mission house and never got up. The oath of office was administered October 16 and, after formal calls from Omaha, Plattsmouth and other candidates for the capital, on the 18th he died. Afterward Burt's son said his father intended to settle the capital at Bellevue, but whatever his intention had been, it was soon apparent that Secretary Cuming, now the acting governor, was open to suggestions. He was from Iowa, a newspaperman, and owed his appointment to the influence backing Council Bluffs and therefore Omaha. Cuming ordered a territorial census, although the population was hard to count with the Kansas-Nebraska line not surveyed and many of the so-called Nebraska citizens about as legally settled there as a flock of snowbirds on the wind. The total finally submitted was thirteen slaves and 2,732 white inhabitants, 1,818 south of the Platte, 914 north. Cuming created four counties on each side of the river and assigned seven councilmen and fourteen representatives to the north counties, and only six councilmen and twelve representatives to the south, although it had practically two-thirds of the population. The southern region was really alarmed. Bellevue, north of the Platte's mouth, objected to being in the same county as Omaha and called a mass meeting to hold the capital. The governor was invited and charged not only with accepting bribes but with actually demanding them from the Omaha town company.

In reply Cuming called the new legislature to convene at Omaha City to select a capital. They came, many from far states or at least across the river. Bellevue joined the South Platters in what was called a program of vilification, led by the twenty-two-year-old J. Sterling Morton, just in from Michigan. As was feared, Omaha legislators were certified instead of those from Bellevue, and although Cuming's decision was contested, all the committees, including the one to pass on election certification, were dominated by Omaha men. Mass meetings were called over the southern section of the Territory, a Nebraska City delegation adopted resolutions written by Morton, denouncing Cuming as an "unprincipled knave" and demanding his removal from office.

But they were not successful and only Peter Sarpy, who had seen the Clark family run the Indian country into vast personal fortunes, could have anticipated that during the few months of Cuming's term as governor he not only would set up Omaha as the territorial capital but would lay the foundations for his relatives like a sort of one-horse William Clark. When Cuming arrived in 1854, he brought his wife, her widowed mother, her thirteen-year-old brother, Frank Murphy, and her sister. The sister soon married Charles W. Hamilton, who built the brick Hamilton House in 1856, became bank president and organized the first Protestant Episcopal Church in the town, with Cuming and several to grow important in the financial life of Omaha as vestrymen. Young Frank, much like the O'Fallon nephews of William Clark, got his start through his shrewd-eyed relative, Governor Cuming, first in a little office job in the county treasurer's office, and spread out into the financial operations of Omaha. He was in the gas and street railway companies, became bank president, a member of the grain exchange and an organizer of the Union Stock Yards that were to make Omaha the world's foremost beef market. He died alone at the Waldorf-Astoria in New York, leaving an estate publicly estimated at six million dollars —all within fifty years from the day he arrived at Omaha City a fatherless boy of thirteen in the household of Thomas B. Cuming.

Other characters in the town grew tall from the roots of those first years. The newly married Dr. George L. Miller came late in 1854, met Cuming and fell into his "forceful hands and generous keeping." The governor suggested that Miller throw his fortune in with Nebraska and Omaha, but there were scarcely twenty people in the town, all young, vigorous and poor prospects for a doctor. Cuming, with a half smile, half scowl, sneered him out of countenance and into confidence, so, with money and a one-room shack furnished by the governor, George Miller and his bride became citizens of Omaha. Through the governor's influence Miller was chosen clerk of the Council (the territorial senate) by one vote. The doctor, disagreeing with many of the medical practices of the time anyway, entered upon the uncertain career of politics and speculation in a new territory. He was elected to the House and then the Council, took part in the capital and railroad fights and in the wildcat banking of the time. He was made nominal head of a company that accepted a bonus of real estate to build a hotel, and then went under in the panic of 1857 that wiped out most of the adventuresome operations of Omaha, including the banks except those of two quiet and industrious competitors, Kountze and Millard.

Most of the legislators spouted warmly about fidelity to their beloved and highly deserving constituents, whose interests were dearest to the patriotic hearts of their public servants. The rhetoric was largely for the amusement of the constituents and the speakers themselves, who remained residents of practically anywhere except Nebraska. D. M. Johnson, still living in Ohio although listed as the member from Archer, got leave from the Nebraska legislature to run for representative in Kansas and almost made that too.

The really fevered struggle, however, was for the permanent territorial capital and involved Omaha City, Bellevue, Florence, Plattsmouth, Nebraska City, Brownville and half a dozen other largely paper communities. Gradually the south region united against Omaha and what was called Omaha's bulldozing. Later some said Bellevue could have secured the capital through a suitable donation of land for the site, but that the Presbyterian Board of Missions had a reserve on the section wanted, and that the Reverend Mr. Hamilton refused the $25,000 offered, demanding $50,000. It seemed he did refer the question to the Mission Board, which also rejected the $25,-000, or perhaps the money couldn't be raised, if anyone tried. Certainly the Omaha speculators could not be expected to let the capital get away now. In mid-January 1855, the new legislature met in the state house built by the ferry company, "without costing the government a single dollar" was the boast, "but in anticipation of a good return." The two-story building was brick, the first in town, with red and green calico curtains at the windows. The local legislators hurried to select their seats, the double school desks mighty small. Some sat on top, perhaps whittling, practically everybody spitting, either chewing plug tobacco or snuff.

The members from other localities swooped into Omaha in revengeful mood, wrapped themselves in red Indian blankets and announced they would break up the assembly. Cuming saw the halls fill with excited, desperate men and moved swiftly. Resolutions for a joint session were rammed through, and the moment this was convened the governor entered, delivered the certificates of election, pronounced his message, declared the legislature organized and directed the two bodies to withdraw to complete their organization. In half an hour the opposition was vanquished.

Or so the victors seemed to think, as other victors in other capital fights on the Plains thought, one time or another.

It was winter, the river frozen over, the whole country snowed in, but gradually news did spread that a bill establishing the permanent capital at Omaha was passed in fighting debate February 22, 1855. Later the few resident constituents heard various stories of a place called Scrip Town, a tract laid out by the owners of the original site of Omaha as one of their "precautionary measures." It was perhaps half a mile wide and ran along the north and west of town. The stock was frankly created to "induce" members of the legislature, as General Estabrook, the territorial attorney, explained, the scrip to be distributed where it would do the most good. When one more vote was needed for Omaha, a leading member of the legislature was given an important block of shares, about a twelfth of the site, to buy his co-operation. Indiscreetly he let it get out that he was still going to vote against Omaha. A wily, shrewd and cool man, later prominent in merchandising, was delegated to meet the holder of the scrip as if by chance and say that there was a mixup in the numbering of the shares on the books.

"Let me have them and I'll make the correction at once," he said.

The scrip was handed over and never seen again by the treacherous legislator. "An honest man is one who stays bought" was the sour comment around Omaha, and then south of the Platte too, but out of the other side of the mouth.

Toward the close of the capital fight, Mitchell of Florence, a bitter enemy of Omaha, was also "induced" to abate his hostility. In return for his vote and influence he was appointed a committee of one to locate the capitol within the city. He drove his stake on what became Capitol Hill, and the next summer he had sixty town lots to sell at public auction. Another member who was given shares in Scrip Town to buy a South Platte legislator's vote for Omaha decided he could use the scrip himself, and so he advised the man to take nothing but money. They agreed on $1,000, which a ferry company man promised in return for the vote. By the time it was recorded for Omaha the ferryman had taken his boat across the river, across the territorial line, and the money was never paid. The legislator with the scrip kept it, saying he had been most doubtful about the Omaha capital location himself, and so he used the shares to buy his own vote.

Glenwood, Iowa, backed Plattsmouth to the end, but their legislators didn't hold together. Those who switched to Omaha had to face an indignation meeting of Glenwooders, among them the president of the Nebraska Council representing Richardson County. For the usual inducement he had promised his vote to Omaha, but faithfully recorded it for Plattsmouth, and was furious with others who didn't. One man who reneged on Plattsmouth never went home to Glenwood, afraid of being lynched. A Nemaha County representative who voted for Omaha narrowly escaped a horsewhipping from his outraged Iowa constituency for misrepresenting them. There is no record of what the Nemaha settlers thought.

Two Missouri residents claimed to represent the same Nebraska county. One, a preacher who wanted to act as chaplain, promised Speaker Hanscom to vote for Omaha, and after he got the contested seat said his conscience compelled him to vote against the town.

"You're a damned infernal lying old hypocrite," he was told. If there was to be any more praying to be done, the Speaker would do it himself.

It had ended in a brawl, with any refractory member, meaning against Omaha, who refused to take his seat and shut up on orders from Speaker Hanscom, warned he would be knocked down. In the crowded lobbies the factions armed themselves with bludgeons, brickbats and pistols, but the killings, if any, had to wait for another day.

The new territorial governor, Izard, had reached Omaha February 20, 1855. He was from Arkansas and suspected of plans to swing Nebraska for slavery. In his address he suggested that the laws of Iowa be adopted temporarily, since "so large portion of our citizens at present are from that state."

There was an executive ball, the only one Omaha was ever to have, it seemed, and the stories of it vary, all edged with sarcasm and acid. Dr. Miller described Izard as physically stately and impressive, but mentally rather weak, even puny, some thought. Izard had never known the honor of a governorship and he wanted his advent suitably celebrated. The facetious and wily Cuming suggested to the small number of permanent population that this be a grand ball at the City Hotel, a small one-story frame buiding not yet finished. The two rooms were hastily plastered with a single coat that turned into frozen mud and ice; the floor of rough unplaned lumber was scrubbed, but with the afternoon and night well below zero, the water froze on it and could not be thawed by the one puny stove, no matter how red-hot. The benches along the walls were rough cottonwood planks laid across sawed-off stumps, the more elegant ones at the head of the room covered with buffalo robes.

At seven the grand company began to assemble. His Excellency Governor Izard, and Jim the fiddler, Council Bluffs' entire band, arrived about the same time. Izard was very polite to Jim, who was just oiled enough to be polite to the governor, the guest of the nine ladies, all that could be gathered for even such a state occasion that winter. These included Mrs. Cuming, Mrs. J. Sterling Morton and Mrs. Miller, all, like their men, very young. Two of the ladies couldn't dance and their places were taken by gentlemen, with, some reported, handkerchiefs tied around their arms to indicate their gender in the quadrilles.

After the governor's son James, his father's secretary, arrived in white waistcoat and white kid gloves, the fiddler climbed up on a rough table, some said a whisky barrel, tuned his fiddle and began to saw away. The floor was slippery with ice, but at least it needed no waxing, which would only have been candle scrapings or cornmeal. There were several accidents in the swing of the dance. One lady, to become very well known later, fell flat on the icy boards, her skirts flying up. At midnight there was coffee with brown sugar but no milk, certainly no cream, and sandwiches that were chunks of very dark bread cut thick and ragged as though hacked with a pocketknife, with fried bacon—sowbelly—between. The dessert was that staple of the frontier and pioneer regions, dried apple pie. The coffee was passed around in a washtub, the sandwiches in a willow basket made by the Indians. The governor, from a warmer and more civilized climate, shivered, but he made an honest effort at a speech, thanking all for the high honor paid him.

By the next winter things had changed, including the schemes around the capital, this time to move it, which would require something a little more imaginative than merely steamrolling the opposition out of its just representation, or the crude buying of votes, mostly by pieces of the public domain. Cuming, who had convened the legislature at Omaha City instead of Bellevue and euchred the South Platters out of their proper representation, was now against Omaha.

"Seems he's milked that cow dry," one old-timer wrote back to his brother in Maine.

Anyway Cuming seemed ready to help jerk the capital away to Douglas City, apparently Bellevue. Sarpy, Morton and a lot of those south of the Platte had about practically everybody outside of Omaha committed to the removal and were optimistic. The problem now was to get Izard out of town so Cuming, once more acting governor, could sign the removal bill.

These men had abused the governor ever since he came, calling him Granny Izard, but now Morton and some others introduced a couple of very complimentary resolutions about him and asked him to go to Washington on territorial business. Izard was pleased and promised to go, but Dr. Miller, representative and editor now, attacked the resolutions vigorously. The governor, disturbed that his backing from the local men seemed to be weakening, whispered to someone to stop Miller, so Izard had to be called out to have the plot explained. The gaudy resolutions were passed, but the governor refused to go anywhere.

By 1857 new towns were appearing thick as mushrooms around an old straw pile, growing up everywhere, at least on paper. A few men—three, four or half a dozen—formed a company, laid claim to a tract of government land, gave it some name with "City" attached to it as a tail is added to lift a kite. Then a hundred or several hundred stock certificates were printed over in Iowa somewhere and the sale started—fancy little stock deals worthy of any Wall Street heading for a crash. Not until 1857 did Omaha lose her tail, her "City." But many other things were lost that year.

The next session of the legislature the capital removers came up with two-thirds of the members pledged against Omaha. This would permit suspension of the rules and overriding the governor's veto. The mythical Douglas City was now definitely located on Salt Creek in Lancaster County, near the salt basin of the romantic legends and where the buffalo had died of the whistling disease. The new town site was laid out and shares issued to the members favoring the removal, their pockets all well lined. Nearly everybody with any power had been sweetened with scrip, including, it was said, some of the Omaha men, perhaps because they knew that only eight votes of the thirty-five in the House were left on their side. The rules were suspended; the new speaker, Decker, ignored parliamentary procedure as Hanscom had; and all that the Omaha backers could do was talk against time, eat up days and weeks in trivial argument. Hanscom, the most adept, did most of it.

The session was stormy. Once the Speaker ordered the sergeant at arms to arrest Hanscom, who shouted, "Come no farther; you are safer there than you will be if you come any nearer!"

Apparently the sergeant agreed, and made no move. By this time most of Omaha, including some river toughs, had gathered in the legislative chambers, and drove the Speaker from the chair, abused him so he became sick, or pretended to be. The members from south of the Platte demanded that the governor call out three hundred militiamen to protect them from the mob jamming the capital and the chambers. Instead Izard addressed them in joint session. It was not necessary to call out the militia, he said calmly. If they behaved themselves their grandmother, their Granny Izard, would protect them.

Opposition votes were demanding $20,000 apiece to flop to the Omaha side, and while land and land scrip were cheap, cash was getting mighty tight in the depression. The removal bill passed and, as expected, was returned unsigned by the governor, but now suddenly the south lacked the votes to override the veto, with much guessing at the price those few votes got for their last-minute shift.

Next session, Hanscom, only a lobbyist now, was asked to marshal the defense of Omaha. He said that he, for one, had paid out enough money for votes and from now on he proposed to do a little whaling. Word got around that the new Speaker of the House had armed himself with a pistol and that his party was doing the same. It was a lively session and furnished many lurid stories of what happened. Hanscom, with no right on the House floor, was perhaps the most active man there, his brows jutting in the anger that set his voice "roaring with fists in it," his admirers said. He was backed by a mob of irate Omahans beyond the railing, more often inside it. In joint session he seated himself on the step near the speaker's stand, and when Decker tried to take over from the chairman, Hanscom yelled his war cry: "Hit the rascal over the head with the gavel!"

Half a dozen pushed in to protect Decker, but Hanscom had already grabbed the Speaker by the neck and seat of trousers and dumped him under the table. Now everybody was up, and jumping into the free-for-all, fists flying, eyes blackened and teeth knocked out, mostly by roustabouts fetched in from the bars and the livery barns, and well armed with knucks and guns. Hanscom was still running everything like a leader of the border ruffians soaking Kansas soil in blood, beating down every legislator who tried to take the floor against him.

The next morning the legislature had adjourned to Florence, away from the legal capital. Governor Izard refused to recognize them, their acts or their payroll. So the session ended like the others, but with much more noise, violence and fury, more mob action by outsiders, with their persuasive brass knucks and drawn pistols.

The general anger against the outlaw tactics of Omaha stirred the old desire to cut loose from the whole northern outfit. With the Platte too shallow for ferries, too full of quicksand for fording, and too wide for bridging by the poor communities, it seemed a clear and natural boundary. Morton, who moved to Nebraska City permanently after Bellevue's defeat, had tried a resolution asking Congress to move the Kansas boundary up to the Platte. Mass meetings were called and delegates sent to the Free State convention down there, but when the abolitionists saw they wouldn't need the Nebraskans to win, they cooled.

Omaha was the most successful of all the speculator towns. Many of the others never existed anywhere but on paper—a map and prospectus offering lots cheap, with perhaps an account of dozens of fine homes, a bank or two, a newspaper, schools and churches, all where even a ground squirrel would have felt lonesome. Often the purchaser was never completely disillusioned, because when the deal was made and the money handed over, he never heard of the site or the salesman again, and the purchaser of ground, site unseen can hope eternally. In the East, real estate peddlers sold lots in such Nebraska territorial towns as Hudson, Brooklyn, Neapolis, Cuming City (named for the governor and with an actual college chartered there and some real houses built), San Francisco, Amherst, Buchanan, Delaware City, California City, Curlew and even Platonia.

One town that should have prospered was Niobrarah City, located on a most beautiful timbered site near the mouth of the swift, clear river, a site admired long before any white man's eye found it. Historically the Poncas lived there, and the Mormons came to camp in 1846. Ten years later speculators from Omaha, Council Bluffs and Sioux City organized a town company, staked out 3,000 acres, put up a little log fort and several houses, houses that the friendly Poncas somehow managed to burn the next winter. But a fine six-foot map was made of the town, superimposed upon a purported railroad survey, the lots laid out neatly and numbered along the tracks, labeled "The Great Pacific Route from the east through Chicago, Dubuque, Sioux City, Niobrarah, Fort Laramie and the South Pass to the Pacific."

The sites mentioned were all put in a practically straight line west, on the railroad, with engines probably already tooting just over the hill, racing from Chicago to Niobrarah, the distance telescoped so it looked not over 150 miles. A three-story hotel accommodated the hopeful buyers tolled there by the map, at least for awhile. A railroad did come to the Missouri, but it did not cross to Niobrara, as it was spelled by then. Later tracks passed within twelve miles of town, the train whistles plain on cold mornings. Finally, in 1902, forty-five years after the map was distributed and lots sold, the first engine roared into town.

There was plenty of speculation in land too, but usually not by the homeseeker, who couldn't sell his preemption of 160 acres until it was paid for at $1.25 an acre, due any time during the first year of residence or before it was surveyed or offered at public auction by presidential proclamation. Then the entryman had better come running with the cash or his place and his improvements would go to the highest bidder, and the money into Uncle Sam's till, as Buchanan tried to do with the settlers of Nebraska Territory in 1858 because the government was hard up, and the settlers plainly harder.

All this time there were soldier bounty-land warrants, assignable after 1852, and bought up at cut rates by speculators. Better than a million and a quarter acres in federal bonus to soldiers from wars long before Nebraska was born were paid out of her lands, largely to speculators, the land often unimproved, unproductive, untaxable for years. Then in 1863 the Agricultural College Endowment Act gave vast acreages to the land-grant colleges all over the nation, to come from the public domain either by location or by the agricultural college scrip sold like the soldier warrants. Only two states east of the Mississippi River—Michigan and Wisconsin—selected their lands within their own borders. All the rest, New England and the other states with the best educational facilities in existence, financed more education out of the public lands of the West, often where education could not be financed at all. They not only took the best areas from these western regions but often put the patents, the eternal control of large tracts, into the hands of eastern and foreign speculators and financiers, into the hands of powerful forces against taxation, against every local improvement, particularly schools, whether district, town or state, and against all other public improvements in the West or national to serve the West, all improvements except roads to their lands.

Nebraska lost almost a million and a quarter acres to out-of-state agricultural college scrip, money taken out of a struggling territory to enrich other, older regions powerful in Congress. That is why the man from the Plains, practically a hundred years later, still finds himself growing an inch taller in contempt when he is expected to show admiration for the great accumulations of wealth—financial, cultural and educational—in the East. He knows where much of the wealth came from, not only from the riches of his earth but by high-handed appropriation of great chunks of the very earth itself.

Now it was the railroad.

Cuming had died in 1858, two years before the telegraph came through, built by the energetic Creightons who got their start in Cuming's day too, and later established Creighton University with money made from Nebraska and the Plains. The war that hastened the telegraph to hold California eliminated the North-South struggle for the transcontinental railroad, but locally the fight between the river towns for the Union Pacific terminal was noisier than a herd of buffalo bulls fighting in a canyon. Omaha frankly offered land and privileges and piled them on, as Omaha knew so well how to do. Omaha won.

Ground was broken in late 1863, with a thousand standing around in the raw cold to stare at the silk hats and look for Durant, the railroad promoter, usually in frontier dandy dress—velvet coat, slouch hat and top boots. Hanscom presided, Governor Saunders used the shovel and everybody important made a speech, including the stocky George Francis Train, the fabulous show-off man, who erected a large hotel in sixty days across the street from the one where he had been offended, the man to attempt building streetcar lines in London, be called an anarchist while he claimed to own thirty million dollars in Omaha real estate, and to get himself jailed in various countries on various silly charges. The newspapermen rated him the best orator at the ground breaking but wondered if he was played out at thirty-three. He had been everywhere, done practically everything. What now? "The Train of ideas sometimes lacks coupling chains."

In 1865 Omaha's elation over the railroad was chilled by rumors that President Johnson had ordered the U.P. to start at Bellevue, and many Omahans sneaked down there to buy lots under assumed names, coppering their bets like so many faro men. Later it seemed that the Missouri bridge was to be built near Bellevue, and Omaha would die like a hedge orange on a broken twig—tough but done for. Some said that Kountze and Millard read the gloomy telegram about the bridge in the parlor of the First National Bank and hurriedly gathered up sixty solid townsmen to a determined conference. After several trips to New York and a lot of national maneuvering, the bridge was relocated and the U.P.'s Durant, already with three, four million in his back pocket, was given $50,000 in Douglas County bonds by Kountze, Governor Saunders and Millard. Durant was said to have declined the gift, but plainly Omaha did know how to get things done, everything except keeping the capital.

With the war over the old issue popped up like a skunk when the cellar door is lifted. Statehood had been rejected twice and then the state constitution was approved in the 1866 election, although scandal and charges of fraud clouded the triumph. Omaha was determined to maintain the topheavy representation of the north side of the Platte. They lost, although the last session of the territorial legislature ended in gunplay, silent and odorless, but surely a pistol to the head. A capital commission of three men was named to pick the site, and Omaha made a last attempt to break the unity south of the river, where some Democrats still smarted under Rebel defeat. The Omahans suggested that the name of Capital City, whatever the site, be changed to the Rebel-hated one of Lincoln. But the Democrats hated Omaha more and Lincoln was located near the salt basin of the legends.

There are still accounts of the moving day, with rifle-armed men hidden just outside of Omaha to hold off any mob that might try to recapture the state records on the way to Lincoln, and similar forces at other strategic points in addition to the armed riders guarding the wagon all the way, prepared for any ambush. There are stories of last-minute attempts at bribery, bribes offered, bribes asked, and one account of Omaha men spurring out of a brush patch along the route to discover that the wagon they were stopping was a wedding party, shotgun and all, looking for a justice of the peace. But whatever the truth, the records reached Lincoln, although some still insist that the horses were lathered and panting in their collars from a chase.

Dr. Miller's new paper, the Omaha *Weekly Herald*, had expressed the town's determined note when the capital relocation bill was passed: "Omaha is erect in her own strength and if such small potatoes and potato balls . . . suppose that they are going to keep anybody awake nights hereabouts by removing the capital into the interior, he is as much mistaken as though he burnt his chemise."

Omaha grew and prospered, became the main shipping point for the products of the upper and middle Plains, and an outpost for the livestock commission houses and meat packers, for electricity and gas companies, and for gangsters fleeing Chicago for a while, all these to be manipulated one way or another by the eastern headquarters, eastern owners. Sometimes, but rarely, the western unit was to outstrip the parent, as in packing and, some thought, in gambling under Tom Dennison, but even that at second hand.

There were colorful mayors, Jim Dahlman, for instance, a Texas cowboy who came north as Jim Murray back when it was customary and safer not to ask a man his name but to say "What name you traveling under?" Then there was Butler, who on his death received his short inch of immortality in *The New York Times* obituary notices for three accomplishments: elected mayor of Omaha and the banning of *Idiot's Delight* and the book *Slogum House*. Not that the Butler bannings were the first in the city. Any good tart has her little pretenses to respectability, as a Lincolnite, perhaps a little envious, said at the time, and pointed out that *Huckleberry Finn* had been banned from general circulation by the Omaha Library years ago. Besides, Alfred Lunt did talk Mayor Butler into permitting *Idiot's Delight* to go on at the last minute.

J. Sterling Morton's attempt to cut his part of the state away from Omaha was not to be the last. As recently as the Territorial Centennial in 1954, signs of the old anger against the proud city on the Missouri ran through the celebrations like a shoddy thread in a lovely scarf. The next year Tom Lally, energetic newspaperman of Bridgeport, out on the North Platte, revived the old plan of joining the Nebraska Panhandle to Wyoming to escape the domination, the contempt and the milking of western resources by the eastern section and Omaha. The Panhandlers, he said, were getting nothing but a kick in the pants. It would be advantageous for Wyoming too, particularly in the golden harvest of new cowboy song lyrics, starting with one to be called "The Panhandle of Old Wyoming." Others advised the Equality State to give some long thought to the push and pugnacity of the Nebraska Panhandlers before accepting them into easygoing, peace-loving Wyoming, or its citizens might find themselves flying for refuge to Montana, petitioning for annexation there to escape their New East, their domineering, contemptuous and mulcting New East.

By 1960 a wider anger centered specifically upon Omaha, the protestors representing what they called Greater Nebraska now, with newspaper headlines like "Warn Against Omahog Deal" denouncing diversion of interstate highway funds to purely Omaha advantage. Yet even the hottest of the resenters were grateful for the vision of Omaha's early speculators who established the Union Stock Yards and welcomed the packing houses. True, for a long time a powerful stench hung over South Omaha and the surrounding country when the wind was right. Perhaps that is why so many flowering shrubs were planted in early Omaha, the great rows of fragrant lilacs still there, and all the bridal wreath that falls in such snowy spring cascades down the terraced and diminished bluffs where two anvils were shot one Fourth of July long ago. In a way the pink marble of the Joselyn Art Museum seems part of this beautification for the senses. George A. Joselyn came much later and perhaps leaner of pocket than the Cuming group, but the bustling, optimistic financial atmosphere of those early men made his swift rise to fortune possible, and his gifts to various institutions, including the young and burgeoning Omaha University. His real monument, however, is the Art Museum, centrally located, where men and women and children in everyday, in working clothes can come to stand before this painting or that one, or slip in to listen to good music, as is fine and proper. Art is for the people who can feel it.

The same people can see plays worked out, future actors and actresses develop at the Omaha Community Playhouse that has sent several Nebraskans to the New York stage and to Hollywood. Henry Fonda, who had preferred journalism, was persuaded to try a bit part by Dorothy Brando before her son Marlon was born. Later Dorothy Maguire worked there, and a dozen others that the people who slipped in enjoyed.

These things of Omaha took speculation, speculation in time and money, not only along the bluffs where a man named Jones kept the post office in his hat, or where a wayward river ate boat and land, but far out on the prairie too, out to the Yellowstone and beyond, where the early settlers grew grain and meat. They were speculators too, with limb and loved ones and life.

VIII   Moccasin Tracks on the
Buffalo Grass

The ancient little patch of mounds on the bench below Omaha was gone. It didn't matter whether it had been an old village of river Indians or a rookery of the mythical Knife-Wing-Bird-That-Never-Lights; all sign of it was lost under the shadows of the wood and brick and stone buildings on the heights of the 1870's. From Indian Territory northward, cattle and corn were pushing westward over the wide fertile prairies. Spike mauls were ringing on the new railroad tracks that crept up along the streams. Yet much of the northern Plains was still legally Indian country to which no white man had a right to go.

The tribes that stood most firmly against white encroachments were the Sioux, the great majority peoples of the region, and the small tribe of Cheyennes, who, like any minority, made up for their lack in horizontal spread of numbers by a sort of vertical string of remembered generations, remembered great ones. The Cheyennes had stories not only of their wanderings west of the Great Lakes and the crossing of the Missouri to the Plains, but of another crossing, long, long ago, over salt water.

It seemed in that old time the Cheyennes had been driven from one place to another until they were coming upon the Last One, the place that a holy man in the far past had predicted their moccasins must one day touch. They had approached out of the freezing mist that shrouded the dark and rocky coast, one figure first, then others, more and more, their tattered skin robes drawn about them, to huddle together in hopeless little knots, nothing but more mist and the salt ocean ahead of them. Back in the grayness a scout or two moved cautiously, watching the way the people had traveled, although if the enemy was upon them now there was no further place to run.

After a while the holy man among them rose weakly to speak. He would go to the high place some distance back, strip himself to the breechclout and, stretched with his face to the sky, wait.

"You will die," the others said hopelessly. "Even now we have carried you."

But the worn old one would go, and so four of the strongest men left among them placed him upon his robe and bore him to the rocky knob. There they spread him naked upon the ground and returned, not one of them looking back. A time of eating passed, and of sleeping, and a second sleep, with nothing for the handful of moss fire that the women still carried, nothing for anyone, not even the few infants left to tug at the breasts dry as old hides. Even the last sinew had been chewed, and so the people pulled their robes over their heads and prepared to die, each in his own way.

But at dawn there was a sudden rumble of thunder, and a scout came running in. Those most able went out to bring back their holy man, who had dreamed. In the dream he saw the hunters of his people fall upon a small herd of the buffalo with the long, long hair. They all came to the hunt at the foot of his rocky hill and ate of the meat and then they made skin boats of the hides, with the heads and the tails left on. Willow sticks were pushed into the cold earth, the other ends bent down into the ground too, arranged in oblongs, each in the shape of the hairy animal's body. The skins were stretched over these willows and small coals placed underneath for the drying. Then they turned the boats up, fastened a strip of strong hide around the top, and pushed them into the mist and the salt ocean, a man strong in holy ways at the head of each, and a reasonable man at the tail to steer, the paddlers and the people and their poor store of dried meat filling the boats.

And as the holy man had dreamed it was done, one boat after another vanishing eastward into the fog, toward the sun. None looked back. When the first touched land, the people started southward, the rest behind, traveling moon after moon, and many winters, the people strengthening and multiplying, following the grasses and the game.

This, the Cheyennes remember, is the way they came to America.

The Cheyennes were latecomers to the American continent, and even they have no story of their first sight of the Plains when they crossed them eastward in that long-ago time. That would be the real story, the finest of all, not of the Cheyenne's but of the first man's coming. How did he come, his hairy sun-darkened body practically bare of all covering, stooping low, slipping from one inconspicuous cover to the next, with perhaps nothing more than a rock to lengthen the reach of his arm, so puny and feeble against the huge beasts that fed on the rank vegetation?

Or was he here even before that? Before he knew the power of a stone grasped in the palm?

No one knows when the Indians came to America or the Plains, or whether they were the first men on the continent. There are some who believe that the Yellowstone valley was the cradle of man and that he vanished for aeons, even longer than the horse, but found the region well suited to him when he returned, if not as completely as the horse, at least well enough to feel the horizon like a warm robe about the shoulder of the first desperate wanderers in the strange new land.

Men, probably Indians, were associated with the great animals whose fossil remains make all the tall tales of tall-tale Nebraska look like pious understatement. Man lived in the region with the mammoth from Lincoln County, the largest elephant* known in the world, and with the mastodons, camels, huge ground sloths and buffalo with six-foot horn spread. Although these early people were skillful stone workers and expert hunters, they went the way of the mammoth and the saber-toothed tiger, or perhaps mixed with later Asiatic migrations and became the ancestors of the modern Indians. A drouth that sucked up the lakes and streams and the vast marshes killed the lush vegetation that the great creatures needed to survive. Man of those early periods lived in caves at such places as Signal Butte of the Scotts Bluff region, with its many layers of habitation, and at Lime and Medicine Creeks in Frontier County, Nebraska, and Yuma, Colorado, with more sites located all the time.

About 400 to 600 A.D. the Woodland people appeared, still hunters but less nomadic perhaps, living in semisubterranean houses with central fireplaces. They gave way to a more sedentary people in rather large unfortified villages, from the Republican across Nebraska to the Loup country and the Missouri River, with perhaps seasonal hunting camps in the sandhills. They were relatively peaceful and advanced in agriculture, and lasted from about 1200 to 1500, almost to the coming of the Spaniards. New influences and perhaps new peoples pushed up from the south—more advanced in the arts, with high-grade pottery, and with stone, bone, horn and shell tools and ornaments. They lived largely from their cornfields and the buffalo, whose hunting must have become a fairly organized undertaking.

Because the buffalo, the American bison, was without serious enemy he had become the most numerous wild ruminant the world had ever seen. He moved in millions over the rich grasses of the Plains, so secure that the weak little eyes under the curly mat of hair were no handicap. He depended almost entirely upon his nose as he grazed into the wind, which, in the cyclonic character of the Great Plains, drew the four great herds in roughly four-hundred-

* In Elephant Hall, State Museum, University of Nebraska.

mile migrations, southward in the fall, northward in the spring. Using care and daring, a lone Indian could sometimes sneak up behind a laggard bull or a cow heavy with calf and plunge his stone-pointed lance or arrow to the heart, or if only to the paunch, he might elude the angry animal by slipping down wind, and then follow until the creature lay down. Usually only one or two buffalo could be taken before the herd was up, tails in air, their heavy gallop shaking the ground. Often they were gone at the first approach of man, warned by the sharp-eyed wolves that followed the herds, or the hoarse cry of alert raven, grackle or perhaps other birds with the animals, often riding on a back to pick the insects from the heavy wool.

An occasional buffalo was not enough to supply a family with the meat, hide and other products needed during the months when the herds were gone, particularly during the long snow moons. Because the large villages of the later Stone Age Indian depended on substantial kills, elaborate ceremonials and rites were devised to bring the herds into reach, the hunt itself the product of long, careful organization and planning, and carried out with the utmost courage, energy and discipline. Deer, moose and elk could sometimes be taken during the winter in some sheltered mountain foothill pocket or other broken country—the moose yards, where the animals had gathered and kept moving to trample the snow down while outside it piled shoulder deep or more. These animals could be approached from downwind on snowshoes and killed as they plunged in panic out into the deep drifts, perhaps by a slash to the throat, the snow suddenly dark with the gushing blood. But moose yards were scarce and the buffalo, his wool often snow-matted, was hard to find in the winter, alert, grazing the wind-swept ridges, practically untakable with spear or arrow, so the Indian had to make his meat in big kills in the summer, dried and stored.

The best places for large killings were plains with a sheer drop-off somewhere, as at Cabin Creek near the Yellowstone, the Chugwater in Wyoming or at some of the bluffs into the White River valley in northwest Nebraska. Scouts watched such places and if a herd came near they signaled with sunlight on flakes of obsidian. Runners flew over the prairie to notify the hunters and others too, including the women and the old—anybody who could shout and run with a robe, to slip behind and alongside the herd, watching to keep out of any wind that would carry the man smell to the keen nostrils. Hidden, they waited ready to jump up and flap the robes to start the herd running toward the drop-off, with more Indians, reckless, willing to risk being trampled, along the route to turn any trying to escape. The herd had to be kept together and running hard enough to push the leaders on when they hesitated at the brink of the bluffs, to send them all over in a great piling up at the foot—the broken, the crippled and the whole in a struggling mass, ready for the swift spear and the knife, the carcasses to be dragged out for the butchering later.

Sometimes, if there was luck, the grass dry and the wind turned in the right direction, the Indians could use fire. If the hunting party was small, women might hurry out to scatter the smolderings from their fire bags along the grass, to be fanned into flame by the high wind. With larger parties, men ran with burning arrows or pitchpine knots to touch the prairie into explosive blaze. Either way, the flames spread together in a roaring prairie fire and the buffalo herd broke into a terrified, earth-shaking stampede, to pour in a dark flood over the bluffs. There might be enough in the kill to feed an entire small tribe for months, the meat dried there and taken back to the village by big pack and travois dogs, whole strings of great wolfish dogs, rough and powerful, emasculated to make them manageable only after they had developed the broad fighting shoulders of the grown male. Then a tight band of green hide was wrapped tightly around the base of the scrotum, to dry and cut off the circulation gradually. So the dogs were tamed, the way the white man tamed his oxen for the great freight loads across the Plains a few hundred years later, but bloodlessly, less crudely than with the white man's knife.

No one knows what became of these Indians; perhaps they abandoned the Plains during the great drouth that drove the cliff dwellers of the Southwest down into the Rio Grande valley and spread its burning blast northeastward, drying up the headwaters of the east-flowing streams. In those desperate years much of the vegetation west of the Missouri shrank so there was very little pollen in the deepening alluvial deposits dropped by the great dust storms on the deserted earth villages of the river valley. The great herds of the Plains must have followed the rain, and man with them.

When the thunder clouds returned the Pawnees were evidently pushing up out of the south and southwest, perhaps on the path Coronado was to follow from water to water a long time later. They had carried the tangible core of their belief with them, their center of the earth, and also their sacred bundles, which contained two ears of corn, their great mother. The most important ceremonials of the Pawnees, including the human sacrifice of the Skidis, were primarily to assure a good corn crop. The fields were small, usually not over an acre or so, in the mouths of ravines or wherever fertile ground was loose and workable with the hoe made from a buffalo scapula.

The corn ears, usually not over four inches long, were generally gathered in the milk, boiled, cut from the cob, dried and placed in skin bags to store in caches. The Pawnees also had beans, pumpkins and squash, and a wild potato from the sandy Platte and Loup valleys.

There were two big buffalo hunts a year, for hide, hair, sinew, horns, hoofs and so on in addition to the meat. The summer hunt came after the second corn hoeing, in late June. The people returned in time to harvest the crops and went on the fall hunt when the buffalo robes were thickening toward winter. The favorite place after they obtained horses was between the Republican and Arkansas Rivers, a trip covering from four to nine hundred miles a hunt. The meat was eaten fresh when possible, with a great prolonged feast and dancing after the hunt. What was left was taken home dried.

When the Plains were well grassed once more, a newcomer, the white man, appeared at the seacoasts bringing his horse and iron and powder. There were stories of pale-faced, bearded men in the region long ago, blue-eyed men, and some with beards black as a buffalo bull's in the fall, and the seers had predicted their return. The great shifts and pressures of the centuries following the drouth brought a formidable Indian enemy pushing in from the northeast. They carried arrows and spears tipped with iron and had a few guns too, and some horses. These energetic and powerful Teton Sioux, who called themselves Lakotas, the People, were determined to move into the hunting grounds of the Pawnees. The small Missouri tribes, mostly Siouan stock but separated long ago, helped their neighbors against the Sioux. Later the Crows and Shoshonis too, and the white man, joined against the arrogant, powerful Indian invader of the Plains.

The Missouri tribes were scattered up and down the river on about five hundred sites during early historic times, not all occupied at once. Many of the upper villages had a rather highly developed culture and were fortified with stout wooden palisades and moats. Perhaps there was some connection between this cultural level, this effective fortification, and the Viking iron still found in the Lake Winnipeg region, near the old home of the Mandans, who had blue-eyed ones among them when the early trappers and travelers came, and what the whites labeled an un-Indian depravity.

No one knows when the Sioux first made summer forages out upon the buffalo plains for meat or how early they began to raid the sedentary peoples of the Missouri. Certainly young men from prominent families took their customary youth journeys all down the Plains long before Columbus reached the western world, as others from the tribe went east, to the Mohawks and the salt sea. It was such young men who had obtained the first horses, the big-dogs, at Horse Creek, to be called Brules, Burnt Thighs, ever since.

The upper Missouri tribes managed to hold off these driving Sioux at their village walls, and although a few of the raiders sifted through the river barrier westward, they never got a foothold at the Missouri until the white man's smallpox of the late eighteenth century decimated the crowded dwellings. Then, after a hundred years, the fortified villages crumbled and the Sioux swept over them and out upon the western prairies like a cloudburst washing over a buffalo trail. Periodically many returned to the river traders until some of their favorites moved down south of the Black Hills, to the White, the Niobrara, the Platte and the Republican Rivers. The Oglalas, Brules and part of the Minneconjou Sioux deserted the Missouri for all time. These, with the other divisions of the Tetons up around the Black Hills, the Yellowstone and beyond, became the dominant tribe between the Smoky Hill River of Kansas to Canada. So vast an area controlled by a nomadic hunting tribe was unique in America, perhaps in the world. Even so, the Sioux wars were usually a series of small or probing encounters to drive other Indians from the buffalo ranges and as a testing ground for the young warriors, the fights usually more for show than bloodshed and altogether not much more fatal than the white man's football. The highest warrior honor, the first-class coup, was touching an enemy without harming him, to be danced with a symbolic scalp by the women later. The coups brought position in the warrior society, gave the young man prominence in the village and in the eyes of the shy young maidens, and their families.

Such domination as that of the Sioux was only possible on a vast expanse of rich open prairie with the great buffalo herds to serve as a continuous self-replenishing commissary. Given iron, powder and the luxury of the horse, and saved the temptations and the pressures of the white man's whisky and ambition, the Plains Indian, north and south, could have lived an enviable life for a long, long time, husbanding his buffalo, developing his gentleman's life and his increasingly close relationship with the earth, the sky and everything between, a deep personal identification with all the universe around him, a oneness with the buffalo, the rock, the cloud, the tree.

Without a written creed or an organized priesthood the religion of any people adapts itself to new regions, new situations, rather quickly. The Pawnees carried their center of the earth along and the Cheyennes their Sacred Hat and Arrows as the white man brought his altar with its cross and its symbols of the blood and body of Christ. The Sioux, however, had left the last concrete symbol of his religion far behind and carried only a few remnants of an agrarian worship, such as the fertility rites within the sun dance, with him. So intellectualized had their religion become for the selfless leaders by 1877 that they were sometimes called the Unitarians of the American Indian.

Unfortunately the white man had to be accepted to get the fine things he brought. His goods demanded many furs and, with the beaver gone, very many robes, which meant killing buffalo far beyond the Indian's requirements for food and shelter. Often the whisky alone took not only most of the robes the women could tan and work while they and their children went ragged; in addition it made their men violent in the villages, and sometimes the women too—this where persistent noise and troublemaking had always brought ostracism. Some chiefs did ban the whisky wagons from their camps and took their people to the Powder River or the Tongue and Yellowstone, but there were Plains chiefs who became as sodden as any of the river villages and traded their prettiest maidens to the fur men and later the soldiers for the same favors.

Through the 1840's the Platte Sioux watched the strings of wagons move westward across their buffalo grounds, heard the boom of the guns and saw their valley bare and white as scattered snow in bleaching bones. Farther east the Pawnees were starving but afraid to follow the buffalo into strong Sioux country after some punishing attacks on their winter villages and summer hunting camps. By 1849 the Pawnees were so hard pressed that they gave up an old village site below Fort Kearny and moved in closer to the Missouri, far from the buffalo, with the people hungrier than ever. Emigrants complained more and more about these rascally show-offs who plundered the travelers and traders with their begging and thievery. They even attacked and plundered an occasional government wagon, and were described by the army as the worst Indians of the West, now that they were no longer quiet and compliant. Often they were contrasted to the tribes farther west, openly or by implication, as in a letter from Fort Laramie, September 18, 1849, in the Missouri *Republican:*

> We were visited a few days since by about two hundred Cheyennes and Sioux, who danced a little, stole a little, ate a great deal and finally went on their way rejoicing. These Platte Sioux, by the way, are the best Indians on the prairies. Look at their conduct during the past summer. Of the vast emigration, which rolled through their country this year, not a person was molested, not an article stolen. Such good conduct deserves reward.

One reward the Sioux received those years was the cholera. And scarcity of game. Gradually they, and the Cheyennes too, began to turn darkening faces toward the trails, demanding pay for the loss of their best hunting grounds, their buffalo herds and their happy camp sites at the Platte, once so fine in grass and water and meat. Besides, old mountain men like Fitzpatrick warned that the struggle for the shrinking buffalo grounds would increase and with the hunger there would be growing thievery and violence along the trails by every tribe. Finally the government moved to obtain a legal right to the Holy Road, as they called the Platte trails, and to bring peace between the tribes, divide the Indian country equitably between them forever. Old-timers in the region were hired to find out the early hunting claims of the various tribal divisions well ahead of the treaty conference called for the summer of 1851 at Horse Creek. The site had been suggested because it was well known from Nez Perce country to the land of the pueblos as a place for trade, for races and competitions, for feasting and dances, a place of peace.

The conference was the greatest gathering of Indians ever known. One group, one tribe after another, came charging up, mounted and in fullest glory of paint and feathers, beadwork and jewelry and dust. Gradually the great camp spread up and down the creek for many miles, the horse herds like cloud shadows over the farthest hills. There was much talk and scolding brought from the Great White Father, and big promises. Then when the chiefs hesitated and disagreed, for no one could tell another what must be done, the whites acted as Lewis and Clark had on the Missouri long ago, and many others since. In each tribe the commission selected a man they could manage and lifted him with power and many presents to sit over the chiefs picked by the people.

It was truly the biggest meeting ever held at Horse Creek, and the last, for within a few moons it was plain that the white man did not intend to honor the promises made at the place that was sacred to peace and the straight tongue. The Senate reduced the years of annual annuity for the Holy Road from fifty to ten, with perhaps five more allowed later, but the change was never submitted to the Indians in a way they understood. They could not imagine actually selling the earth, which belonged to all the generations to come, and considered the annuities as pay for the use of the trails. When the goods failed to appear, the Platte valley reverted to them, the Indians thought, and the whites who traveled on its trails were trespassers, taking what did not belong to them.

Soon there was another anger, one that ran through the Sioux country like a prairie fire in a high wind, leaving the same darkness over the land. Within three years after the treaty was signed at Horse Creek, Conquering Bear, the government's head chief over the Sioux, was dead, killed. The Indians had argued in 1851 that there could be no one headman, that they elected a circle of chiefs on each level, from the smallest camp to the great Teton council fire, the power always in the circle. Each man was selected for a stated period, and could be thrown from his high place any time the people wished. Only the circle lasted.

Now in 1854 while the Indians had waited in a hungry camp for weeks to receive their treaty annuities, already there but locked up, a Mormon cow, loose because she had gone lame, was caught by some hungry Brules and eaten. Conquering Bear had hurried to Laramie to pay for the cow, but Lieutenant Grattan mounted twenty-nine men and with two cannons headed down to the annuity camp of many thousand impatient Sioux, Cheyennes and Arapahoes. He came with too much youth and arrogance, after too long a stop at a roadhouse on the way, and with too much whisky in his interpreter and in some of the rest. The lieutenant halted his cannon at the head chief's lodge and blew it to pieces. Before the thundering echoes had died, he and his men fell, cut to bits, while all around them the women brought the lodgepoles down and fled for the hills. Some of the warriors broke into the trading houses holding the annuities and scattered with them. Those who had rescued the wounded head chief whipped his travois horse toward a medicine spring far in the sandhills, the spring that would surely heal the shell-torn man if they could get him there. But on the Niobrara he died, and was placed on a scaffold* overlooking the river that he had loved and an old camping ground that dated back perhaps to earliest man on the Plains.

The next year, when Harney came to punish the Indians for killing Grattan and making trouble along the trail, the offending young warriors were far away, but Little Thunder's peaceful camp on the Blue Water Creek was handy to be struck, the shelled bluffs left a mass of rock, clothing and torn bodies. For years the Indians told of that day, with the long string of captives Harney had gathered up, all those unable to run away but who could be made to walk—old people, women with small ones on their backs, and the wounded, some so pitiful that many troopers were ashamed.

It was then that one of the men said "Squaw Killer!" as he looked toward Harney. A couple of those beside him nodded, their young windburned faces gaunt.

One story told was of the woman who was cut across the abdomen by a piece of shell so her bowels and her unborn child hung out as she stooped over her clasped arms. Somehow she held herself together with her blanket and struggled on at the command of the mounted soldiers who drove the captives along behind the triumphant commander. He was so elated that he ordered his cannoneer to blow the top off the Chimney Rock that had been a welcome landmark for western travelers for years.

It was here, the Indians say, that the woman with the arms full of

---

* Apparently erected about 100 feet from the Niobrara home of Jules Sandoz, where sixty years later an occasional old Sioux still came to dance a little.

herself stumbled and fell, and did not move. Those who hesitated around her were hurried on, leaving the woman alone in the dust. That night one of the sentinels found two of the captives trying to sneak back. The women stiffened into the shadows, but the young soldier passed by, making a swift motion of the arms meaning "Go! Go!" When he had vanished in the darkness, they crawled into a gully and ran until they were discovered by their warriors come to skulk around, to help if they could. Together they found the dead woman, wrapped her in a robe and tied her into a tree in a far canyon. Years later the Sioux told about the young soldier, hoping that he came to greatness as another youth of that day had— a visiting Oglala who helped women and children get away from the attack and later became known as Crazy Horse.

Harney's troops marched into Fort Laramie with the white's man first victory over the Teton Sioux, singing about wiping out Little Thunder. They hadn't wiped the chief out at all, only the more helpless of his people, but they had put a barb of anger into the hearts of the Sioux to fester there a dozen lifetimes—an anger that would help bring the only two complete wipe-outs suffered by the U.S. Army, first at Fort Phil Kearny and then on the Little Big Horn.

At Fort Laramie, Harney, in his highhanded way, ordered Agent Twiss to have no contact at all with his charges—the Sioux, Arapahoes and Cheyennes whose annuities he was treaty-bound to deliver, whose little father and official spokesman he was. It is told that Squaw Killer did this with considerable satisfaction, bullying the old colonel of the army engineers, the old Military Academy honor man recently appointed Indian agent. Perhaps Harney, not a West Pointer, had suffered from some who were more arrogant than Agent Twiss, known as a gentleman and a scholar. It was not surprising that some time later Twiss chose the people of his gentle young Oglala wife, and, leaving Laramie and all his race behind, went with her out to the Powder River camps, where he was seen, now and then, for years, a fine white-haired old figure. Once at the trail with the Oglalas he spoke of the forts as little islands of whites in the great sea of Indians and buffalo, unaware, perhaps, that a little over twenty years later even the bleached bones of the great herds would be gone, and the Indians only little islands in a great sea of whites.

After Harney's attack in 1855 there were constant small encounters and irritations, even with the Cheyennes, who had gone far west to avoid trouble, taking their angry young men away from the trails. But some slipped down to help the Sioux avenge Little Thunder's dead, making the heart good again, making trouble for their people, the older Sioux and Cheyennes argued. This was very foolish now that nothing could be done about the shrinking game, the starvation and diseases brought by the whites, or about their curious ways. When a white man killed an Indian, only that one could be punished and only by his own people, who never found him; but if an Indian shot a white man, all the Indians the soldiers could catch, women and children too, were shot to pieces by the wagon guns.

Because this was true, a young Brule chief named Spotted Tail came in to draw the punishment for all upon himself. He came singing his death song. Irons were put on his hands and feet and, with some companions and his young wife, he was hauled by wagon to Fort Leavenworth. When he came back he brought insight no other Plains Indian possessed, and some understanding of the strength and number of the white man—powerful as the chain that tied all things inevitably to death, and numerous as the stars in the great white road across the evening sky. The Indian must learn to live with this white man, and yet in 1864 Spotted Tail was one of the leaders to close the Platte and Smoky Hill routes, not because he thought he could win for his people, but because he felt that now they must fight. And if this did not win a chance of life for them, then they would at least die honorably, die fighting.

The troubles of 1864 had been growing like a thunderhead bending from the western sky for months, years, and with more emotion on both sides, more tall tales even in the records, than about any except that later fight where Custer died. The Indians had heard what happened to the eastern Sioux in Minnesota, people who had accepted the white man's god and then were cheated and starved so that they had to fight until many died, whites and Indians.

In April the Platte Sioux were called in for a council. Several hundred arrived in bad humor but in great pomp, fully armed and finely mounted. The chiefs, over a dozen, laid off their weapons and seated themselves in a semicircle on the ground. Then the army officers moved in from among their soldiers and dropped their sabers and pistols in a pile. General Mitchell, in the only chair, a large folding one, was an imposing figure, tall, square, with full curly beard and strong sunburnt nose. The officers beside him were well selected, all six-footers, in blue uniforms and their red dress sashes.

Of course there were large men among the Sioux too, young Touch the Clouds seven feet tall, and others sitting with shoulders high. Spotted Tail, in the center of the chief's circle, drew out his long redstone pipe, filled it deliberately, lit it, sent the puffs to the earth, the sky and the great directions between, and handed it around. Then he rose, the Indians pushing forward to see. He asked what their white brother, the general, wanted with them. Mitchell demanded that the Sioux keep out of the Platte valley entirely. The interpretation of these words brought a powerful young chief to his feet, dropping his blanket, to stand naked in breechclout and moccasins. But he spoke quietly. They had been pushed back a long time, from the lakes and westward over the Missouri. Now it was enough.

Another man rose to tell the story of hunger and a third to protest the whisky and the cheating. Mitchell replied in words that came hot from his beard. "The white men caught selling whisky to the Indians are put into chains." This brought a roar of denial from the warriors, and even the officers beside the general shifted uncomfortably. But Mitchell went right on. The Indian *wanted* the whisky, he said, and this time the interruption was so great that the pipe had to be relit and sent around to quiet the tempers.

Then Mitchell repeated that he wanted a treaty to keep the

Indians out of the Platte valley. They must come no closer than the hills, for they scared the women and children. If they wished to cross the river they must send word to one of the posts, and soldiers would escort them through.

"This is our country!" one chief shouted. "We will not be told where we can go!"

Mitchell went on speaking through the noise, his lips showing red as they moved. The bad Indians must be restrained, and if they were not, the headmen would be held responsible.

"Is the soldier chief put in irons when foolish whites shoot our women and children?"

There was no reply to this, only that if it took more bacon or blankets or corn to keep them out of the Platte valley, they would get more. To this the chiefs sat silent, but not the young men. "Promises!" they shouted. "Our chiefs are bought with promises that are less than the wind on the buffalo grass!"

Now Spotted Tail put his pipe aside and rose again, the one feather of his chieftainship standing in his hair, his blue blanket drawn close about him, his strong womanish face as remote as Cloud Peak of the Big Horns. The Sioux did not care about the Platte any more, he said. The game was scared away, the grass and wood gone, the water dirtied. But they must have places to sell their robes. They had let the white man pass; now he would not let them pass. About this they would see. He wanted everybody to know that they were not afraid of all the whites together.

So the council was adjourned and a feast made of boiled beef, coffee, hard bread and molasses in the tin plates passed around. Not long afterward a wagon was attacked within sight of the troops and set afire, the two men killed, the horses run off. The North Platte River ran in flood eight feet deep and no one followed the Indians, who shook the two fresh scalps at the soldiers and then joined a camp nearby, said to be Cheyennes.

The second council was no better than the first, with another postponement. Spotted Tail took his angry Brules clear up to the Powder; the Oglalas were already away at White River. When some of their young warriors wanted to start on the warpath, they were overtaken, the leaders killed, their belongings in the village destroyed, as must be done to public menaces. In June a great caravan of Mormons passed along the north bank of the Platte, many of them foreigners, moving by every means, from bull train to handcart, everybody carrying something, and not one soldier along for protection. The warriors did not molest them. They were friends.

In July the Indians were called into council again. This time there were more warriors, few women and no small children at all. A new sullenness was plain among the usually affable Sioux, perhaps because they had heard that Mitchell was bringing a battalion of scouts, Pawnee Indians, their eternal enemies, in soldier coats. To avoid trouble Major North camped his scouts two miles from the Sioux and Cheyennes. Some said Mitchell was determined to force the headmen into a treaty. Anyway, he ordered them to a canyon over near the Pawnees, away from their warriors. But everybody went, the wilder young men shouting insults at the soldier Pawnees, who shouted back. The general hurried his escort of sixty-five men up, setting them in a thin line between the enemy Indians, the men facing in alternate directions with drawn sabers flashing in the sun. Then one trooper stuck his saber into an anthill for a talking place, and the general and some men rode out to it as the bugler sounded "Forward!" while behind them a detail moved up with a howitzer hidden in an open arrangement of cavalry, but aimed at the Sioux chiefs.

Mitchell started by speaking for peace between the two tribes, but there were no "Hous!" of approval from either side, only silence until finally a Sioux in a long feather headdress walked out and spoke. He didn't think the Pawnees amounted to much even as enemies, and to please the Great Father and the general he would agree to let them alone.

There were angry snarls to this, and a long conferring among the Pawnees. Finally one stepped forward, in blue army breeches, short hair bared. His people were willing to make peace, he said. Smallpox had come, their land was gone, everything gone that they would fight for. Now all they asked was that the Sioux and Cheyennes let them alone.

For a moment it seemed that someone among the Indians there must understand who the enemy was, the warriors from both sides fall upon the few white men in their army blue and their long knives that flashed. But instead the Sioux warriors were taunting the Pawnees, "Why are you here, with soldier guns in your hands?" the few Sioux women along making obscene signs to the Pawnees, deprecating their manhood, until it seemed someone would shoot, and so Mitchell pushed his horse forward and stopped the council.

The old mountain men and the traders shook their heads when they heard what Mitchell had done this spring and summer. "He's set the country afire," they told each other. "Bringing in the Pawnees was the worst."

After a few peace men, including a couple of Cheyenne chiefs, were shot down coming forward to shake hands with advancing troops, it was plain that the extermination policy started by Harney was still in full force, in spite of the outspoken and active opposition from some officers who knew the Indians and their situation. There were increasing incidents in Kansas, eastern Colorado and from Julesburg down to Kearny on the Platte. East of there it was quieter until the day some friendly Cheyennes let troops come near. When six of their camp were shot down, they realized they were in a war too. They fled, leaving even their horses, and when the relatives of the dead men killed some emigrants, the chiefs took the band deep into Kansas, hoping to keep the angry warriors and the foolish young men of the army apart. But soldiers came there too, and besides the Indians knew now that the goods for the Holy Road, even the little they had received, were to be cut off, and instead of getting the road back they were told to keep out of the Platte valley entirely. Besides no trade for guns or ammunition was to be permitted anywhere, no trade, no sale, no gift, with the people hungry, the buffalo very scarce. But there were ways of getting guns—by raids, and in trade for the good horses and mules one could take from the whites.

Because the soldiers shot at anybody this year, several Sioux chiefs asked for white representatives of the government to come live among them, to tell any approaching troops that they were peaceful. This was not done. Instead several good men were shot, the most peaceful bands so angered that even the white men married into the villages felt in danger. Rumors of secret Indian councils and far signaling reached the generals, but they believed that destroying a camp or two and sending the Indians flying over the prairie like sheep from the wolf would quiet the West.

It was then that the Indians moved. August seventh they struck from Julesburg down into the valley of the Little Blue, getting guns, ammunition, horses, mules, coffee, sugar and sometimes a little whisky. Most important were the guns, too few but good—guns and the power of closing the trail. This time the depredations and the killings were the stories of the whites, the settlers, as those of Harney's attack on the Blue Water had been the Indians'. Here too the innocent paid with their lives, but not nearly as many as with Little Thunder or even in this year's fighting, and no one as important as the Cheyenne peace chiefs down in Kansas.

The Kansas-Nebraska frontier was thrown into a panic, and the few troops along the trail mostly shut themselves up in the forts. More soldiers were marched in, many of them Galvanized Yankees —Confederate prisoners who had taken the oath of allegiance and enlisted to fight Indians. Even so, weeds were sprouting on the trails for the first time in twenty years. No one dared move without a large force of troops riding on all sides, their guns shining, perhaps a black-mouthed little cannon along.

The Indians could not sustain a war without a steady supply of arms and ammunition any more than they could feed their people. Before long the cottonwoods yellowed toward winter and meat had to be made, slow and hard work now. The government ordered the peaceful Indians to separate themselves immediately from the depredators, who would be hunted down and severely punished.

Black Kettle, long a peace chief, took his Cheyennes to the place his agent designated as safe—at Sand Creek, Colorado, close to the agent and far from the trails and trouble. There Colonel Chivington fell upon them with his Colorado Volunteers, hundred-day men who had recently been ordered into a Civil War area where a man could get killed. A little Indian fighting at home would help keep them there until their enlistment expired, so Black Kettle's people, mostly women and children and old men, were slaughtered in the cold November dawn, scalps from the head and elsewhere displayed on the vaudeville stage of Denver a few nights later to great applause and laughter, and some horror and alarm.

The shock of what was plainly a massacre spread over the nation, particularly among those who recalled the Emancipation Proclamation of last year, and the war being fought for the rights of another dark-faced people. Yet so successfully had the public image of the Indian been changed from Noble Red Man to bloodthirsty savage that such slaughter could be planned and carried out in the administration of the Great Emancipator, and without one protest from a voice that must be heard.

Surely more innocent ones would die, this time for those who lay on the ground at Sand Creek. As soon as the mourning ceremonials were done, the war pipe was carried as far as the Powder River to draw the young Oglala warriors and hundreds of the Brules in addition to the Northern Cheyennes, who were grieving for their relations, and angry as only a people who had tried to be peaceful can be when driven to war. These all went down to rescue the bereaved and crippled Cheyennes, who had lost everything—lodges, bed robes, winter meat and the wealth of fine beadwork—bring them to the Powder country, far from shooting soldiers.

Black Kettle, still the peace chief, went south, but many of his followers joined what became the greatest war party known to the Plains. Usually winter brought peace to the region because the ponies were weak and thin, living on cottonwood bark gnawed from the young growth that the women cut and dragged home. But this open fall and winter the horses were strong from the fine cured grasses.

Early in January 1865 the huge war camp started out of Kansas, to cut a swath a hundred miles wide north across the Platte country. The first attack was on Julesburg, by a reported one thousand warriors. The Indians had tried to decoy the soldiers out of the little post nearby and failed, but killed some. The stagecoach passengers, at the station for breakfast, fled to the post, the army paymaster too, leaving his money box behind.

The Indians plundered the station, carrying away sacks of shelled corn and flour, too, which they dumped on the ground to get the cloth bags for shirts and breechclouts. They unwound bolts of bright calico to float on the winter wind, hacked into the paymaster's money box and threw the apparently useless greenbacks aside. One warrior was said to have chopped a stack of these to pieces with his hatchet and tossed them to flutter like summer leaves on the wind. Then suddenly the moon took on a pale snow warning and the Indians struck for the Powder canyons, burning stage stations and road ranches all the way across the Platte, most of the places deserted, the keepers gone.

As was to be expected, many stories are told of that year, told this way and that, with several versions of the greatest prairie fire of the Plains. Some recounters, including the Indians, date this along in January. General Mitchell, hoping to stop the warrior march north, had organized a vast fire-setting crew from Fort Kearny up along the south side of the Platte and the South Fork, deep into Colorado. Swept on by the growing north wind, the little flames spread into one vast blazing front that roared down across the southwest section of Nebraska, west Kansas and eastern Colorado, jumping the frozen Arkansas on the way to the Texas Panhandle, where the flames died naturally. But the Indians were well north before the fire started.

Some say that it wasn't Mitchell but another officer who set the fire, and not in January but in October. If that were true there should have been no Sand Creek massacre in November because there would have been no Indians there, not without grass for the buffalo or the ponies. Nor could there have been the long camping

in northwest Kansas and the slow march of the Indians up from
Cherry Creek to Julesburg and north without forage or game.

But even at its best the Mitchell fire was less than a will-o'-the-wisp
rising from some buffalo bog compared to the one the general had
ignited the summer before with his arrogant councils. These, with
the conflagration started by the government policy of those years,
set a blaze that was to sweep over the Plains in war whoop and
scalp knife, one that still smolders in angry breasts, Indian and
white.

The size and determination of the war march astonished the
government, and the next summer troops for a large three-pronged
expedition marched into the Powder and Yellowstone country.
That this was illegal concerned no one. "Receive no overtures of
peace; kill all males over twelve," Connor ordered Cole as they
started. But no one told this to the Indians, who, in their innocence,
led the troops a tantalizing chase through the wilderness until the
soldiers had lost most of their horses and equipment, found the
game all scared away before their line of march, and finally were glad
to get back to Fort Laramie, walking, practically barefoot, and
starving, but otherwise unharmed. It was a good story, whether told
in the camps of the Powder River, east among the Indian lovers of
New England or deep in the South, where war defeat was heavy
upon the people. For a long time nobody told them that cannon had
to be turned on the Galvanized Yankees at Fort Laramie to get them
to move out against the Indians at all. They argued that their war was
over. Besides, other troops mutinied too, until the cannons faced
them.

In 1865 the idea of a transcontinental railroad was still such a tall
tale that all the derring-do, the vice and crime, of its building was
like a Plains thunderstorm, with dust and noise and great bolts of
lightning to tear the sky and drop a few spatters of rain in the road.
The alarm of its coming spread into the farthest Yellowstone
country. A fire wagon, a monster, roared westward on an iron path,
with a big eye like the sun and a stinking smoke and shaking noise

that scared the people and the game. Plainly the Holy Road had not been sold for this. Small parties swept down on the graders and track layers, stampeding the horses, putting arrows into the herders and anybody caught beyond the reach of the good rifles always there.

One of the stories most often retold was Turkey Leg's wreck at Plum Creek. With rawhide ropes the Cheyennes tore out a culvert and from a rise watched a freight engine stretch out over the hole a second like a giant caterpillar reaching for the next leaf. Then it crashed, the cars piling up against it with a great noise and hissing of steam and spinning of wheels. Some said that the fireman was thrown into the firebox and burned, the engineer lost between the churning drivers. In the confusion the conductor got away to the telegraph at Plum Creek. The Indians attacked, left five men on the ground and broke into boxes of groceries and dry goods, tied bolts of bright ribbon and cloth to the tails of their ponies and raced over the prairie, the fine streamers whipping out in the wind behind.

Later one of the men on the ground regained consciousness, his face bloody, his head torn bare, the scalp nearby, dropped after the coup was witnessed. He put the piece of hairy skin into a bucket of water and took the rescue train to Omaha, hoping to have the scalp sewed back into place. But by then it was slimy and stinking, so he dried it and carried it in his pocket the rest of his life to prove his story.

Up in Wyoming the Oglala Sioux chief Red Cloud was leading the siege against the Bozeman Trail forts and, with the rising young war chief, Crazy Horse, the annihilation of Fetterman. The treaty of 1868 gave the Indians what had always been theirs—most of the west half of Nebraska north of the Platte, with hunting privileges below the river, their old hunting grounds of Wyoming, the Dakotas and Montana for "So long as grass shall grow and water flow," as they were told at the time, although events soon denied this.

With the Platte country free of depredations, once more important visitors came. In 1871 James Gordon Bennett of the New York *Herald* arrived for a buffalo chase, bringing his French chef, waiters in full dress and two wagons to carry the ice and the wines. At North Platte he saw a handsome young Long Hair named Cody, called Buffalo Bill, the nickname, like most on the frontier, from some unfortuitous circumstance. Cody had been set afoot and running by an enraged buffalo bull when he was shooting meat for the Kansas Pacific. The name stuck and became an asset after Bennett saw Cody's possibilities.

The next January a more elaborate hunt was arranged for Duke Alexis of Russia and his gold-braid retinue, Russian and American. Spotted Tail, the same wily Spot who less than eight years before had helped close the Platte and Smoky Hill trails brought about a thousand of his Brules to put on a great show of Indian life and buffalo hunting, making certain that the Duke got a fine large head, one that the Russian swore looked phenomenally larger in camp than when he shot it. That was one of the truths that Spotted Tail would know, also that the credit for the big heads must go to a white man, preferably one of those darlings of the army, the men they called scouts and guides, in a region where everyone knew the location of the smallest Indian camp, where trails were plain a mile off.

By treaty the Sioux and Cheyennes were free to roam their old hunting grounds of the Powder and the Yellowstone, but the government tried to toll them to Indian agencies, the one for the Oglalas called Red Cloud's Sod Agency, on the north bank of the North Platte, just west of the Nebraska line. The warriors had resisted all pressure to put this up on the White River, even considering its present location illegal because no whites, not even agency employees, were permitted in Indian country. The wild young Oglalas with nothing to do liked to whip their horses through the dusty little agency, whooping and shooting, scattering the whites like their chickens. The Indians found this particularly amusing after a few drinks of whisky, always handy here, where lawless traders and the breeds could carry it across the river in the night.

"Move back," the agent and his Great Father in Washington kept saying to Red Cloud. "Move back from the trails, to the White River."

Many of the Sioux remained in the Powder River country, with fine little fights against Crows and Shoshonis. To keep the young men of the agencies from running away to these great goings-on, and to help fill in the subsistence cuts by Congress and by the grafting of the contractors, the agency Indians were allowed to hunt down in the Republican valley. Settlers were pushing in there very rapidly, and while there was little trouble with them, there was friction between the Indians and the buffalo-hide men, who scattered the country with millions of naked, rotting, stinking carcasses, killed by their fine rifles when even the poorest guns or ammunition were denied the Indian to feed his hungry family.

"Killing our cattle," Spotted Tail protested. When his young warriors shot a white man's cow, they got a bullet.

The year of 1872 brought new anger to Spot's people. In February, just after they helped make the big show for Duke Alexis, a killing blizzard destroyed thousands of range cattle, almost all the Texas stock, unaccustomed to deep snow, to rustling on wind-swept ridges or to the furious freezing storms that caked the eyes and drove them into bottomless drifts. Because there were Sioux in the region, living off the remnants of the buffalo herd, John Bratt, cattleman of the North Platte region, devised a scheme to make the Indians pay for the dead stock. Spotted Tail was apparently very hard pressed, for it seems he touched the pen to a paper saying his people had killed thirty head of Bratt cattle in the blizzard. According to rumors, two ciphers were added to the paper and presented to the Indian Bureau for 3,000 cattle at $30 a head, $90,000 to be deducted from the poor thin goods due the Indians. When the Oglalas and Brules heard of this, they were in an uproar. On investigation* years later, it came out that the claim was for $20,000 and $9,801 actually paid from the Indian funds. The chiefs proved in court that they killed no cattle, could not have killed even the thirty head of Spotted Tail's paper. The money was refunded to the Sioux, not hastily, of course, not

* By Justice Bayard H. Paine, Nebraska State Supreme Court.

until 1879, but it was money paid back to Indians.

On top of the anger about this theft from their funds and the rapid destruction of the buffalo by the hide men came the shooting of the peace chief Whistler, by Wild Bill Hickok and his partner. Whistler, an Oglala chief married to a Brule woman, was with the Sioux down on the Republican trying to make a little meat for the winter. The country was full of the skinned carcasses and very few live buffalo, all too wild. Hickok was well known to the Oglalas and Brules from back in 1861 on the Oregon Trail, when he killed McCanles, later around Fort McPherson, and particularly the last five years in and out of the Republican valley hunting buffalo. The Indians knew every hunter's camp around, and when Whistler and two relatives didn't get home from a visit with friends, the chief's horse was tracked to a stop at Hickok's outfit, probably for coffee, as he had done before. The place was deserted, plainly in haste, with blood patches on the ground. The Indians followed Hickok's wagon tracks to the bodies, and the hoofprints of Whistler's horse to the Platte, where they found Hickok's partner riding it. Those who followed the loaded wagon away from the camp ended at Sidney, where they were told Hickok had sold all his hides in the wagon and out on the Republican and left, never to return to his old hunting grounds, as the Indians knew, for they would be waiting.

Swift distribution of troops between the Sioux, the hunting camps (all suddenly deserted now) and the white settlements discouraged the hot young men who pointed out that it was always the peace chiefs who got the shooting: Conquering Bear, the villages of Little Thunder and Black Kettle, and now the white man's best friend, Whistler.

Realizing that there would be avenging, and that other chiefs would hesitate to turn friendly, the War Department sent out investigators to run down the murderers, drive them from the Indian country for the sake of peace. Obviously no white man would be punished for killing an Indian, no matter how friendly, not by a government operating on an extermination policy since 1855. After the investigation blew over, practically everybody except Bill Cody claimed to have killed Whistler, including Doc Carver, out of the region at the time, and Bill Kress, a buffalo hunter, who, according to his Indian friends, took up with a young woman among Whistler's relatives, where the chief's murderer would not have lasted over night. Kress was later driven out for stealing Sioux ponies, but by then Whistler's killer had been avenged. The chief's peaceful adopted son had vowed a red blanket on the ground, meaning his blood at sundance time, for the death of Hickok. He had to wait almost four years. Then he danced his vow in the ceremonials near White Clay Creek and gave all his good horses to the needy in gratitude to the Great Powers.

Ever since the Tall Bull fight in 1869 the Sioux itched for revenge upon the Pawnees. Several Sioux visiting in Tall Bull's camp had seen the savagery of the Pawnee scouts among the women and children, a savagery those Indians had had little opportunity to wreak upon Cheyennes until the army put them into uniform. Finally, in the Pawnee hunt of 1873 the Sioux got even, although both tribes had their acting agents along. Perhaps the Pawnees had become soft in the years with the soldier coats, overly secure. When they were warned that the Sioux were hunting nearby, they thought the hide men were trying to scare them away from the last little bunches of buffalo. When the Sioux attacked, the Pawnees fled down the canyon, dropping baggage, cutting loose from the travois. The unlucky, the slow, went down under the Sioux charge. The whole band would have been wiped out if troops from McPherson hadn't galloped to the rescue. Even so, many died, some say seventy or more, and hundreds wounded, crippled. It was probably the largest slaughter of Indians by Indians on the middle Plains, and long regretted by the Sioux.

"We let the white man split us," they said. "We should have stood together in a row like the hard face of the Big Horns against all the whites. We tried a little, once, but not enough."

Because hunting was now impossible for the Pawnees, and the white man would not keep his treaty promises to feed his charges, the children he had made of that brave warrior people, they let him send them on the unhappy march to Indian Territory. Soon they were shaking with malaria and gaunted by starvation dysentery. In two years half the tribe was dead—in less than two years.

February 1874 a North Platte paper close to Fort McPherson reported that there was no Indian unrest, and Generals Sheridan, Ord and Reynolds had all gone east. Army men might not grasp the Indian situation, but they all understood the possible effect of the panic of 1873 upon their investments, their military careers. Military curtailment would be ordered by the economy Congress and every man wanted to be in Washington to look after his interests.

The hard times that drove the generals east and sent thousands of the unemployed and the lawless west to the buffalo ranges shook banks and businesses so they fell like overripe plums in a wind-swept thicket. Big speculations like railroads were rocked. Track laying stopped on the Kansas roads. The Northern Pacific, headed up the Yellowstone where the nontreaty Sioux under Crazy Horse had attacked the surveyors the last two summers, ended in rusted rails east of the Missouri. New investors with billions of dollars were needed fast, and the only way to get them seemed by publicizing the gold long known to lie in the Black Hills and to pretend that the Hills were on the N.P. route. True, white men were excluded from all that region by treaty, but Indian treaties had never been more than a Missouri sandbar in flood time. Custer, as the most flamboyant military figure and a writer who thumped his own tub, was sent into the Black Hills, and although the Indians burned the prairie for his stock, they could not fight the guns and cannon of his large expedition.

As the Indians anticipated, a messenger whipped out of the Hills with the news of gold found at the grass roots, but not for the Indian's enrichment. Once more the gold seekers came, this time thick as the grasshoppers that were skinning the crops and the prairies of Kansas and Nebraska. With pick and gold pan the miners swarmed over the sacred Black Hills of the Sioux, his before the

American Revolution, and reguaranteed by the treaty of 1868, or so he thought, by that promise: "So long as grass shall grow—"

The angry hostiles from the Powder River country buzzed around the hills and the tamer warriors slipped out to raid the gold outfits, but the miners were too many and came from all directions, bringing a new anger to the agencies that had been forced back from the Platte to the White River. Many warriors turned against Red Cloud now, calling him a sold-out chief as they rode toward the Powder River and the stories of great exploits. The young men who remained were ready for any trouble. When the foolish agent decided to raise a flag, Red Cloud sat on a pile of poles, watching, smoking his pipe, silent, still the politician, risking nothing until he saw which way the warriors jumped. They charged in to chop the pole to pieces and he still said nothing, not even to their angry defense: "We will not have anything of the soldiers here!"

The commotion spread. Suddenly the agency was thick with whooping, painted Indians, the few whites cowering behind their barred doors, more and more Sioux riding in from the camps around, shooting, swinging war clubs. Long animosities between the Oglala factions began to break into the open, between the Loaf-About-the-Forts and those who felt they were sold out by Red Cloud, and from back when Red Cloud, in a drunken fit, had killed the chief of another band. Then there was the anger gathering around Conquering Bear's son. He was torn from his horse, knocked down, a bowstring set across his throat. "Your father started it all! Becoming the white man's chief!" one shouted as he stood on the bow.

But he was thrown aside by Sitting Bull, the Oglala, as a small detachment of troops came galloping from Camp Robinson nearby. The Indians charged around them, at least a thousand against the handful of soldiers, tearing at them, anticipating the first shot that would start the killing. But Sitting Bull came forcing his horse in, swinging his three-bladed war club, ordering the warriors back, knocking them off their horses, making a path through which the soldiers spurred to the stockade, the gate slamming behind them. Outside, with his powerful roaring voice, Sitting Bull commanded the

Indians away, and they went, slowly, but went.

Next spring when the Sioux chiefs were called to Washington, there was a gift rifle engraved "SITTING BULL from the President For Bravery & True Friendship," for the one who was now called the Good, to set him off from Sitting Bull, the Hunkpapa, who was making trouble up north. What the whites wanted was to buy the Black Hills. Red Cloud and Spotted Tail shook their heads. They must council with their people. Only the white man did it the other way. So there was a conference in September in the White River valley, with many of the hostiles down from the north to threaten a bullet through the heart of any chief who rose to speak for selling the Hills. Many from the agencies were painted and armed too, ready. Suddenly the Commission found that they were cut off from the small handful of soldiers along, surrounded by angry Sioux with guns against every back and upon the chiefs in the council circle. Behind them all were more Indians, thousands, angry and roaring. One shot and the massacre of the whites would begin. There was a paleness upon the faces of the commissioners, senators and generals both, and a silence that was not of the will.

Then one man rose from the chief's circle, daring the bullet to the heart, waiting silently for it to come, his chest bared. But there was none because the brave one was Young Man, Afraid of His Horse. Now he ordered the angry warriors back, and when none moved he repeated the command, snarling it out. This time they went, first one and then another pushing back, until there was a path for the white men to get to the ambulance, the prairie wagon, and start for Fort Robinson, the driver whipping the horses into a lunging gallop, much of the way lined by jeering mounted Sioux.

For days the telegraph and the newspapers spoke of the young chief's daring, his quiet courage, his power over the wildest warrior to save the Commission. They did not know that they spoke of a member of the most honored family of all the Sioux, not only of the Tetons but of them all. The family went back to when it was called Man, His Enemy Is Even Afraid of His Dog, before there was a horse on the continent, or one white man. It was the father, Man,

Afraid of His Horse, who refused to be made a government chief after Conquering Bear was killed in 1854. The Sioux selected their own chiefs, he said, and could throw them from their high place any time. He was a Sioux and not to be bought by the power and presents of the white man.

"They are the Adams family of the American Indian," one who knew them said. "Brave and wise in war and in council, peaceful, judicious, and responsible, modest and incorruptible."

Early in December 1875 the government ordered all the Indians to the reservations, although by treaty they had the right to roam the Powder and Yellowstone country so long as there was hunting. All Indians not in by January 31 would be considered hostile and struck by troops. Evidently this was planned to further the extermination. No messengers could penetrate the farthest reaches of the Powder and Yellowstone in the snows of midwinter, locate the camps scattered for protection, for wood and a little game, get them moving in time. The ponies were gaunt and stumbling from nothing but cottonwood bark for two months, the weather falling to forty below zero, the route back long for the old, the sick, the infant—from three to five hundred miles.

"It is planned that many shall die," the older ones said.

February 1 the entire Teton Sioux nation was turned over to the War Department and Sheridan tried to launch a winter campaign, as he had eight years ago in the south, into Texas. There was sour laughter all over the country from those who had felt Little Phil's spurred heel, or the heels of Phil's boys—Custer at the Washita, Carr at Summit Springs, and certainly more to feel them before it was ended.

This was real extermination, bullets and starvation up north, with the buffalo about gone there too, and sickness and starvation on the agencies. Many preferred to die on their feet, which might be soon, because there was only one year left to the Grant administration that let the Plains army show-offs ride so high. They would surely make the most of this year.

Events moved swiftly now. The Northern Cheyennes were struck first. They had always kept north, considered themselves at peace with the whites, even during the war of 1864. But now they were shot out of their winter beds in their own country and sent running, those who could, to the camp of Crazy Horse, whose people divided what they had: lodges, robes and meat. This attack brought rising anger at the agencies where they were eating their ponies to keep alive, the younger, the stronger, slipping away north, bringing what they could—not the coffee and sugar and tobacco that the Northerners missed so much with the trade cut off, but a few guns and some powder from the illegal traders around the agencies or captured on the big gold roads into their Black Hills.

General Crook had to retreat from the Rosebud fight because finally one man among the Sioux realized that they could not win against soldiers with good guns, and standing in a solid row. Not so long as their warriors, badly armed, fought in the old Indian way, when and how it suited each one, anybody free to stop in the midst of a battle to rest or roast a little meat. Crazy Horse, the war chief respected by both Sioux and Cheyenne, managed to get some organization into the repeated attacks on Crook's force that June 17, and when evening came it was the general who left the field. A week later Custer and his men lay scattered on the ridge at the Little Big Horn, but there was no joy in the Indian camps. Crazy Horse and the others knew that now soldiers would really come running through their country thick and angry as the bumblebee from a tramped-on nest.

It was time for the treaty-stipulated summer hunt, and with no beef to issue at the agency it was hard to hold the Indians, particularly a band of Northern Cheyennes who had been peaceful and kept their young men out of the fighting. They were told they could not go, but they knew they must if the children were to be saved. Carr, who had struck Tall Bull's camp at Summit Springs and shared in the general glory that Sheridan's boys reaped at the expense of the Southern Cheyennes, was scouting the Mini Pusa, across the old lodgepole trail to the Powder. July 1 Merritt took over the troops

and after the news of Custer's defeat he was ordered to hurry to
Laramie for supplies and join the waiting Crook up in northern
Wyoming for a swift thrust against the Indians. Instead, Merritt
swung around east toward Red Cloud to intercept the Cheyennes.

"Seems safer than chasing Crazy Horse," the old troopers said.

In the surprise of the Cheyenne camp, three young warriors, including Yellow Hand, rode out to hold the soldiers off while the
people, mostly old ones, and women and children, got away. Yellow
Hand had clapped his war bonnet on, to draw the eye and the fire.
There was a volley from the troops, smoke puffing out in sudden
blue rows, then again, bullets whistling around him. His horse went
down. Coolly, in the old-time warrior way, he drew the bridle off,
tucked his war bonnet under his belt and started to walk quietly back
while the Cheyennes cheered, the women sang strong-heart songs.
Then he was hit and fell. A soldier spurred up, dismounted, grabbed
the war bonnet and shook it in the air while another man came to
squat down beside Yellow Hand. The grass flared into fire and the
Cheyennes fled back to the agency, the troops never catching up.

That fall Cody held up a tuft of hair in his show, shouting, "The
first scalp for Custer!" with a fancy story of killing Yellow Hand
in a duel with knives, large posters advertising the show portraying
the tall tale. Years later the Cheyenne woman Cody usually hired
to make his beaded buckskin shirts laughed at the story. She had
seen the killing and their friend Buffalo Bill was not there. They
would have made no beadwork for any civilian who killed Yellow
Hand any more than the Sioux would have made any for Hickok
after he shot Whistler. Killing by soldiers and warriors in battle was
honorable. A killing by Cody, a civilian, a friend, would have been
murder and the heart could only have been made good by blood
afterward.

Miners, mine equipment and boomtown accounterments were
cutting deep trails into the Black Hills from the Missouri at Pierre,
across northern Nebraska, from Kearney northwest through the
sandhills, out of Cheyenne and, the shortest route, from Sidney, that

trail passing within whooping distance of Red Cloud Agency, past dark and sullen faces. All these trails were illegal and all the activity in the Black Hills too. The army drove out a few miners and missed the thousands. The gold seekers, mine promoters, railroad backers, cattlemen and all kinds of investors had money and lobbyists working for the sale of the Hills. A second conference was called, the Indians to be compelled to sell before Grant was out of office and the matter became complicated. This time the conference was not held in the open, but in the Red Cloud Agency stockade. When the chiefs said they couldn't sign the paper, that they were too few by the treaty of 1868, and could not speak for all those north with Crazy Horse, the stockade doors were locked. Then the chiefs were told there would be no food for their women and children on all the reservation until the paper was signed, the Black Hills sold.

"They have let them steal our Pa Sapa!" the young men shouted when the stockade doors were opened and the chiefs, suddenly very old, walked out on dead moccasins. Not Sitting Bull the Good. He had been a peace man since 1868, but now it was enough. He had whipped the other chiefs in scorn, shouting, "Go north! Maybe there a man can still live in honor a little while!" Out, he headed for Crazy Horse, as many others did, even Red Cloud himself, it seemed. He moved his camp farther and farther away until one dawn troops and the Pawnee scouts came upon him. The horse herd was swept away, the guns taken from the hands, even that of the great Red Cloud, who eight years before had forced the United States government to dismantle the Bozeman forts. Now he walked the sorrowful miles back to his agency, his followers and his family afoot too, helpless, even the bows gone.

This winter the Sioux and the Northern Cheyennes at Red Cloud learned what slow extermination meant, while those with Crazy Horse had to run over the frozen hills of Montana, cannonballs bursting among them. The buffalo was gone, too wise, it seemed, to stay on an earth where such things were done, for surely the great herds could not have been killed by man. So, as soon as the thin ponies of Crazy Horse were able to travel, he brought his starving, ragged people in. To save them he had to believe the promise of a reservation up in the Tongue River country, where they could rest and have peace.

But that was one more promise gone like the wind on the buffalo grass. As soon as the guns were handed over they heard that every-one must go to Indian Territory. Spotted Tail had taken a trip down to see and returned saying that even the Pawnees, the favored friends of the whites, were dying of sickness and the thin belly. The Cheyennes, with no agency, finally agreed to go, on the promise they could return if they wished, to their beloved Yellowstone. They started, looking back toward the White River from the ridge before they went down the other side, the women keening as for a thousand dead.

Before long there was a death at Fort Robinson, where the soldiers looked down the throats of the Oglalas. All summer envy of the young chief Crazy Horse had been growing. Red Cloud's warriors were deserting him for the new camp, following the plain, unadorned, silent man with their eyes and their moccasins when he came in to the agency. The army officers, even General Crook when he came through, liked to go to the lodge of Crazy Horse to talk about life in the north and about the fighting on the Rosebud and against Reno and Custer. It was plain from the stories around the agency and the reports to Washington that the officers found the young chief very interesting, not only as warrior and field general, but as a man.

Then another kind of rumor swept through the agency like dust on a whirlwind. Crazy Horse, it seemed, was to be placed over the old entrenched government chiefs. This was met by misinterpreta-tion and lies of planned treachery, both from the Indians and from the scout, Grouard, who feared Crazy Horse because he had come to the chief's camp on the Tongue River when the officers were looking for the murderer of army mail carriers in Montana. Crazy Horse knew this and, also, that Grouard was the Sioux, white and Negro mixed-blood named Brazzeau who had fled Missouri with Cadet Chouteau after a murder at school. Perhaps Grouard suspected Crazy Horse would expose him—a most unlikely prospect. More probably the scout was backed by a combination of Red Cloud followers and others envious of the young chief's power and prospects, men who wanted him out of the way. Responsible interpreters protested the mistranslations, but it was too late. Crazy Horse was arrested and taken to the guardhouse, with a wagon waiting to hurry him out in the night, to the railroad and Dry Tortugas, perhaps to die in irons far from his beloved Plains. But when the chief saw the prison bars he jumped back and, held by an Oglala, was bayoneted through the kidney by a trooper, and a second time. That night he died. The real tall-tale man of the Plains, their very essence, died.

With Crazy Horse gone the resistance of the Sioux crumbled and they were moved out of Nebraska forever, or at least their agencies were. Eighty years later many would be back in the state but without reservation there—unlanded, largely unwanted, without education or training for a livelihood—displaced persons living in a starvation and squalor not to be tolerated for people of any skin but red. But that fall of 1877 the troops pushed the disheartened Indians northeast toward the Missouri. They went sullenly between the blue-coated soldiers, the Crazy Horse parents carrying the body of their son along, to be hidden and rehidden until it seemed no alien eye could ever see it again. Without verve or spirit these remnants of the once great Teton Sioux went, defeated by iron things—guns, wagons and railroads, but mostly guns in the hands of the buffalo hunters. No greatness showed in these Sioux now, although within the last eleven years they had wiped out two arrogant men and their trained troopers. The only humor left was in the wild young warriors driving loaded wagons for the first time. Not understanding or caring about brakes down the hills, they stood up, whooping and whipping their horses to keep them ahead of the pursuing wheels, perhaps to upset or to pile together at the bottom. The cheap contract wagons broke down all the way, the troops cursing and sweating in the fall wind to get the long sad file moving again while the Indians sat and smoked.

By the next year both Red Cloud and Spotted Tail were desperate enough to defy government orders and return to their home region. Red Cloud stopped his moccasins at the place he would live, later called Pine Ridge Reservation. By then Little Wolf and Dull Knife were bringing what was left of their sick and dying Northern Cheyennes from Indian Territory across practically fifteen hundred miles of open plains with army posts all along the route that was crisscrossed by telegraph and cut by three railroads. At one time eleven, twelve thousand troops were moving to intercept the little band of Indians, less than three hundred, only eighty-three of them males between twelve and eighty. The stories of that desperate flight are still multiplying, and vary from those that make the path one bloody trail up the Plains to one that pictures the Indians as curiously arid superhumans who could see their people shot down all the way and not shed one drop of white-man blood in return. Actually the chiefs, responsible, peaceful men, were only trying to get their people back home to the Yellowstone country as they had been promised they could if the south did not please them.

But troops came shooting, shedding the first blood. After that even the strength of Little Wolf, the bearer of the sacred chief's bundle, could not control the angry warriors completely. Three years earlier, in north Kansas, Medicine Arrow, Keeper of the Sacred Arrows, had been shot down under his flag of truce, his party of Southern Cheyennes destroyed by a few troops and a lot of buffalo hunters. Now, in 1878, the warriors killed a white man for every male Cheyenne shot in that attack, and stopped. There was no way of paying for all the women and children dug out of the holes and slaughtered by the buffalo hunters on the Sappa that day in 1875.

After avenging Medicine Arrow's band, the Southern Cheyennes returned to Indian Territory and the northern chiefs took what was left of their people and ran very fast, for the troops were hot over the bloodshed that Little Wolf had worked so hard and long to prevent. In Nebraska, where none of their people had ever been massacred, no whites were to be harmed if it could be helped. "Shoot only to save a Cheyenne life," Little Wolf ordered. They kept away from the settlements, and although a train was ready, with steam up, soldiers and horses loaded, the Indians got across the Platte River before anyone could stop them. But they were still very far from the Yellowstone, the people worn out, many old and sick, many crippled from the fighting, and already there were fingers of ice along the morning river. So the people divided. Dull Knife, with those who could not hope to get north through the winter snows, would try to slip in to Red Cloud, unaware that his friend was surrounded by soldiers to intercept the Cheyennes. Dull Knife was captured in a blinding blizzard on Chadron Creek, taken to the barracks at Fort Robinson, locked up, and ordered back to Indian Territory.

The Indians refused to go. To break their resistance, the fuel was cut off in subzero midwinter, then the food and finally the water too, from the old, the sick and the small children. Everything was cut off. Rather than die there, they broke out of the barracks the night of January 9, 1879, to run across the moonlit snowdrifts at twenty below zero, the soldiers shooting them down, their falling bodies marking the trail like winter buffalo fleeing before the hunters. Those who reached the bluffs were dug out and pursued across the snow of the breaks north of the post for thirteen days, to the final hole out on Hat Creek flats; the firing continued until nothing moved.* Only a few escaped, including Dull Knife, who was hidden, first by a white man and his Indian wife and then by the Sioux of Pine Ridge.

Little Wolf's party lasted longer. They hid in the sandhills in a small valley called Lost Chokecherry, only a few miles from the Niobrara crossing of the Kearney-Black Hills Trail. With troops searching for them every few days, the Indians had to live half underground, watching every twist of smoke that might betray them,

* This was excused by saying that if the Cheyennes survived this jump from their reservation, every other tribe would try it. In 1877 the Nez Perce had made their magnificent flight. The Poncas left Indian Territory hard behind the Cheyennes. The massacre of Dull Knife's people brought so many protests that a writ of habeas corpus was obtained for Standing Bear, the Ponca chief, on the ruling that "an Indian was a person within the meaning of the law." It was momentous but too late for the Cheyennes.

every moccasin track of the hunters. Somehow they survived, waiting to see what happened to Dull Knife's band, hoping to help them get away. When the news of the massacre at Robinson came, they mourned a little while, all they dared, and then left for the north, swinging out around the Black Hills. By April they reached their far destination, the Yellowstone, seven months on the way.

Up around Fort Robinson more and more dead Cheyennes were found as the snow thawed off and the buzzards began to circle. In the end the post led all the Plains in the number of Indians killed around it. But the dying was not yet finished. In 1890 a new hope rose in the Indians, a hope nurtured by the desperation of hunger. Thousands came to believe that if they danced long enough in a certain holy way—crystallized from a curious blending of Indian and Christian symbolism—the white man would disappear and the buffalo and the Indian once more own the earth. But although the Ghost Dance was a nonviolent movement, the newspapers managed to profit from their lurid tall tales of the frontier running red in blood, and there was fine business for the army contractors. In the end Sitting Bull, the Hunkpapa, was killed by Indian police, and the hot chatter of Hotchkiss guns cut down Big Foot's band, men, women and children, at Wounded Knee, South Dakota, after they were disarmed.

So it ended, with all the white men who generaled the wars of the Plains except Custer dying in bed. Four of the high-up Sioux leaders of those years were killed, all while at peace with the whites.

In 1931 He Dog, brother chieftain of Crazy Horse, cast his trachoma-blinded eyes back over the years. "Perhaps," he said, "it would have been better to die fighting."

IX   A Few Bad Men and Good—

There were perhaps more stories told about the American Indian than about any other people except the Hebrews of the Old Testament, and most of them seemed to be about the Plains tribes. When the noble child of nature was turned into the bloodthirsty savage, the white man of the region became the romantic figure, standing stalwart and tall upon the prairie, no matter what his stature elsewhere, or what traits and dimensions the time demanded of its heroes.

The great invasion of the Plains came after the Civil War. Many of the men, North and South, had seen four years of ruthless violence against their own countrymen, their brothers. Often with no niche in their home community to welcome their return, and no desire for one, they drifted to the buffalo and Indian plains, to the vast regions with no law except that of the rifle and the pistol against the belly in some bar, gambling den or other place of chance.

Postwar society is always reluctant to give up the emotionalism stirred by the great bloodlettings, the great heroes of the butchery, and the great bereavements. It is unwilling to settle down, particularly after the hysterical excesses of a civil war, to the dull mundanity of peacetime. Relieved of most decisions by a wartime government, the public refuses to take up the responsibilities of peace, preferring to turn them over to some figurehead and occupying itself making heroes of the most irresponsible, the most violent of men. Writers who provided escape from the problems of Reconstruction with lurid fantasies of the frontier in the 1860's and 1870's flourished, and from them came the gaudy characters who still ride the Plains.

Although the three gaudiest, Wild Bill Hickok, Buffalo Bill Cody and Calamity Jane, actually existed, their actuality vanished with practically the first word of the mythmakers, who, ninety, one hundred years later are still at work and, curiously, with perhaps greater impact. Once the illiterate, with a suspicious and healthy skepticism, could ask of the politician: "If I believe you, whose mule will eat the corn, yours, mine, everybody's, or yours?" To reports and accounts he could say, "I don't believe nothing I hear and only half I see," which seemed sufficient protection, for after all he couldn't read the papers. But that time is long gone and now the eyes of the illiterate, and of the great mass of misliterates, are bombarded by total falsehood most of the day. And where should disbelief, even in what one reads, begin? As an old grandmother* out in Nebraska used to say in her German-Swiss dialect, "*Weis' Papier ist j̇' 'dultig.*" White paper is indeed patient, compliant.

While Hickok, Cody and Jane Canary were all born elsewhere, they got their start along the Overland Trail in their teens. Calamity came out of Missouri with her parents and, according to the records, on a trip through Sidney married a soldier from the Barracks. But at sixteen the life soon palled and she hit the road. According to some writers she went scouting for General Crook—romantic writers who thought of scouting as the showy, big-bugging of the fringed buckskin boys, and usually between the Smoky Hill and the Platte River.

* The author's maternal grandmother, from Schaffhausen.

That region was crisscrossed by trails and overrun by tallow and hide hunters, by visitors, troops, railroad builders, cattle trailers and settlers, all during the 1860's. Even in the southern regions any knowledgeable army man depended on real scouts like California Joe, who was with Custer at the Washita. To men like Joe scouting was not riding in fine style beside the commanding officer under the guidon but a hard, dull, and dirty business of breaking most of the rises on the belly out five, ten miles ahead of the column.

Of course Calamity Jane did not scout for the army, particularly not in the dangerous Indian country above the North Platte, away from the Black Hills Trails, nor for General Crook, who had no room for the show-offs in his expeditions, preferring men long in the region like Little Bat Garnier. There seems no doubt Calamity was discovered in the bull train of an army expedition or two. There were usually prostitutes hidden in the canvas-topped wagons. It was when a special ambulance was provided for the women, or for one officer's woman, that the government protested, and not then unless the failure of a campaign had to be explained, as Custer's of 1867.

Hickok and Cody were horse tenders at stage stations on the Overland Trail, living in dugouts as most tenders did. Hickok shot down an unarmed Southerner, McCanles, when the first anger of the Civil War was breaking over the West with the news of the first defeats and the lengthening casualty lists. His trial was the first for murder in a new county, with a new court. How could such a northern court find a man guilty of murdering a North Carolinian right here in their midst, one trying to collect money, not from Hickok—even in 1861 that was known to be futile—but from Wellman, who owed McCanles for the stage station? Besides, it seemed the Southerner had not only brought his family to live here among them but a girl called his mistress, one who was offering a little entertainment at the station under the Wellmans, as was common at the coach stops. She seems to have been a rough woman, deplorably short on constancy but handy with her eyes, and her hands on a hoe. Or perhaps the wielder of the hoe that finished off the killing Hickok began was the woman called Mrs. Wellman.

James Butler Hickok came out of the trial with little inconvenience except a change in his nickname from Duck Bill, for his protruding upper lip, to Wild Bill, because he told such stretchers, such wild stories, in court. Bill grew a fine drooping mustache to cover his lip and followed the usual path of the petty bad man of the period, into the army, some say into the more profitable business of raiding and bushwhacking. After the war George Ward Nichols' tall tale in *Harper's Magazine* made Bill a hero and whetted the morbid postwar appetite for more such lurid characters. Judson, as Ned Buntline, went out to kick the brush over the West, hoping to scare out somebody he could build into a heroic plainsman to compete with Nichols' Hickok. Apparently he was advised to stop off at North Platte and take a look at Bill Cody, handsome, a Long Hair, with a taste for western costumes and showing off. It was easy in those times to make a bloodthirsty Indian scout of perhaps the least observant individual to survive on the frontier, a man who, it was said, never deliberately harmed another human being, unless, perhaps, one asked his wife Louisa, Lu, for an opinion.

Cody became what Judson saw in him there around Fort McPherson: a great showman, but never really able to make expenses for very long, and more Sioux Indians from Pine Ridge became acquainted with parts of Long Island than anyone would have believed likely. That was where they were stranded when Cody went broke.

The Plains nurtured if not produced the scouts and hangers-on of Phil Sheridan's boys, as the old-timers called Custer, Carr and the rest around Fort Hays and the campaigns of 1867-69, from the Platte to the Sweetwater and back. These included Cody and Hickok, California Joe and Lonesome Charley Reynolds, the latter two preferred by Custer, perhaps because they were not showy and knew their business. The quiet, gentle-spoken Lonesome Charley died up on the Little Big Horn with Reno's men because he joined Custer up at Fort Abraham Lincoln. California Joe of the ragged red hair and beard, and the rope-tied old coat, was an early plainsman before the Seventh Cavalry was created. He had covered the region from Texas to the Musselshell, scouting and hunting. He was killed up near Fort Robinson, but not by an Indian. Not even a Cheyenne from the Washita would have harmed Joe because they saw him as a man who had lost himself, a strange one, set off from other men for some purpose, a holy one, perhaps, and lost. Besides, he wasn't much given to shooting at Indians. It just happened that he was one scout worth the name. He knew the country and kept his eyes open.

Perhaps the greatest braggart and blowhard of all the Plains was Doc Carver, who learned to hunt buffalo in the Republican valley in the early 1870's and tried show business as Hickok did and even Calamity Jane. Carver was a newcomer and his exaggerations offended the Plains. It was one thing to be made the center of fairy tales by a Ned Buntline or a Nichols or Buel, something else for the hero to try it. Cody didn't tell those stories about himself, not to old-timers, and Hickok was a quiet man except in dress. Carver came from a lusher region, where a Paul Bunyan could overcome every obstacle, where a man could brag. The tall-tale characters rooted naturally in the more austere Plains had wrier success. Jim Bridger struck the true tone in his story of his fight with the Blackfeet:

> Seventeen Blackfoots run me up a box canyon. We fit all day and we fit all night, and the ground got slippery with blood an' just when I was about a goner, the last Injun busted down. Then seventeen more Blackfoots comes tearin' up the box canyon—"
> "How did you get out?"
> "I didn't."

That rueful twist, in one form or another, shows up in the stories most commonly repeated on the Plains, even in the recent Feobold Feoboldson tales, with Feobold's friends the Dirty Leg Indians on the Dismal River, which is a real and lovely stream rising in the Nebraska sandhills. Then there is the story of the Pawnee rainmaker. In the drouth years it was true, as visitors used to say, that if one saw a Nebraskan he was looking up into the sky for rain, and if there were two Nebraskans together, they were both looking up into the sky. In the great drouths rainmakers like Wright, with his dynamic stovepipes, and the Melbourne Miracle, who made rain for Goodland, Kansas, appeared. The best Plains product was an old Pawnee who operated with as much ballyhoo as a medicine show and offered to bring a good shower for $10, a real soaker for $20. Some desperate settlers, down to their last nickels, got together to make one final try. They managed to raise $20 and a jug of last year's corn liquor for the Indian. He went into his rain medicine with genuine enthusiasm, and everybody was hailed out.

While Hickok was the most flamboyant and publicized killer of the middle Plains, many other bad men came through the region, actually or in fancy. The Thompsons, fighting Texans, got as far as Ogallala. Slade, with, some claimed, twenty-six dead men to his final credit, was division agent for the Overland stage line out of Julesburg, where he killed Jules and was said to have cut his ears off and dried them with a pebble inside each for rattling watch charms. He did his rope stretching up in Montana when the vigilantes caught up with him.

Jesse James was all through the region, and apparently hid out with the Santee Sioux near the mouth of the Niobrara for a while, using the name of Jesse Chase, although the Indians all knew who he was. The mixed-blood Chase family there are said to be the descendants. Sam Bass and his gang made their one big train robbery out near Big Spring and scattered down through Kansas with the money.

But these were transients. By this time there were more settled outlaws on the Plains. Big Nose George was considered a Wyoming man. Fly Speck Billy, a slight, almost beardless youth with a splatter of tiny very dark freckles across his nose, apparently ran with several gangs of road agents working the Black Hills trails. He seemed to prefer the one out of Sidney through Red Cloud Agency, with many good hiding places among the Sioux and in the bluffs, badlands and breaks of White River and Pine Ridge, and the whole Black Hills. Billy was in jail at Ogallala for horse stealing for a while, but the evidence must have been mighty slim or he would have danced at the end of a rope. Released, he boldly took the stage he had robbed and went back up the trail to join Lame Bradley or perhaps Dunc Blackburn.

Gradually some believed that Fly Speck really was the custodian of several big gold and money hauls and that finally he and two others buried the accumulated $300,000 in bullion and gold dust when the law and other robbers got too close. Apparently the men hid out in a cave in the Niobrara River bluffs, fell to quarreling until one or two or all three were killed. Actually Fly Speck (James Lawton or James Fowler, whatever he happened to call himself) was lynched by masked men up at Custer City early in 1881, some time after the cave story got out. It seems that a freighter from Kearney overtook Fly Speck walking into the Hills, let him ride in a wagon to Custer, even loaned the youth his pistol, and was killed by it in a saloon. The mob took Fly Speck from the sheriff and strung him up.

Now the story of the hidden gold spread, but, with the Niobrara canyon three hundred miles long, there had to be some special identification, said to be a row of three small pine trees standing like horsebackers along the bluffs above the cave. There were three such trees, and a cave, near the Sandoz crossing to Mirage Flats the spring of 1884 when the settlers came. Periodically the next thirty years treasure seekers worked the cave and the slope around it, some secretly, some openly with their Winchesters handy. Two of the three trees were cut down, perhaps became ridgepoles of settler soddies, but the stumps and the dying old trunk still tolled the diggers. A Polish immigrant homesteaded the place and, it was said, kept stolen chickens in the cave, protected by a stout wooden door and an old ten-bore loaded with buckshot. After the settler moved away the cave smelled of chicken droppings and feathers on damp days, but new test holes appeared inside and along the bluff. Often at night lights moved around the cave, sometimes openly, perhaps picnickers daring the ghosts said to haunt the place. Several times fleeing outlaws and escaped convicts were said to be hiding there. If the treasure was ever found, the news was kept very quiet.

It is curious how many of the western outlaws, gamblers and gunmen were really slight and boyish, from the long-haired, delicate-featured Hickok in his foppish silk-lined capes to the mildest, least conspicuous of the lot, Doc Middleton. Doc was soft-spoken, in a time when even ministers and sky pilots ran to strong language, in their sermons, of course, with their shouted threats of hellfire and damnation. Sometimes they were lawless in action too, as the Reverend Ware, indicted and imprisoned for land fraud and settler intimidation, with many saying that the intimidation included murder—hired—but murder.

Middleton's name was just one "to travel under," as the Plains expressed it. Some said he was the Riley kid who killed several, perhaps even nine, men in a saloon in Newton, Kansas, in 1871, and vanished north, never to be heard from again. Later a slender, mild-mannered boyish man known to the Texans as Jim Riley or Jim Cherry turned up as Doc Middleton, freighter and night herder with a P. & F. outfit to the Black Hills. His first real trouble up north seems to have been in Sidney, in a saloon full of gold seekers, cowboys, freighters, old buffalo hunters, gamblers, badmen, soldiers and dance girls. On soldier nights, usually after payday, no one was allowed to dance there unless in uniform. It was a boom time, the crowd roaring. A girl with a drunken soldier flirted with Middleton and started a fight, other soldiers joining in. The music stopped, everybody pushed up to see the quiet man half-knock, half-push the soldier down. But when other troopers started to kick and punch him, the sharp report of a revolver drove them back. The waiters flapped the lights out before the soldiers could get to their guns, the crowd trampling, fighting to get out into the open and away.

Doc was followed by the soldiers far over the bluffs, but escaped, with a price on his head for killing a soldier. Friends offered money for a lawyer, since it was plainly self-defense, but he refused, perhaps because he was the Riley kid of Newton, or of other killings. But now he was an outlaw. When he tried to work, the law showed up and he had to run, so finally he collected a bold gang around him and went into horse stealing on a large scale, gathering up good stock around the Missouri, running them up the Niobrara valley to sell to the ranches spreading out in Wyoming and in the North Platte valley. There his outfit stole other horses for the drive east, picking up Indian ponies on the way. Before long Doc showed his Texas fondness for good horseflesh and began to slip around the racing circuits of the settlements, sweeping away a winner now and then. He was becoming a sort of Plains Robin Hood. A lone horseman might appear at a settler shack at evening and ask to stay overnight. The man was young and good-looking in a polite way, with a gold tooth plain when he talked or laughed, his horse a good one but worn out. After supper he went straight to bed and was gone the next morning, the settler's horse gone too, if he had one, the tired saddler in its place and usually more valuable. Perhaps later the stranger sent pay for the horse he took, double its value; sometimes, if the man was hard pressed and had to stay at a dugout or other very poor place, he might leave a folded bill in the palm of a bewildered small child, a bill that turned out to be twenty dollars, or the penny picked from behind the ear of a little boy a gold piece. Then the settler would know that he had fed Doc Middleton and he would have no information to give any pursuers coming by.

In 1878 Doc was working the Platte too, well past Grand Island and down into the Lincoln region. Early the next year he made a flying visit to three towns along the railroad and got twenty of the best horses in the region, well-blooded stock. Rewards totaling several thousand dollars were posted for his capture, enough to tempt any settler with his children barefoot in January, but somehow nobody turned Doc in. When the Sioux started after him for horse stealing, he circulated a story that he had been killed. Gradually his gang built up refuges in the Niobrara canyon and some of the steeper tributaries, places where a small force could hold off an army and, if pressed, scatter into the breaks and timber, or hide their trail in the bed of the swift river.

The Oakdale *Pen and Plow* carried an interview with a sheriff who had made a foray into Middleton country. Carrying a warrant to serve on the gang, he had started out with eighteen men, including some who had lost stock. They rode to a point thirty miles from the town of Niobrara, on Turtle Creek:

> and came upon the real headquarters of this nest of horse and cattle thieves. They captured eighty-one head of cattle and eleven head of horses, all of which have been since reclaimed. Sheriff Hopkins supposes that there are about fifty men engaged in this nefarious business of horse and cattle stealing who have headquarters on Turtle Creek. They are Freebooters, bandits, like those of Italy and Spain. No United States Marshal dares to penetrate that nest, although they can have, if they wish, the whole United States army to back them.

Apparently it was not a settler but a larger stockowner who gave the site away. Besides, the gang was getting too big, too careless. Middleton and some of his men went to a dance at North Platte, and the sheriff raided the hall and caught three of the outfit. The rest scattered, Doc taking to the bridge. With the bridle reins in his teeth, a revolver in each hand, he spurred his horse to a thundering run over the planks, firing as he came. It was all wasted; nobody had thought to guard the bridge.

The story was worth telling, whatever the truth, and the region from Le Mars, Iowa, deep into Wyoming went into a curious, unfrightened panic. As always, every crime was blamed on any conspicuous outlaw of the time and Doc was accused of robbing a post office. That brought the government down on him. Deputy U.S. Marshal Hazen and a helper were ordered to capture Middleton. They sent word to him that they wanted a conference, would give him a place on the detective force if he surrendered quietly. Doc went and was riding between the two deputies, talking the proposition over, when a third man, Texas Jack, planted to dry-gulch him, fired, but only once, and fled. Doc, wounded in the hip, slid from his horse, shooting. He hit Hazen twice but the other deputy spurred off, with one of Middleton's gang firing at him. Doc, thinking he had killed Hazen, crawled away, but if he had turned to look back he would have seen the grass move behind him as from some great crippled bull snake creeping off in the other direction. Doc got to his father-in-law's place and was taken to a timbered canyon with guards at its entrance. There, in a tent, he healed while Hazen was recovering with a doctor.

Now Doc saw it was time to surrender. He pleaded guilty to horse stealing, was sentenced to five years, and with a year and a half off for good behavior was out in time to cause another flurry of newspaper stories. It seems he eloped with his former wife's young sister and that her father threatened buckshot. Doc got off at the depot with a gun in one hand and an arm around his bride, straight into a hilarious delegation. The couple were hustled up the street between men bristling with guns, to meet the bride's father waiting with a rifle on his arm. Instead of a funeral there was a big blowout with dancing and beer, even coffee and doughnuts for the temperance ladies, or so it is remembered.

The next year Doc worked around the new ranches spreading themselves on the upper Niobrara since the Indians were removed. When the new county of Sheridan was organized, Middleton was appointed deputy sheriff—to protect the cattle and horses of the ranchers, the settlers said sourly. But Doc Middleton was tamed. He opened a saloon in Gordon, offering soft drinks at the front when local option overtook him, but even then he had a gun on his hip and, it was said, whisky by the drink, the bottle or the keg in the back room. He buried his lovely fair-haired little daughter there and took part in the thousand-mile horse race from Chadron to Buffalo Bill's Wild West Show at the Chicago World's Fair in 1893. Doc didn't win the race, hadn't intended to, because he rode the cushions most of the way, but it was fine publicity for everybody. Perhaps he regretted the obscurity of those later years. There were stories, some said that Doc started them himself, of taking part in a Black Hills gold robbery, the booty cached in a hole of a prairie dog town, but although the dog towns of a hundred miles around were searched, apparently nothing more special than rattlesnakes and dog owls turned up, so the gold, if it ever existed, may still be there.

Although Kid Wade, who took over Middleton's gang when Doc was sent to the pentientiary, was hanged, Doc died more quietly, in jail up in Wyoming but apparently only for drunkenness. Many remembered that the Sidney *Telegraph* had carried an editorial when he was first arrested, back in 1879, assuring him that public sympathy was on his side. "Doc Middleton . . . has proved a gallant foeman and all we ask is that he shall have a fair trial. . . ."

Many a great public hero who got much more deserved less.

There are Plains stories of violence and lawlessness apparently less fitted to romantic musical comedy than the activities of the blue-eyed, mousy-haired Middleton. Or even of Fly Speck Billy. One of these involves a woman, the accounts of her life and her end little more than scarce whispers, and of such nature that she is not the center of any television series, as even Hickok has become, and probably never will be. She was Elizabeth Jones Taylor of the Welsh settlement of Clay County. The Jones family included the mother, three sons, one daughter—Elizabeth—her husband and their two sons and small daughter. There seems to have been trouble in the community over land and timber and perhaps other things. In 1881 Elizabeth's husband was found dead in the field under suspicious circumstances, some saying he had married into the wrong family, others that he had been as bad as the Joneses. It seems that an organized gang of hard characters hung around the Jones and Taylor places, the outsiders as bad as the owners, people who wouldn't stop short of murder, if that. Fires had plagued the neighborhood, barns burned, stock was killed and other atrocities were committed. It was said that Elizabeth Taylor threatened Roberts, another Welshman, if he cut any more timber on a tract of land she claimed down on the Blue. Then early in January 1885 he was killed and the two Taylor sons, twelve and fifteen, were jailed for the murder. They were brutal-looking youths, the papers said, bad eggs who had shot at neighbor boys several times. But many blamed their mother, perhaps forty, short and thick-bodied and tough as the murdering Bender women down in Kansas.

After her sons were jailed, Elizabeth Taylor refused to spend the nights alone on her place but went to her brother Tom's homestead, about a mile off, around dusk, always returning in the morning, armed, generally with both pistol and rifle. Tom Jones, about thirty-four, was single and had his mother and now usually Mrs. Taylor's small daughter with him. He had a bad reputation too, but got along with the neighbors fairly well until Roberts was killed. Then he was also suspected, perhaps from the stories the Taylor boys were telling in jail. When a Texan who had been bulldozed by the Jones outfit disappeared right after the Roberts killing, a posse was formed. No telling who would be next.

The story from that point was never very clear, although there were many who knew at least most of it. Even the number of the posse varied, from fifty to seventy-five as told by those in the Jones home when the men came, to from twelve to fifteen by those who had "heard" about it. Anyway, the mob appeared at the Jones sod house around one o'clock in the morning, with clattering hoofbeats in the pitch dark and loud shouts ordering Tom Jones and Mrs. Taylor to come out. There was commotion of many people inside the small house, with the sound of barricading at the door and window. The posse threatened to throw a dynamite bomb down the chimney if they didn't hurry. There was a lot of low talk inside and finally Jones came through the window, without arms, followed by Mrs. Taylor. Their hands were tied with rope and then they were taken behind the house while the outsiders, four men and a herd boy, came out one at a time and got their hands tied behind their backs too, leaving only old Mrs. Jones and the five-year-old Taylor girl inside. Later one of the men from inside was turned loose and told to hurry off, creating the suspicion that he had been a spy of the mob inside the Jones house. The rest of the outsiders were locked up at a neighbor's place to be guarded there until morning.

Then Mrs. Taylor and her brother were taken to the bridge of the Blue about a quarter of a mile off. There they were told they would be hanged and now was the time to clear their consciences. Some said Mrs. Taylor admitted that her brother had hired a man to burn the Llewellyn barn, but there was little but rumor about that night. It seems the two pleaded, apparently promising reform, promising anything, but they were told to pray and make ready. They prayed loudly in Welsh for some minutes and then were led under the bridge and hanged with Mrs. Taylor's mule halter ropes.

Afterward the men returned to the house, to beg Mrs. Jones's pardon for the interruption, and left. Although the bodies were seen the next morning by a woman crossing the bridge, the coroner didn't get there to cut them down until in the afternoon. A jury was impaneled for a secret inquest. The men caught in the Jones house left the country. Late in March about half a dozen men, some with good Welsh names, were tried for the lynching. Old Mrs. Jones, sixty-six and shaken by her experiences, was the principal witness, but although it seems that none of the mob was masked, the night was dark and her testimony was considered insufficient evidence. She could not swear which of the men being tried had hanged her son and daughter, or if any did. The sooner the matter was closed, the better.

By now the usual sensation seekers gathered to see the Jones house, to judge whether the sod walls were actually four feet thick, the door heavy planking. The dark interior seemed more like a hide-out, a den, than a home, with a row of posts down the center to hold up the ridgepole. One side was divided into stalls for sleeping; the other had two beds, an old cookstove, a rough pine table and one chair and a box. The old woman sat on the bed, her face bent, the bright little girl dark-eyed beside her. And then they, too, were gone.

There was much finger pointing from nearby states, nearby counties, less from Dawson and Custer, however, with the recent lynching and man-burning by Print Olive and his cowboy gang. The same papers that carried the story of the Taylor-Jones mobbing reminded their readers of the range war still strong in Custer County, with news of homesteaders there finally organizing against the Brighton Ranch—ninety-two men, armed, ordering Allyn and Brighton to get out of the country. Some of these settlers had been brought in with the Cozad colony by the gambler and community builder John Cozad. He had contracted for 40,000 acres of Union

Pacific railroad lands for his community and for speculation. He held the settlers together through drouth and grasshoppers and depression, at least most of them, defending his community against starvation with work at a sod bridge he planned across the Platte, and against both range cattle and gunmen with pride, arrogance and pistols. Paternalistic, dictatorial, arrogant and violent, with the pride of the faro man, he fought with enemy and friend until he finally had to kill a man in self-defense. Then in one large gesture he left his town of Cozad, his past and his name behind, and the names of his sons. The second, Robert Henry Cozad, who spent his formative years from seven to seventeen as youth and as budding artist in his father's town of Cozad, became Robert Henri, the noted painter, the great teacher of painters. It seems fitting somehow that the affectionate and penetrating portrait he painted of his father twenty years later, the man he must call Richard H. Lee to his death, should be brought to Nebraska by one with roots deep in Cozad and the region of the hundredth meridian.

While most of the Plains settlements grew out of the great land hunger of the world, not all were established primarily as homes or even financial speculation. From the beginning the region was part of the territorial prize between Spain, France and England. After the Louisiana Purchase the Americans took over the task of driving the British out of the Missouri country, with the overambitious Yellowstone Expedition that never got to the Pacific or even past Fort Atkinson, although it was planned against the encroaching traders and empire builders from Canada. The struggle was still alive in 1847, when Fort Kearny was established by the Oregon Battalion that never got much farther either.

In the 1870's Nebraska became a sort of private outpost against Canada, a base from which the province was to be split off the British Empire, not by the U.S. government but by a romantic Irish soldier of fortune who had annexed the title of general. John O'Neill was born six weeks after his father died of the black plague in Ireland, and when his widowed mother migrated, the boy stayed behind with his grandfather to be tutored, for he must not jeopardize his faith, not in the national schools. At fourteen the rise of Young Ireland into revolt stirred John. He came to America, fancying himself like Washington's four Irish officers. But the times were less propitious, and the summer of 1857 O'Neill found himself with Johnston's expedition to Utah and deserted, as he said later, because there was no fighting. He joined some emigrants to California, found that too tame and enlisted in the cavalry. When the Civil War broke out he was a sergeant. Dissatisfied, O'Neill moved around in the military service, told of harassing Morgan's raiders and of capturing three of his guns. He finally resigned, feeling he had been passed over for promotion, but requested a captaincy with the colored infantry and was put on the examining board. Later, as pension agent at Nashville, it seems he accumulated a fair fortune, which was fast work in one year, even for a carpetbagger.

Early in 1866 O'Neill resigned and joined the Fenians, the Irish fighting patriots, for an invasion of Canada, and had trouble with his superiors. The Catholic clergy was condemning all societies requiring an oath to destroy government or religion, and the Fenians retaliated by protesting that the priests were going beyond their jurisdiction when they tried to dictate politics. To his further disgust, O'Neill found the American Fenians as far west as Denver divided about attacking Canada, one wing scornfully predicting failure. The men and money raised should be used in Ireland, where it counted for freedom.

At the end of the war many Irish veterans either found no jobs or preferred to fight. Some non-Irish veterans, angry that England had sided with the Confederacy until Russia showed her battle fleet in northern harbors, also joined. The grand several-pronged invasion to cut Canada from England started the spring of 1866, with O'Neill in command out of Buffalo. He got as far as Fort Erie, cut the telegraph connections, raised green flags and even had a little fight or two, but the main body of Fenians promised to him never arrived and so he had to retreat and was captured by an American gunboat. President Johnson ordered the Fenian soldiers dispersed, the government generously paying their way to any part of the country.

O'Neill undertook a second invasion of Canada from Vermont, but at the first shots his slender force fled; he was arrested and released after three months by presidential pardon. His third attempt was farther west, where he managed to seize the Hudson's Bay fur post at frontier Pembina, was arrested by U.S. troops and turned loose again. Evidently the Canadians couldn't take the man and his activities very seriously. Not that John O'Neill gave up. He excused his failures by blaming those who backed the first invasion. The Chicago Fenians hadn't arrived in time; the wealthy Irish who proclaimed themselves willing to sacrifice their last dollar and last drop of blood for Ireland's liberation on St. Pat's day failed in June. He had hoped for at least 5,000 of the 100,000 men promised, and got only 500. He said he spent $60,000 converting 5,000 Springfields into breechloaders, which were still in transit somewhere, if not seized by the U.S. government.

Apparently O'Neill thought about those guns, and his future plans for them, when he went around seeking a place for his settlements, for his colonies of city Irish, to remove them from poverty and misery, get them at least the freedom of American land. He was pleased with Nebraska, with the healthy climate, pure water and fertile land, millions of acres free for the homesteader, and great railroad and speculator areas from which a man could make a little profit. Besides, it was an easy, an unobstructed prairie march to west Canada.

O'Neill selected a location in what was to be Holt County, up the Elkhorn River. At Plattsmouth the general, as he now called himself, talked about his plans to Fitzgerald, grade contractor for the Union Pacific and Burlington railroads. O'Neill complained about the problem of arms in the invasions, his guns that got as far as the border but found him without the money to pay the freight. Fitzgerald gave O'Neill $300 to pay the railway charges and was surprised when the boxes of arms arrived at his home. He stored them, and when the family moved to Lincoln the boxes went with the family goods and were stacked in the basement. The house burned, the boxes were discovered by the firemen, opened, and

Fitzgerald was accused of plotting an army to overthrow the government. Insisting that the guns belonged to General O'Neill didn't improve the situation, not with that Irishman's reputation for private armies and invasion of foreign soil.

The early seventies were panic years all over, and John O'Neill, even with his fine military figure, good voice, flowery delivery and blarney on his tongue, was having trouble getting finances for his new colony. Finally the *Irish World* saved him by donating space for publicity and, early May 1874, O'Neill's first settlers came, by wagon, a week on the prairie, disheartened by the flat, empty site, a hundred miles from civilization, about fifty from a post office, with no priest, doctor or teacher. All the provisions, every palmful of tea, had to be hauled from the railroad at Wisner, over a hundred miles away, a two-week round trip by oxen.

But O'Neill pointed out that the soil was good, game plentiful, even antelope, and that the occasional Indians were friendly. He traveled the region, stopped at the government surveying camp, slept on the ground with the outfit and ate camp food. In 1876 he reached out toward other locations; one of these, west of O'Neill City, was named for Colonel Atkinson, who was anxious for Irish Catholic colonization, and furnished part of the money for the settlement. Now colonists could choose between the two sites, but even so dissatisfaction against John O'Neill grew, some saying he was in it all just for the money, and when it was pointed out that his family lived in the town too, he was called a visionary fool, to bring his wife here, to dream of invading Canada. The province was far away and the hard times looked permanent, or did until the gold in the Black Hills brought a boom to O'Neill, suddenly a supply station for bull trains. The one large store building began to burst with supplies, others were erected, the ten to twenty clerks kept busy. One store took in $1,000 a day for awhile.

Late in 1876 O'Neill wrote to Bishop O'Connor describing his community with a father's fondness. Around the settlement lay a vast area of free land, while in the cities men by the ten thousands were idle and hungry. He proposed that the Bishop use his influence to bring in half a dozen Irish colonies before summer. The Bishop acknowledged the possibilities of the region, particularly for settlement on railroad lands, to help develop the country. He would take a special interest in the spiritual welfare of all colonists within his jurisdiction and would send priests until resident pastors could be supported. John O'Neill hastened to make a circular of this correspondence and the promise of a railroad from the president of one surveyed through the region. He sent a copy to each member of the Nebraska legislature, reminding them of what he had done, adding that his personal resources were gone, that he was in debt.

The legislature was overwhelmed by similar requests from a hundred communities. They made no appropriation for O'Neill. No offer of an appropriate public office came to him, nothing like those the Irish from the Revolutionary War had managed to snag for themselves, or like Meagher, an Irish Civil War veteran who got himself appointed Secretary of Montana Territory. Then there was McGee, the Fenian who went to Canada from Ireland, deserted the cause, became a Canadian politician and condemned the invasion and O'Neill as a participant. True, Meagher vanished on a Missouri River boat, drowned or murdered, at forty-four, and McGee was shot down, just past forty-three.

O'Neill got $1,000 from the Irish Catholic Immigration Bureau toward traveling expenses. The Omaha *Herald* praised him and described his colonists as fine and intelligent, industrious and sober— men who were breaking the prairie and planting corn on good land. But fine words made no barley and the settlers felt tricked by the community builder. They had been promised an increase in population that did not come, civic improvements that were not made. They did not get the county seat that the politicians wanted, and the railroad they expected was still far away.

John O'Neill knew how to ignore complaints. Early in the year he announced that Bishop O'Connor's name was being given to a new settlement. He made more trips. At Little Rock he picked up a cold that aggravated his asthma. He came home, suffered a slight stroke and in the hospital at Omaha he was found on the floor beside his bed, chilled. He died of pneumonia, about the age of Meagher and McGee, not quite forty-four. He was buried at Omaha, and although his body was offered to O'Neill, it seems the community ignored the overture. Finally his town did put up a monument to him, with an Irish harp on the side, but that was a long, long time afterward. It was the treatment community builders should expect. Horse thieves are more generally loved and mourned.

Although O'Neill's town never became the capital of the world, as the general sometimes hoped, or the outpost of the invasion to be armed with the boxes of guns found in Fitzgerald's basement in Lincoln, the town was called the Irish capital of Nebraska. It was an energetic community from the first. The settlers built up a brass band and encouraged those of the towns around them. Several Protestant churches were erected and a Keeley Institute for those wishing to break free of alcohol and tobacco. Lawyers flourished, not only for their own lawless region, but for the towns farther west. The drouth and hard times of the nineties struck the region hard. Several capitalists organized a chicory factory to process the root crop into a coffee substitute, particularly welcomed by the French settlements. It provided a market for farmers and work for factory hands, but the boom busted when coffee prices were cut in half. Lion Head, Arbuckle and similar brands sold for ten to fifteen cents a purported pound, with coupons for such premiums as a stereoscope or an elegant blue velvet table cover if anyone ever lived to collect that many lion heads.

But O'Neill's outstanding product continued to be lawyers, frontier lawyers. One, Harrington, defended the Sandoz mob after they hanged and released a community troublemaker who shot through the night windows of the settlers out in Sheridan County. The next generation there were even more lawyers, men and women, several doing very well in Washington, notably Arthur Mullen, Democratic party leader who helped get Franklin Roosevelt nominated and then broke with the President, splitting the party in Nebraska down the middle, the second time in one generation—too soon after Bryan's resignation from the cabinet over Wilson's policies toward Germany during World War I. Apparently the party was not to recover from these splits, at least not for many years, in the state of the Bryans.

The small towns of the Plains are a sort of tall tale in themselves. Often they grew from the first sod-breaking to the nuclear age in one lifetime—sometimes a long life, but Nebraskans, at least, live a long time. Here and there someone rose from such a town to leave a mark. At Cozad, Robert Henri learned the courage and the techniques required to fight the battles for his brother artists in New York many years later. Willa Cather's finest books are rooted in the Plains around Red Cloud, her prose like sunlight on a swale. Both of these artists came to their towns in childhood. Perhaps man, like the apple tree, improves with early transplantation.

Then there is Wahoo, Nebraska, a kind of essence of the Plains, a town with notables like a vast lone cottonwood on a river bottom spreading in every direction. From the beginning the unusual individual was welcomed. One of the first was Per Axel Rydberg, who came to America from Sweden in 1882 hoping to be a mining engineer. A mine accident stopped that and he became a teacher of mathematics at Luther Academy at Wahoo from 1884 to 1893. During the summers he earned two degrees at the University of Nebraska and, on the recommendation of Dr. Charles Bessey, was selected by the U.S. Department of Agriculture to make field trips. He became the authority that described many, many plants of the West—one of the world's best botanists.

A town that attracted and encouraged such men when scarcely a dozen years old became a sort of hotbed for fine seedlings of its own. In those days Wahoo had one business street with Victorian façades, its white frame dwellings set back among oaks and elm. Behind those lace curtains and out into the poorest shack there was the same enthusiasm for music found in the soddies up on the table-lands, with their dwellers scrimping to buy band instruments, and in Lindsborg, down on the Smoky Hill in Kansas, with its famous *Messiah* chorus. Howard Hanson was born in the midst of music in Wahoo, receiving his early training there and at the University

School of Music before he struck across the Atlantic for extensive study and became the goateed and ebullient world-famed director of the Eastman School of Music.

Perhaps the Victorian façades and white gingerbread houses of Wahoo also influenced Darryl Zanuck, who looks more like a dandy from Franz Josef's empire than the moving picture producer that he is, and certainly not like the boy from a wind-swept trans-Missouri town grown up and coming back to stroll the streets where Rydberg, Hanson and Wahoo Sam Crawford walked. Perhaps Sam's rise to National League home-run championship and into the Baseball Hall of Fame was even less likely than the prominence of the other Wahooans. It seems a town barber who couldn't bear to see the boy waste his time loafing and smoking cigarettes encouraged him to try sandlot ball.

In 1958 Wahoo added another scientist to her notables. George Wells Beadle grew up on a farm near town with his father and a succession of housekeepers. He went to school to Bess McDonald, whom he remembers as one of his best teachers. She had played in the orchestra with Howard Hanson, had a deep appreciation for the arts, and taught science with a dedication. She drew young Beadle from behind the plow where his father tried to keep him, insisting that the boy go to college. At the University he studied under Dr. Pool and went to Oxford on an Eastman Kodak Company grant. Eventually Dr. Beadle and a colleague found themselves among the Nobel prize winners for their study in genetics, which, it was hoped, might eventually lead to a cure for cancer.

While Abilene, Ogallala, Dodge City, Cheyenne, Deadwood and Miles City were getting lurid names, some towns off the trails enjoyed their sinning a little more privately. One of these was Hastings, Nebraska, said to have been settled in the bad years of the early 1870's by English immigrants who couldn't walk home. The first hotel was the Roaring Gimlet, soon faced by the InterOcean, built by a salty old sea captain who got as far from both seas as he could. Soon there was a third hotel, nicknamed the Howling Corkscrew. Those early years included stories of stuffed ballot boxes, a county seat steal in the night, mob battles, lynching and the most notorious trial of the Plains, that of the Olive man-burners, with threats from Print Olive's cowboy gang to kill the judge, clean out the court and burn the town to the ground, until the governor sent the militia in.

Early Hastings was a town for a boy to grow up in, with the men and women of those daring days still walking the streets beside him. But Otto Rinderspacher, the son of a pioneer meat packer in the town, was not interested. Apparently sausage, salami and the special Rinderspacher liverwurst did not concern him much either until they became the proper companions for a good glass of beer, and the source of funds for his hobby. Music was Otto's love, and he grew into one of those big-boned flabby men who seem so drawn to the tiny chairs of the chamber music ensemble. His interest was in old music, from 1450 on. Hastings heard he was oboist with the Philadelphia Orchestra, before he went to Europe, to spend years searching out early manuscripts. He collected early instruments too, and organized a Collegium Musicum to play the early chamber music on the old, old instruments all over Europe. Among his originals was a flauto d'amore of the seventeenth century and a flat-back violin from early in the same century. He gathered many copies too, including a chitarrone or theorbo from about 1550 and a chest of six viola da gambas, 1600-1750. In addition he commissioned a clavichord and a harpsichord from John Challis. In 1952 he gave his entire collection of thousands of manuscripts and all the fine instruments to Hastings College, in Fuhr Hall of Fine Arts, not more than a good pistol shot from the sites of the mob battles and the courthouse fights that are only one good healthy life's length back in time.

A small academy and a college, an orchestra, a barber and a teacher of science in one place, the stories of violence and the money of a sausage maker in another—these and similar fertilizers in the towns of the Plains made them the rootground for so many talents, much like the early communities in the American colonies, teeming with that first ferment of settling, the first turning of virgin sod.

Perhaps it was to be expected that many would be stirred to tangible make-believe by the vast horizons, the deep nights and the summer whirlwinds, heat dances and mirages, of the high country.

The Wizard of Oz from the imagination of South Dakota's Baum fitted neatly into a Kansas tornado. The marionettes of Bil Baird are creatures dancing in a mirage. Bil, born William, son of a chemical engineer for the sugar company at Grand Island, built a puppet population for a miniature city for his friends, later assisted Tony Sarg and started the Bil Baird's Marionettes for the Chicago World's Fair. When he married he added his wife's name, Cora, to his Marionette Theater and together they became the world's most famous puppeteers, with whimsy and humor overlaying the often tragic and powerfully evocative extrareality. Some of this seems to spring from the bit of wild man, of the natural man, that the tinge of Cherokee blood has brought to the blue-eyed Bil Baird.

Perhaps there is something in the slender legs, the lithe build, of those who grow up in the iodine-leached earth of the Plains, and in the distances for flying leaps, that produces dancers, dancers varying from Maria Tallchief to Fred Astaire. Some time before the First World War the Omaha *World-Herald* reported that Frederic and Adele Austerlitz, two local children, had been graduated from a "well known art school," made appearances in New Jersey and were presented by Keith in New York, but because the new child-labor law prohibiting appearances of children in public houses was to be enforced. Keith had to let them go. Billed as The Astiers, toe dancers and acrobatic tumblers, they were booked for Europe, with Paris in May. More than fifty years later Fred Astaire, as he finally called himself, was still dancing on those lithe and slender legs.

For a region less than a hundred years this side of the buffalo and the Indian there are remarkably few tales of great duelings with the aborigines, practically none except Buffalo Bill's purported knife-to-knife combat with Yellow Hand. Not that the Plains lacked strong men; every section has stories of muscle exploiters, with Antoine Barada perhaps the strongest of all. Barada, by the accounts, was a halfbreed, and there were Baradas in the fur trade, with a romantic tale about one of them coming to America in search of a beautiful Indian girl he saw in a window in Paris and then spending twenty years of his life wandering over the country to find her. This is perhaps the tallest Barada tale of all. Any Indian girl he might have seen in France in the early eighteenth century would have been very easily traced.

'Toine Barada stories were told as far as the upper Yellowstone. He pulled a steamboat off the Missouri sandbars and lifted a 400-pound boulder to his knees. When he got tired of watching a pile driver working along the Missouri, making the up-down, up-down with the hammer, the driver yelling "Git up! Whoa! Back!" to his horses, 'Toine got so impatient he picked up the Johnny Jump hammer and threw it clear over the river, where it bounced around and tore up the earth for miles, making the breaks east of the Missouri. They finally grassed over a little, the soil poor but it seemed to satisfy those who never crossed over the river to know anything better. The piling that was left standing Barada gave a lick with his fist and drove it into the ground so deep water flew out like from a bunghole fifty feet across and would have flooded the whole country if he hadn't sat on the hole mighty quick.

There were always iron men on the Plains as far back as legend goes, skillful men, strong men. The old traders used to tell of a Blackfeet who wrestled the wind, but it was clear that, being a Blackfeet, he used the traditional guile and trickery. The Northern Cheyennes produced a noted wrestler and "hill builder," called Little Hawk in his mature years. Stocky, powerful, it was said he could bend his knees outward, arms akimbo, shoulders squared, and hold up nine men, two on each thigh, two on each shoulder and one on his head, nine of the heaviest.

Wrestling seems to be a favorite sport in new communities. To much of the Plains the scientist, the artist of the mat, was "Old Jawn" Pesek of Ravenna, Nebraska, the cow town whose main street was originally named the Appian Way. Pesek was unbeaten, it is claimed, for eighteen years and recognized as a world's champion. On the side he bred and raced greyhounds, a little like Old Jawn himself in his good years.

The eastern settlers brought in harness racing, with practically every little crossroads on some circuit, perhaps to be raided by Doc Middleton or his kind. But running races had come in when the Indians first got horses, and the interest grew as the military and the cattle outfits arrived, particularly the British interests in Wyoming and above. Perhaps the two best-known races were up in the White River region. Jim Dahlman, Texas cowboy and later mayor of Omaha, was involved in both. He was mayor of Chadron during the thousand-mile race from there to the Chicago World's Fair in 1893, and rode in the other, the earlier one. He had brought a blood bay named Fiddler up on the Texas trail, cleaning out the cow camps all the way, and prepared to skin the sports and horse owners from around the Dakota Indian reservations. The race was a big affair, at White Clay. Fiddler ran against a ragged, rough-haired gray that had been traded for the homestead where Hot Springs, South Dakota, was built. All the cattle outfits and the army sports from as far as the upper Missouri were betting on Dahlman's horse. It seems that the medicine-making of a Sioux named Little Horse (for his proficiency with the pony herds) threw Fiddler off his stride and the wild-maned gray won.

The Plains were the maturing ground, or the playground, for many transient army men. In addition to the solid, serious officers like Atkinson and Leavenworth, and Crook later, there were those who exploited the region and the Indians for their romantic and professional aggrandizement, men like Sheridan, Custer, Carr and half a dozen others. John J. Pershing was, however, more closely tied to the region. Fresh from the campaign against the Sioux in the Ghost Dance troubles, the young West Pointer was sent to the University of Nebraska as military instructor, with time to take his law degree. Drill had been mostly a joke, spit and polish unheard of, but the stiff-backed young Pershing changed that. The second year he instituted a Company A, which drilled several hours daily, won competitions and grew into the Varsity Rifles, the crack outfit that became the Pershing Rifles, established in 135 colleges and universities.

The name Black Jack probably started from Pershing's command of Negro troops in Cuba, but it stuck because of the dour visage of the man, known as a tough commander, unloved, at least overtly, by his troops, although no one could say he did not take care of them, did not fight for their supplies, their fitness, their welfare. The death of his wife, daughter of Governor Warren of Wyoming, and their children, except the son Warren, in a San Francisco fire did not lighten the man's face. After World War I the general bought a home in Lincoln, where his two sisters and young Warren lived. He refused to run for President. He was an informed man and appreciated the importance of preparation and training for a task, hard, thorough and specific training. He knew what happened when a man trained all his life to carry out the policies of others suddenly undertook to make the policies himself. One might wish other generals had been as wise.

The Plains Indians were an artistic people and, without an alphabet, they became very proficient recording their history in pictures, with a fine eye for decoration by quilling, paint and beads. Their pottery, often decorated, and their ancient shapings of stone and bone rival most of the very small amount of sculpture of the white man's years. True, Gutzon Borglum, the sculptor on living mountains, spent much of his life on the Plains and executed his figures with scope and independence. After the difficulties at Stone Mountain, Georgia, he returned to cut the massive heads of noted presidents on Mount Rushmore, in the Black Hills.

In recent years painters sprouted like sunflowers over the prairie country, particularly in the farther, the newer reaches still rather close to wilderness days. The greens, duns, tawny yellows and russets of the prairies, the mauve and blue hazes, the grays, yellows and gleaming whites of the bluffs and buttes against the black-dark of pines and cedars in the breaks and hills, the blazing skies of the sun's rise and set, do stir the eye. Even before the horse began to disappear, an occasional old cowboy tried to picture his favorite cutting horse on perhaps a chunk of old wagon sheet or tarp from his bedroll, sometimes with leftover wood paint. Later the stripped-down Model T and the jeep, which became a sort of iron pony on the range, were as likely to have a paint box and easel in the back as a saddle for an emergency cow chase. Restaurants and Legion halls began to accumulate the work, like cottonwood fluff catching on thistles and in cactus patches, displaying it. Some painters aimed at more ambitious showing in towns like Sheridan, say, or Billings, Minot, Goodland, or Las Animas, and perhaps even Chicago or New York.

To be sure, much of this was not art, but young painters with some training moved to Cleveland, Chicago or the Art Student's League and Paris. They were unaware that they followed the path of Henri, the leader of the Ash Can school, the motivating spirit of the art world for years, the challenging teacher, the fighter for the artist against the hidebound system of judges that had blocked the way of any new eye, new brush. They did not know that it was in the brilliant sun of the Plains that the boy learned to see like an artist and, in the darkness of those violent years, to feel as an artist must feel. At twelve he had stood off gun-armed cowboys and their Texas Longhorns from land belonging to his father and his father's settlers, heard his father and himself promised a bullet in the gut if they crossed the line of the cattleman-controlled county seat, saw the bodies of the settlers hanged and burned by the outfit making the threats. These young painters could not know that what makes the artist, Indian or white man, Henri or the stiff-kneed old cow puncher, was something that lies deep in all men, something like a vein of red stone, to be bared by the winds or thrust out by the eruption of violence.

While the Kansas artists Sandzen, Curry and Poor worked with spatula and brush, a curious and unpredictable spurt of cartooning was being produced by Nebraskans out of the 1910-20 period. Herbert Johnson, commenting on Clare Briggs, Rollin Kirby, John Cassel, Hy Gage and himself, said: "With five cartoonists from one corner of it, the Cornhusker State must have much on its artistic or inartistic conscience to answer for." Most of these men were rather good-humored, even gentle, particularly Briggs, with his "When a

Feller Needs a Friend," but Kirby had a real sting that won him the first Pulitzer prize awarded for a cartoon, and then won it twice more.

The most surprising artist of all the Plains was Jackson Pollock, whose work started a feuding and fighting in the art world comparable to the Johnson County Cattle War in his Wyoming. His canvases were less surprising to some who had been caught in an early blizzard between Rawlins and Rock Springs, say, the sixty-mile-an-hour wind cutting the face with as much black grit as sharp snow, to settle eventually in thin, streaked, twisted drifts. Apparently no man escapes the symbols skulking in the depths of his childhood's alarm.

The University of Nebraska, called the seminary in the cornfield by the jokers, opened its first class in 1871. There seems to have been some chancellor trouble in the early years, with the complaint, rather common to the Plains institutions of higher learning, that none held the position more than five years. December 6, 1879, *Frank Leslie's Illustrated Newspaper* carried an advertisement that faculty members, and students too, copied and read to each other:

> THE CHANCELLOR OF THE UNIVERSITY OF NEBRASKA CURED
> Dr. Fairfield is well known all over the United States as a man of high standing, learning and great eloquence in the pulpit. He is at present Chancellor of the University of Nebraska. Prior to the use of Childs's Catarrh Specific, he had utterly lost the use of his voice and was compelled to suspend his daily lectures. . . .

> Rev. T. P. Childs: *Dear Sir*: I think you have the true theory and practice for the cure of Nasal Catarrh and also for the treatment of the respiratory organs. My throat is now so well restored, that I lecture daily without difficulty, and I find no difficulty whatever in preaching. You are at full liberty to use my name for the benefit of others. Yours very truly, E. B. Fairfield, D.D., LL.D., Lincoln, Nebraska.

Plainly the testimonial business is not new. Perhaps it paid well enough in money or publicity; in 1882 an acting chancellor took over and Dr. Fairfield's well-restored voice was heard elsewhere.

By January 1890 the great period of the University had begun. To the potential student, welcomed to take entrance examination, and offered the preparatory Latin School, because many would arrive without much beyond a few months in a district school, the University announced, as others did all over the Plains: "Advantages are offered to all *free of charge for tuition*, without regard for sex or race or place of residence on the sole condition of possessing the intellectual and moral qualifications requisite for admission to such an institution."

Dr. Charles E. Bessey, filling in as acting chancellor in addition to his regular duties as dean of the College of Literature, Science and the Arts, and teacher, set the tone. It was heightened by the new chancellor, Dr. James H. Canfield, whose evenings with music and good and challenging talk welcomed such plow-footed youths as Alvin Johnson. Alvin was charmed by the chancellor's dark-eyed, Kansas-born young daughter Dorothy and her violoncello, and deeply involved in the scholarly discussions and the arguments over the menace of Bryan and the Democrats to Populist ideals. These talks helped turn young Johnson toward economics and eventually to the founding and the directorship of the New School for Social Research in New York, epitomizing his beliefs that the groves of academe belong next door to the public forum.

Dr. Bessey was busy with such students as Rydberg from Wahoo and Howard Taylor Ricketts, who was to give medicine its first knowledge of Rickettsia, the cause of such diseases as Rocky Mountain spotted fever and typhus, which he was to contract fatally during further research in Mexico. There was Hiram Winnett Orr, to become a noted orthopedic surgeon, and Hartley Burr Alexander, poet and moving swiftly toward philosophy. There were half a dozen others, all arguing to settle the relative importance of the arts and the physical sciences. And always there was Pershing, drilling the awkwardness out of the feet on the parade ground, and out of the mind too, with mathematics.

During those years the gates of the iron campus fence clanged shut at night to keep the spooners out, until the time that U Hall caught fire and nobody could find the custodian with the key. The fire horses thundered up with bells clanging and iron hooves shooting sparks on the cobblestones, to stand there, stomping, as the flames rose high. Afterward the fence was moved out to Wyuka, the cemetery, to keep the dead safe.

In those early days a small but special group of students passed through those iron gates, including four young people perhaps unmatched at any time from so small a school. They varied in age. The oldest was Roscoe Pound, admitted to the bar in 1890, at twenty, now working toward his Ph.D., honorary curator of the Herbarium, instructor in American history and jurisprudence, and to become the most famous dean of the Harvard School of Law. Another was Roscoe's sister Emma Louise, to drop the Emma and become the famous philologist and folklorist Louise Pound.

The Pounds were born in Lincoln, taught at home by their mother until they entered the Latin School at the University. Louise became what was called a "world-beater" at the time, with a diploma in music (piano) in addition to her scholarly degrees. She was a figure skater, champion golfer and winner of University tennis titles over the men. She organized the Golden Fleece on the campus, with the handsomest thick auburn mane of the lot, one that stayed with her to her death at eighty-five. Although she had her doctorate from Heidelberg and many excellent offers, nothing could draw her from her home town for long. She talked of her mother, her sister and the old house built by Judge Pound at the edge of a cornfield and prairie, to be overshadowed by the new capitol tower with its Sower looking down where the fields had been. Her duty to these held her, she said. Perhaps she really fooled no one. She was a woman of the Plains, not the geographical Plains so much as of that other vast Plains country—language. In her case it was the widest language of all, English, from Anglo-Saxon to the speech of the homesteader, the cowboy, the wildcatter, the ex-convict—all of whom appeared in her classes and were all made welcome. The more the speech of her students varied, the more it pleased her. To her language was a growing thing.

"Tell your stories in your own words, in the words and expressions that the people used, in the talk that is natural to the material," she advised a student who had been struggling against the insistence of another professor that she write of her raw homestead childhood in Barrett Wendell English.

Another of the four inspired ones, the youngest, was the daughter of the chancellor, the future Dorothy Canfield Fisher, so much a part of her Vermont hills in her maturity, although she reached there by way of Kansas, Nebraska, Ohio and New York, a sort of western emigration in reverse. She was already writing very well at fifteen, sixteen, and sometimes collaborated with the fourth of this group— Willa Cather, only three years older—for the campus literary magazine.

All four of these young people came from well-managed, well-bred and well-read homes, from settled, stable communities. Willa Cather, born in Virginia, in the proudest region of the defeated and humiliated South, was moved at eight to the little town of Red Cloud, near the Kansas-Nebraska border, on a railroad then, but near the site of the settler stockade thrown up in the 1870's against the Indians. In the home of Governor Silas Garber she heard stories of those days. There were still Indian artifacts scattered on wind-swept spots, the anthills colored with their beads. Occasional lone buffalo heads bleached in isolated spots. Little fence-corner cemeteries cradled men who had died of blizzard or bullet, women lost in childbirth or to typhoid, and many children, perhaps swept off by summer complaint, scarlet fever or diphtheria. The young Willa saw the homes, perhaps little soddies growing naturally out of the ground like the mushrooms that her Bohemian settlers collected and dried. As Dorothy Canfield Fisher was to say of her:

> No matter how widely she rode, in all that unfenced prairie, the only people for her to see were transplants; and for the first few years most of them half drunk with the exquisite and unforgettable elixir of frontier hopefulness.
>
> The tragic souring of that wine coincided with her growing up. By the time she was twelve the tide had begun to turn. Successive

drouths had brought terrible crop failures to those farmers from rainy climates, pitifully unprepared for a hot, dry land.

In 1955 Mrs. Anna Pavelka died in Bladen, at eighty-six. She had lost her father when she was eleven and went to work in Red Cloud homes and was immortalized in Willa Cather's *My Antonia*. Afterward came *The Lost Lady* and *Death Comes for the Archbishop* and the rest, written in the style touched with that "exquisite and unforgettable elixir."

The hard times of the nineties killed many things, including the literary ferment in the new colleges of the Plains and their little magazines that provided an outlet. Since then scientists, lawyers, financial and industrial wizards and successful politicians have come from those schools. There was a moderate stirring in the arts on the campuses of the Plains in the 1920's, less than in some parts of the nation, but a stirring. One of the results was a new crop of little magazines. At Nebraska Dr. Lowry B. Wimberly started the *Prairie Schooner*, to draw manuscripts internationally ever since, outliving all others of its kind. The quarterly offered consistent encouragement to a large number of writers, sometimes a first publication that started a substantial literary career, as its predecessor of the nineties had started Dorothy Canfield and Willa Cather.

To be sure there is usually a tinge of queasiness, of priggishness and evasion, about university quarterlies, particularly those in tax-supported institutions. Apparently a certain weather eye must be kept out for officious wives of legislators, or the legislators themselves, and others, perhaps pressure groups, who do not understand that art flourishes in freedom and that everything that can happen in life or that can be imagined is proper material for literature.

Perhaps it is futile to hope for another period of such freedom, such ferment as that of 1890-96 at Nebraska, when, it seems, the only fence around the campus of the University was the one of iron grill that could be closed to fire horses, yes, but hid nothing, and could be climbed by any one with vigor and ambition and an inquiring mind.

There are without doubt new writers rising out of the Plains, even money makers, and some with poetic sensitivity and narrative skill, but where is the writer with the gusto, the wild immeasurable power, the wide horizons, the sense of the universal in man, and his infinite variety, that the Plains might have produced, should have produced?

X   *The Water, the Grass and the Tree*

The Sower on top of the capitol tower at Lincoln strides his solitary way against the pale sky of the eternal spring. The tall white pinnacle with its golden dome and the Goodhue building of it rise from the edge of the old, long-vanished salt basin, rise from the corn lands, the wheat lands and the beef lands in a sort of modern tall tale. The black bit, like an eyelash floating on the warm morning air, is not an eagle soaring but a jet plane and gone almost before the noticing, halfway to Chicago.

Around the tower, in bas-relief, march those gone-before ones, the buffalo, the Indian, the fur men, the pioneers. The great figures of humanity, such as law, justice and mercy, stand watching or depict their significant victories, from those of the Old Testament down through the Independence and the Constitution with its freedom of speech, and of the body and the heart. These figures and those of the vast rotunda inside, and the domes and the mosaic floor, with all the ornamentation inside and out, and the noble inscriptions, these are all part of the symbolic scheme of Dr. Hartley Burr Alexander, one of those young people from around the University in those portentous 1890's. Artistically he seemed to feel an affinity between the old Indian and buffalo Plains and classicism—in the cleanness of line, the balance, the symmetry and repose of the prospect; the vitality of space, the elegance of its sweep and coloring.

And while authorities from far off praised Dr. Alexander's conception, there was very little thanks from his home state, not until long after he had gone to pleasanter fields.

There were some who believed that the Sower of the Nebraska capitol should broadcast not only seeds upon the fertile earth but ideas in government as well. One of these ideas, the unicameral legislature, was started long ago, back in 1914, through an extensive study and report by Addison E. Sheldon. He had been brought to Nebraska as a boy, was an early homesteader west of Valentine, a newspaperman at Chadron and elsewhere, a Populist member of the legislature and a fighter for improved government and the preservation of the state's school lands. As historian, writer and longtime superintendent of the Nebraska State Historical Society, he died with more of the political history of the state in his head than has ever been written down. But he lived to see the one-house legislature. John Senning, chairman of the Political Science Department at the university, pushed it, and, with the great influence of Senator George Norris behind it too, the state adopted the idea in 1934, the same year that pari-mutuel betting on horse races was approved by the voters. Some said, acidly, that the Omaha gamblers, not confident that their voters could differentiate between two such alien words as *pari-mutuel* and *unicameral*, ordered them to vote for both. Both won.

The members of the unicameral are nonpartisan, to be elected solely on qualifications, the annual salary unaffected by length of session and considerably higher than the old bicameral pay. Opponents question the lack of party responsibility and discipline, while proponents point with pride to the high level of the members, generally higher than the state's national representation has been since the days of Senator Norris. Some recall the venality and pathetic ineffectiveness of the last two bicameral legislatures, back in the depression years, when Nebraska was in tragic straits, still almost completely agricultural, with farm prices on a panic level if there had been anything left by the drouth, grasshoppers and dust storms. The paralysis in the legislative chambers brought a farmers' march to the capitol to force a mortgage moratorium before the national one was enacted, before many men were killed in the forced foreclosures, as happened in states around.

In times of extreme privation and hardship, of great public unease or after a war, when people refuse to face the dull realities of peace, they build fairy tales for themselves, tall tales, and if the times are right, these can run over the nation like prairie fire in a high wind. The rage for spiritualism had spread like that after the Civil War, when so many grasped at any hope of communication with those gone in their youth and vigor, or even momentary contact with some portion of the body amputated. The *Atlantic* published a story of a man who walked on his amputated legs at a spiritualist séance.

Suddenly, in the 1890's, when it seemed that the rains would never sprout corn again, tall tales started, not like those of bald-headed Indians, mummified pigmies in Wyoming, or the petrified mermaid of the Loup valley. Now the public demanded something romantic, something to challenge the imagination, chill the heart, something to make them forget the dead fields, the starving cattle. Beguilement for the rain-desperate eyes came. Flying boats appeared. Back in the hard times of 1857-58 there were stories of a flying serpent that hovered over a Missouri River steamboat slowing for a landing. In the late dusk it was like a great undulating serpent, in and out of the lowering clouds, breathing fire, it seemed, with lighted streaks along the sides. Then the middle 1860's brought at least one song:

> 'Twas a dark night in Sixty-six,
> When we was layin' steel

We seen a flyin' engine come
Without no wing or wheel.

It come a roarin' in the sky,
With lights along the side . . .

And scales like serpent's hide.

Now, in the middle 1890's, reports of such flying serpents or craft came in from several towns until the torchlight parades and the hope of Bryan and the Populists engrossed the public, but neither Cleveland nor the hard-money Democrats supported Bryan, the party papers boomed McKinley, and employers circulated the word, or posted signs, warning that a Bryan victory meant no jobs the next morning. All the Plains except North Dakota went for him, but he lost, and a gloom thick as a black blizzard settled over the region, even though the rains came again. What good was corn at ten cents a bushel, or even up a cent?

Then early in February 1897 the papers reported an airship or something near Hastings, moving at about eight hundred feet up. Next a dozen people from a prayer meeting near Inavale saw the bright light of a flying craft about forty feet long, conical, with two sets of wings and a great fan-shaped rudder, so low they could hear voices from the craft and a man laughing.

"Maybe them prayer meetin's changing?" an old sot wondered.

After the moving lights were reported over York, a moderate community, the epidemic was really on the wind, and nearly every newspaper carried similar stories, the earlier towns taking on a second turn: Hastings, Omaha, North Platte, Kearney and Grand Island, sometimes the viewers in crowds of a hundred or more. Skeptics began to organize airship parties, particularly as the nights warmed, and were denounced by the new crop of sky pilots that gather like buzzards to any ailing time.

"Sacrilege!" they cried. "Pray and make ready for the Day of Judgment!" Plainly the flights were a warning, a foretelling of the end of the earth, the craft perhaps a new ark come to pick up the new chosen people.

Then it seems a Beatrice paper carried a letter signed by Anton Pallardy, announcing that he was one of the builders of the airship seen everywhere, and was just waiting for his patent before announcing the details of his large, umbrella-shaped craft with a pair of wings. Nights they took experimental trips from the hiding place up in the bad lands near Crawford.

The letter was reprinted all over the region, and although Father Rigge, professor of astronomy at Creighton, suggested that what people saw was probably the planet Venus, nobody listened, particularly not after a ship or a flying serpent was seen down in prohibition Kansas. At Topeka it was watched by over two hundred, including the governor, who, it was said, hoped this would solve the railroad problem.

As the sightings spread to Washington and elsewhere, the fun picked up on the Plains. The Albion paper gave the dimensions of one of the ships as 37 feet 3 inches by 11 feet 13 inches, described by a man who was three inches away while the owner unfolded it. Next one of the ships was found wrecked at Waterloo, Iowa, although a sour-mouth claimed it was just a big crate that some pranksters made and pushed off a cliff. Perhaps to prove that it was still flying, the airship appeared out toward Wyoming to some select observers, and close enough for one of the men to recognize his runaway wife in it. Others claimed that the woman was Judge Gaslin's wife, who had skipped out with a brother lawyer years before and gone, it was believed, to Wyoming, from whence few returned. Finally a Grand Islander claimed he took a ride in the airship, which was not supernatural at all but was built up in the sandhills and run by the wind collected by following Bryan in the great campaign. A Texan had a better sense of denouement. He said he lassoed the flying serpent from his catch horse, dragged it down out of the sky and chopped it up for his hound dogs.

Thomas Edison, asked what he thought, had labeled all the flying-object stories fakes, but six years later the Wrights did fly a little. Long before that, however, the *Maine* had been sunk and there were other stories to fill the papers, and a little wartime boom to line the pockets.

In the meantime there had been other hoaxes, mostly up around Chadron, around John J. Maher. Later very civic-spirited, and an excellent businessman as well as president of the Friends of the Irish Republic, in his earlier days John Maher was court reporter in northwest Nebraska, and correspondent there for the New York *Herald*. He engineered the casting and finding of the petrified man up near Chadron, exhibited all over the country as genuine, prehistoric. A little farther down the railroad the man was dismissed as a settler who had sat down to wait for the Indian uprising and petrified waiting. It is true that Maher and others of the *Herald* had whipped up national excitement over the Ghost Dancers and helped bring troops to Pine Ridge. After 1900, when things got dull, Maher began a series of stories about finding the Spaniard who sank the *Maine*. This time the U.S. government got more interested than in the Indian scare that brought on the butchery of the Sioux at Wounded Knee. Maher and his companions in the hoax had to buy up a corpse, take it to an old southern fort and burn the place down, producing the charred body as that of the Spanish prisoner who started the war with Spain.

This didn't cure Maher. When World War I was over, the government got out from under the wheat peggings. The price went to the bottom, and broke people all through the wheat districts of Kansas, Colorado, Montana, the Dakotas and the Nebraska Panhandle. The time was ripe for more tall tales. Every region seems to have its Loch Ness monster in one guise or another. The most widely publicized one of the Plains is at Alkali Lake, up near Hay Springs, Nebraska. From the Indian days there had been accounts of a great creature there, but the stories never caught on until the price of wheat went to pieces. Then they appeared in the western newspapers and spread farther, many reported as firsthand accounts:

"Its head was like a oil barrel, shiny black in the moonlight; its flashing green eyes was spitting fire."

"When it roars and flips that powerful tail, the farmers get sea sick."

"It grabs and swallows a dozen calves when it comes ashore."

One story told of a skeptical Omahan who drove out to spend a night alone at the lake. When he returned, his hair was white and his voice gone. Three days later he recovered, to say that the monster was at least three hundred feet long and its mouth large enough to hold the Woodmen of the World Building in Omaha. There were some who suspected that the man's hair was powdered with the stuff that the Community Playhouse actors used.

A picture was displayed in the large center window of Magee's store in Lincoln. A crowd pushed up to see the photograph of a lake with an old truck off to the side, and resting on the water was a dragonlike creature at least ten times as long as the truck. A university student elbowed in to see and, surprised, exclaimed in a needlessly loud voice, "That's a fake! That's a picture of a sandhill water puppy, superimposed on the lake picture!"

But she was shushed, crowded to the curb with angry looks and growls. There was a campaign under way to raise money for a seining out at Alkali, and at least $3,000 needed. It seems that a large caravan of cars, and people by train, did go out to Hay Springs. They trampled the grass around the lake and were threatened with a suit by one of the owners.

There was bantering and broad wit all up and down the railroad towns about Maher's mermaid, although at least a dozen others had taken part in the publicity. In the meantime the eastern papers picked up the story. The *Pathfinder* ran a series of letters on it, the *Boston Transcript* carried several items, and the London *Times* reportedly printed an account, comparing the Alkali monster with the perhaps gentler occupant of Loch Ness. A fantastic drawing credited to the *Times* was copied around the United States. But the most fun was the four-column picture of "The Plesiosaurus Which Grew to Be Forty Feet Long," swimming with a school of small fish around him, in the New York *Times*, Sunday, August 5, 1923:

NEBRASKA'S "SEA SERPENT" RESEMBLES REAL ONES
"Monster" Reported in Alkali Lake Like Those Alive There
Long Ages Ago
. . . . Once more a monster of antediluvian proportions has rolled across the bewildered vision of modern man and, according to report, "lashed the water with its tail, suddenly dived and was seen no more."

The theory of one eyewitness, the *Times* reported, was that there are subterranean passages leading to underground lakes where other reptiles of kindred tastes and habits consort, coming up only occasionally. The one seen, forty feet long, had a hornlike projection between the eyes and nostrils. Perhaps an "army of monsters" is undermining "the peaceful farmlands of our western states." An authority from the American Museum of Natural History was quoted as saying that Nebraska "was once the home of amphibious animals similar to the one described. Is it possible that the earth has another secret?" After much discussion of such things as Nebraska's geological formations, and some old monster stories, the article ended: "The Great Sea Serpent is still abroad in the world—still unconquered—bearing his mysterious secret in his scaly breast."

Well, the writer of the article had fun for the moment, but by the time his work appeared it was overshadowed by pages and pages of eulogy to a dead man, to President Harding, who had died August 2, and so there were new stories, newer tall tales to be half-told.

All this time the Plains harbored a more fabulous creature than any conjured up by John Maher or the New York *Times* for Alkali Lake, or by the mythmakers anywhere. This was the cow, the cow in her partnership with man. Twenty, twenty-five thousand years ago he was already paying her and her kind his highest tribute in magnificent cave paintings in France and elsewhere, caves whose great vaulted chambers served as the first cathedrals, the greatest of these chambers, the Hall of the Bulls, in the Lascaux caves. Cattle, bulls, cows and calves run through much of the mythology and religion of man; in Egyptian art and stories some of the gods were

said to have been born of the cow, and all through the Mediterranean
world the cow was deep in the symbolism of the arts and religion.
Cattle appear in the first chapter of Genesis and were so well rooted
in man's mind that when the story of Moses was told, the idol his
people cast from their golden ornaments and vessels was not the
ruler of the skies or the king of beasts; out of their deep mystical
identification they cast a golden calf.

The true cow came late to America, none to the Plains, apparently,
until Coronado walked his commissary north in 1541, and there is
no evidence, only a possibility, that any got away to reproduce from
his expedition. Certainly some escaped soon afterward, to build up
the great wild herds in the brush country of Texas. The buffalo, the
bison, had been plentiful on the Plains for a long, long time, in company with man at least as far back as the days when he carried a
six-foot horn spread. But this was an independent creature and never
anxious for domestication. He would carry no burdens, pull no carts.
Some wonder why the American Indian never developed the use
of the wheel, but what man did without the patient cow brute to
draw it? Certainly the Indian knew the wheel—not only the Inca
his wheeled toys, the Mayan probably his potter's wheel. The Plains
man moved stones by rolling just as surely as the European or the
Asiatic; he sent felled trees spinning down hill; he tossed the willow
hoops laced with rawhide whirling in his prairie games. Besides, if
he hadn't grasped the advantages in the rolling process for himself,
he could have seen the dung beetle with his lump of fresh buffalo
dung that was far too large to carry or drag, watched him roll it
home to hatch the egg laid inside.

While a few cattle may have seen the Nebraska region earlier, the
first herds that really grew there were those at Fort Atkinson on the
Missouri, the herds that were the pride of the commanders and the
tenders and so scorned by the military inspector because they made
graziers instead of soldiers of the troops.

When the trails opened, work cattle by the thousands began to
plod their way across the Plains and over to Oregon and California,
mostly oxen, but cows too, because they might furnish a little milk

for the small children along or for those with bad stomachs, sent west in great numbers because it was known that even bleeding stomachs sometimes healed themselves out there, perhaps through the physical labor and the fresh meat, still warm from the kill. Besides, in the new regions the cow could start new herds. Then the Texas Longhorns began to walk their swift-legged, lean-flanked way northward. At first there were only a few, crossing the Missouri into Iowa, but later the trails were dark with summer herds headed up to the railroads and northern grasses.

Under experienced trail drivers the Texas stock usually fattened on the way, but they brought a fever to the American, to the stock brought from the eastern regions. If a milk cow or an eastern bull train grazed or settled down for a short cud on the ground where Texas cattle had passed, they often sickened and usually died from the fever. The Longhorn, like a Typhoid Mary, was immune to the disease his ticks scattered from the Gulf to Montana, sooner or later. This alone would have brought trouble in all the increasing settlements from the Arkansas northward as it did in Missouri and farther east. But when the trail herds, usually a thousand to two thousand head a piece, came by the hundreds a summer, the grass was eaten into the ground, all the crops and gardens cleaned out, the women and children scattered by the wild and terrifying horns. Sometimes a Texas steer ran out over the prairie with a quilt or a bedsheet from some clothesline hanging to his horns, bellowing and dodging to escape his burden. Sometimes a whole bunch charged into a washing laid out on rosebushes or the grass to bleach snowy white in the sun. They attacked the family dog, or the children, or stampeded over the well and the dugout, falling through. If a place was left unguarded an hour the lousy Longhorns might scratch the soddy down at the corners.

When the herds became more familiar, the women shouted and scolded, their skirts gathered up to flee. The children were ready to kick the old plow mare into an awkward gallop to drive the Longhorns off, sometimes to find that they held their ground, pawing, bellowing, lunging. Usually the men who tried to stand against the gun-armed trail crews were as helpless. But some, perhaps with old muzzleloaders, might scare up a little lead, and shoot a steer or two, and then be found face down on the prairie for it, although the stock had been trespassing on the settler's land, with no law but his gun to protect it. Even after law came, often the cattlemen controlled the sheriff and the courts.

Most of this was out toward the hundredth meridian and beyond, although there was some trouble even around Beatrice and Lincoln from the more drunken lawless cowboys. Then, when cattle prices went to pieces in the early seventies, rumors reached Nebraska that perhaps a hundred thousand head had found no buyers at any price around Abilene and were to be thrown north. Most of these reached the Republican valley for their first northern winter, coming thin as washboards from the summer on overgrazed range. When the blizzards struck they died by the tens of thousands, many frozen standing up in the snow. It was some of these dead that were later charged to the Indians, who scorned the white man's cow as long as they could, claiming that the meat stank and was never as sweet as fat buffalo hump rib roasted over the coals.

It was soon discovered that Longhorns grew larger in the more rigorous climate, the more nutritious range, of the upper Plains, the meat worth more per pound on the market. As fast as the Indians were driven out the ranchers moved in. With their armed cowboys a private military, they spread over the public domain as though taking a kingdom, and held it as long as they could by gun and rope against the settlers, the legal claimants. For a long time the leading cattlemen held the range against the highest courts of the country.

The Texas trail hands and the ranch cowboys often included men called G.T.T.'s, meaning Gone to Texas, one jump ahead of the sheriff or the U.S. marshal. When these men got into trouble there they might become G.N.'s, Gone Norths, perhaps from the law or to escape an avenger. On payday the trail herders hit town with throats dust-dry, ready for whisky, practically the only drink sold, their heavy pistols the symbols of their potent maleness, the loading of them and the draw important male acts to many who needed such assurance very much. Some of the ranchers were happy to pay for store fronts, bar glass and other bullet damages for the effects that the gun wildness might have on any ambitious little fellow hoping to horn in on their range, and, more important, for its intimidating impact on any homeseekers around, and on settlers and their wives.

Towns from Wichita to Hastings, Minden, and a dozen others. were terrorized, Kearney particularly, until a cowboy put a bullet through the dress of a small girl trying to drive the range cattle from her father's crops. The settlers around organized and promised quick homemade justice to any unruly or shooting cowboy and to the employer of any man who injured settlers. Scornfully calling the town "Hoeman's Heaven," the cowboys and their money went elsewhere, carrying their noise and lead and death with them. Some towns were taken over completely. Plum Creek became Olive Town, headquarters of Print Olive and his gang within a few months after he moved up from Texas with a dozen or more murders behind him. He pushed into the rapidly settling Custer County with his cattle and his hired gunmen, although the ranchers had been moving out. Olive had seen the open, ungrazed sandhill region farther on, where no settlers had taken root, but he picked Custer County because, like in Texas, he demanded conflict, murder. He ignored the Nebraska Herd Law, which made any stock running at large subject to corralling, the owner liable for the damages to crops. But this enclosing, this taking up, was an absolute requirement for a damage case and was often used as proof of theft where the cattlemen controlled the courts, as it still is in western stories, moving pictures and in television.

Print Olive found that neither his reputation nor that of his brother Bob, who had to skip Texas for too many cold-blooded murders, scared the settlers off their homesteads. Plainly their mainstay was Ami (Whit) Ketchum, young Iowa blacksmith and mighty handy with a rifle. The fall of 1877, when Olive was in the region less than a year, one of Ketchum's brothers, government scout

at Fort Laramie, received a letter* from a man in Custer County
suggesting that he warn Whit that certain ranchers planned to make
an example of him to scare the other settlers off their claims.
Whether this was a sort of secondhand attempt to scare Whit himself out or a genuine warning seems not clear, but Olive proceeded
according to his usual well-worn plan. He had some of his stock
thrown over into Ketchum's field and hay, to be taken up for
damages. When this was assured, he sent an armed gang over at
dawn, but something slipped, went wrong. Perhaps Ketchum was
too fast with his rifle or there were complications with the Mitchell
family, who lived in the other end of the long sod house set across
the homestead line. Stories differ, but the usual shooting down, or
dragging away to a cottonwood and a rope, didn't come off. Instead,
Olive got a warrant issued against Ketchum for cattle rustling and
sent his gunmen, headed by Bob Olive, with a price on his head
down in Texas, as deputy sheriff, to ride out of the early morning,
shooting. Old Man Mitchell, his wife, two young daughters and
Ketchum were just getting into the wagon to return a borrowed
bull to a neighbor. The Olive bullets splintered the wagon box, with
the Mitchell family cowering down inside, the old man trying to
hold off the mob by quiet talk. When this failed Ketchum began to
return the fire from behind the wagon wheel until he was hit in the
arm. Then he shot to kill and brought Bob Olive down. The mob
picked him up and spurred away.

Now the settlers knew they would be lynched, as several others
had been in the region lately. The family fled, but nobody dared
help them, not even in far counties. No doctor dared dress Ketchum's
bullet-torn arm, swelling thick as a stovepipe, the man in fever. They
sent the women on in the wagon; the men struck across the prairie
afoot and were ridden down, brought back to Plum Creek and
turned over to Print Olive and his mob, hanged, dowsed in coal oil
and set afire. For a long time nobody came for the bodies, even for
burial, and nobody arrested the mob strutting the dusty street of

* In possession of Mrs. Maud Ketchum Rouzer, daughter of Lawrence
Ketchum.

Plum Creek while the newspapers as far off as New York and Paris denounced the inhuman American man-burners. Then the Ketchum brothers, with District Court Judge Gaslin and others, decided it was time to challenge this mob rule in the heart of the state. The Ketchums were deputized and with a few followers they went to Plum Creek and arrested Print Olive and his men without firing a shot. Because, through a legislative oversight, Custer County had not been attached to any judicial district, the trial was called at Hastings, followed by the threats from the Olive outfit to burn the town. Print Olive and his foreman were sent to the penitentiary. Now one of Nebraska's finest crops of stories sprouted, stories of whole herds of cattle changing hands, and much money too, everybody from a ranch chore boy to a justice of the state supreme court offered a bribe, and many takers. It is true that every member of the mob except the two in the pen disappeared for a while, and every witness, a few of these to turn up dead later. On the strength of the activities of one justice, it was said, the state supreme court ordered a retrial in Custer County, even though it had only a county judge, also a cattleman, one who owned a whole new herd the day after his Olive trial. He had called for anyone desiring to make a charge against Print Olive, and for witnesses to any wrongdoing on the man's part. None came forward, court was dismissed and everybody went out for a drink.

For years Nebraska was the Man-Burner State. In the meantime Print Olive had found himself ostracized by even the more ruthless cattlemen and finally left the region.

"When you control the courts like he did you can convict any settler you want to get rid of by claiming he stole your cattle. You don't have to hang and burn him," many people said, one way or another, glad to see Olive head for Kansas, to push into a cattle pool there.

But arrests and convictions wouldn't scare out as many settlers as the horror of a burning, nor would that have satisfied the twisted needs of the man who, although he came from a religious home and an overfond mother, at last found the end he seemed to seek so long in the bullets fired at Trail City, Colorado, by a cowboy who called himself Joe Sparrow.

The troubles of the late seventies brought more settler organizations like that of the Kearney region, to order the small but powerful
percentage of lawless cattlemen out of the country, letting them go
alive, without bullet or burn. By now the settlements were pushing
the cattle trail westward to Ogallala, the outlet for Texas beef to the
Indians of the Dakotas, and young she stuff to the spreading ranches
of the West. Much English and Scottish money was making Wyoming a sort of financial colony of the British Empire, with an absolute power far beyond that of the British fur traders of the upper
Missouri at their height.

The big Die-Ups of the blizzard years, 1884-87, with the increasing
thievery by employees who saw no reason why they should not
make money for themselves from their knowledge and the American
free grass rather than for their foreign employers, were bankrupting
some of the financial combines. To account for the great losses in
cattle and hold their jobs a while longer, the ranch managers blamed
the settlers, whom they called rustlers indiscriminately, no matter
whether a man ever owned even one cow critter or got his hands on
one.

With Wyoming Territory controlled by the employees and the
debtors of the British financiers, settlers were shot down and hanged,
but not even the hanging of Jim Averill and Cattle Kate seemed to
stop the rush of homeseekers or to scare out very many. So it was
decided to clean the center of settler resistance, Buffalo, up in Johnson County. A large-scale invasion was organized and train-borne,
with gunmen raised wherever possible by the promise of $500 for
every settler killed. No Wyoming cowboys would join but the cattlemen and ranch managers, with a motley lot of loafers and badmen,
mostly from Texas, managed to get a few settlers by bullet and fire.
In the end they had to be rescued by colored cavalry charging in,
just as the settlers, led by the Scottish sheriff of Johnson County,
were pushing a hay go-devil up to the ranch house to burn out the
invaders, trapped there.

With the settlers aroused at last and gunning for any member of
the invasion who had killed homesteaders, none of them stayed
around northern Wyoming very long. Many moved into the last

region with any unclaimed free range left, the last and the best—the long-grass, well-watered, well-protected sandhills of Nebraska. The area, roughy egg-shaped, was between 200 and 250 miles long and 100 to 150 miles across. Surrounded by rougher chophills, the center was a series of high sandy ridges, grassed over, laid across an old lake bed, the valleys mostly down to black dirt, with meadows, marshes and a thousand and more sweet-water lakes. These drained gradually eastward, some northeast to the Niobrara, but mostly to the southeast, forming the many branches of the Loup Rivers.

In 1892 there was a scattering of settlers in the sandhills, but before the end of 1894 the newly arrived Wyoming outfits were cleaning them out. Within a few months four homesteaders were found dead, shot at the plow, the mower, anywhere, but always on their own land, to make it clear that it was the claim-holding, the homesteading, that was the death offense. Soft-handed gunmen appeared on the ranch payrolls and were left strictly, and contemptuously, alone around the bunkhouses by the working cowboys. Big ranches like the Spade, down from Wyoming, and running cattle over a region at least a hundred miles long, and the U.B.I., farther south, were British-financed. Both of these fenced the government land, their range protected by slick fingers, who were to clear out the settlers inside the range and to keep them out.

The cattlemen claimed special concern for the potential settler now. He would only starve himself and his children on the Godforsaken government claims. In the meantime they promoted schemes to get what remained of the public domain permanently into their grasp, working for long-term token leases and for large grazing entries, such as ten sections, 6,400 acres, to facilitate covering the free-land areas quickly with cowboy filings, get them safely patented in big chunks at small cost. It should be easy, with most of the Plains senators, some of the National Republican committeemen and several large financial interests involved in the cattle syndicates of the West. Besides, McKinley was in the White House.

The fences were tightened and, because some cowboys began to keep their homesteads for themselves, the ranchers hunted up old soldiers and soldier widows, with special priorities and privileges, and no desire to settle on the land. These they located on the good hay flats and the water. When Roosevelt, a rancher himself, became President, the cattlemen felt particularly secure and prepared to grab what was left of the public domain. In 1903 they received a shock. Indictments for illegal fencing of government lands were returned against several of them, including the largest outfit, Richards and Comstock's Spade Ranch, an agglomeration of smaller holdings. Of course nothing more would come of this than of similar indictments against Richards and others in 1884-85, but it was an annoyance.

Finally in 1904 the Kinkaid Homestead Act was passed and this, with the related Reclamation Act that brought the federal government into irrigation, changed the whole picture of the farther reaches of the Plains. Congressman Kinkaid, one of the later but certainly no less energetic citizens of General O'Neill's town, secured passage of the 640-acre homestead, subject to the same conditions as the original one, and encompassing it.

Once more a sort of boom struck the Plains, not one that drew a hundred thousand running through, but a land boom, and after the land-hungry of the world had thought their time was surely past. This too came in the midst of a recession, with many driven westward by tight money and jobs gone to mechanization. Excitement hit the land-office towns around the sandhills. Weeks ahead new saloons were hammered together and soft-spoken men, with knife-creased, peg-topped trousers and beautifully kept hands, appeared. A little weatherbeaten church might suddenly be overshadowed by the house next door, gay in new yellow paint, a mechanical piano, a crystal chandelier and flower-globed lamps, with women in lace blouses and pinched-in belts lolling about, chaperoned by a practiced madame, perhaps from Deadwood or the Klondike, in wine-colored satin and a dog collar of imitation pearls.

Two weeks before the opening, covered wagons, horsebackers, men afoot and finally railroad trains long with extra cars for the boomers toiled into Alliance, Valentine, North Platte and Broken

Bow. The more serious, the more intelligent homeseekers got information at the land office and vanished into the sandhills. Many turned
back at the first soft yellow chophills pockmarked by blowouts and
warted with soapweeds, yuccas, their elegant spikes of waxy green-
ish-white blossoms standing tall. Others kept on through this pro-
tective border, into the broad valley region, with the high ridges of
hills reaching toward the whitish sky. Many came in hired rigs and
generally went away again, for the drivers knew how to keep in
the bewildering border all day. So stories spread through the East
of a new Great American Desert, the sandhills of western Nebraska.
The cattlemen should have been paid for living in it.

Locaters like the old-timer Jules Sandoz and the newcomer, O. F.
Hamilton found every good flat either covered by an old entry or
cut up by newer filings, with no one living on any of them. Because
the law required residence within six months, they went to contest
these claims at the land offices for their homeseekers. They found
the towns booming more every day, rows and rows of rough board
shacks thrown together, eked out with canvas and tar paper, mighty
hot in the sun of late June. Inside were solid rows of cots and beds,
extra landseekers sleeping on the floors or in parties out on the
ground. Tents and covered wagons fringed the towns, with pasture
and hay sky-high. Old-timers, recalling the land booms of the seventies and eighties, were surprised to see so many homeseekers not
young any more, many defeated old men and, around the hotels and
the more genteel boarding houses, many women with graying hair
and fuzzy cheeks, perhaps women who spoke meticulous English
and seemed to have their tiny lace handkerchiefs to their mouths in
alarm much of the time.

The day of the opening long queues of homeseekers waited at the
land offices. They stood in two lines, the shorter the preferential—
men in the uniforms of the various wars, and sweating mightily in the
heat. The longer line was of men and women who discovered they
must wait hours in the sun, boys going up and down with buckets
and dippers selling water, or soda pop and lemonade. Most of the
people had few extra nickels and dimes and so endured the heat and

dust as well as they could. And as they passed into the little land offices most of them found even the sad choice of land that had been free yesterday evening had been filed on earlier in the day, and when there was a swift polling of those first in line, it was found that they had been told the same thing. Rumors got around that cattlemen agents had made up whole baskets of entry papers ahead of time and ran them through before the land offices opened, everything worth the paper covered. One woman was said to have filed on forty sections, under forty names, at five dollars a throw.

"But you have to make personal application," the homeseekers complained. They had spent a great deal of money coming from as far as Maine and Washington state.

"You don't if you're taking the land for the ranchers," they were told, but outside.

So the Kinkaid Act was a cattleman law after all, as was certainly intended. The locators and surveyors and some angry landseekers did not give up. They sifted through the sandhills, making plats, writing hot letters to Washington, watching the claims, for in six months every unoccupied Kinkaid was subject to contest. They carried their rifles with them every moment and did a lot of target shooting out where ranch hands could see and report.

The thousands of protests to Washington brought government investigators in shiny top buggies, and some more quietly, afoot, like any homeseeker. Often they carried rolls of the semitransparent bluish maps, records of the original surveys, and pored over them with the local surveyors, the old-timers concerned over obliterated corners, old-soldier widows and fraudulent filings. But many recalled that bucking the cattlemen was dangerous and spoke of the settlers found dead on their homesteads through the sandhills back in the 1890's.

Then more stories got out. It seemed that when the illegal fences around government land were ordered down, the cattlemen were certain that this was just another case of an officious underling stirring up dust as Sparks had in the 1880's. They went to Washington for a friendly visit with their fellow rancher sitting in the White

House. They returned a little quieter, and after a while it was told around that Old Four Eyes had showed his teeth and said, "Gentlemen, the fences come down."

They did, and where the rancher was too slow, soldiers came to cut the wires, throw them back and pull up a lot of posts. Because loose barbed wire was dangerous to man and animals, the ranch hands rolled most of it up and dumped it by the wagonload into blowouts, to keep it from easy sight of settlers wanting to fence their own places. There it rusted like great pincushion cactuses, piled up and turning brown in the sand.

The indictments for illegal fences ran on for years, with increased pressure to pass a land-lease bill, particularly when U.B.I.'s Reverend George Ware, Episcopal clergyman from England, was charged with the same illegal fencing as any of the more godless. He appeared, gave bond and waited for public inertia, public shift in interest, just like the rest. And the usual disappearance of witnesses.

When the ranchers were finally confronted with the proof that government land had been enclosed in their pastures, they changed their pleas to guilty, were fined $300 each and sentenced to the custody of the U.S. marshal at Omaha for six hours. Stories got out that he took them to a fancy champagne dinner, with toasts and promises of a great future for the cattlemen in the free-range regions, particularly the sandhills.

When the settlers heard this, their tongues turned mean as cactus thorns. "Don't butcher a scrub range steer to feed your hungry kids, after the cattlemen been eating up your crops and there ain't nothing left for the family to eat. Gobble up a whole county, and drink champagne!"

Back in Washington, Roosevelt struck like a North Dakota blizzard in January. He fired the marshal, removed the U.S. district attorney for insufficient vigor in the prosecution of the cattlemen, and snorted that he would fire the federal judge, too, if he could. Next Old Four Eyes had the whole bunch of ranchers and their land agents rounded up and got indictments against them for conspiring to defraud the government of vast tracts of the public domain and for subornation of perjury. He appointed Charles A. Goss* U.S. Attorney, but not until he had called the man to Washington to look him over, decide whether money or threats could reach him.

Although the U.B.I. ranch near Mullen, Nebraska, wasn't as large as some in trouble, the Reverend Ware's case brought out some fine new stories, partly because both he and the British syndicate that owned the ranch recalled the long foreign stranglehold on Wyoming. Besides, everybody seemed to know that Hamilton, the locator at Mullen, and partly responsible for bringing Ware and the other local cattlemen to trial, was in constant danger from bullets that spurted up sand around him while on the range, as happened to other locators. Somebody had already tried to burn Hamilton out, his harness and team to go too, but the fire died. Then his two fine Galloway cows were gone, stolen. There were rumors of a deal with Ware to get the cows back. Hamilton was to "forget" the things he knew against Ware, and to make no mention of the attempts against his property and his life.

But the Ware trial dragged on anyway whether there was a deal or not. What everybody had known came out—that the U.B.I. manager had brought carloads of soldiers from the Old Soldiers' Home in Grand Island to file on government land, at first in 160-acre homesteads, illegally stretched out in forties along the hay flats and waterways and where the unlawful fences stood, later by the larger Kinkaid homestead. Each filing required an oath of intended residence, actual establishment of that residence to hold it and make final proof in five years, less the soldier's service period, but everybody had been taken straight back to the Home. Little one-room shacks were built by the ranch carpenter and hauled out to the claims, some on wheels to be moved from one place to another, with witnesses to swear to whatever was needed. Later Ware, like several others, had just used names for the filings, names of live people, dead

* Later, when he was chief justice of the state supreme court, he and Justice Bayard H. Paine transferred some of the records of the cattlemen-settler cases, including those of the Olive hanging and burning of Mitchell and Ketchum, to the Nebraska State Historical Society "to make them more readily available to the serious researcher," Chief Justice Goss told the author.

people, people who had never lived at all.

The government under Four Eyes had, if not all the evidence against Preacher Ware, at least enough. He was found guilty, sentenced to a year in prison and $1,000 fine. Ware appealed all the way to the U.S. Supreme Court and finally, October 1907, lost. He paid the fine and served a short sentence, but not in the cold hard stone of Lancaster prison like any common criminal. He was given quarters in the Grand Island jail and treated like the gentleman he was, with every comfort that the syndicate's money could buy except an open door.

Then in April 1908, Hamilton, the locator, the early witness against Ware and other cattlemen around Mullen, disappeared. Rumors were thick as summer buffalo gnats. One thing was clear: Hamilton was dead and there seemed no doubt in anyone's mind that Ware and the U.B.I. owners had managed the killing. Not the gentlemen themselves, of course, but their hirelings. Apparently it was a well-attended murder, with at least four of the men connected with the ranch one way or another present and perhaps a dozen others aware of the details. All the next year was a farce of charges and countercharges, of threats and blackmail and gun carrying, guns that were drawn at strange moments in a group of men who had left their honor and some of them their names far behind. The settlers learned to stand away from them on the street and to run for their guns when any of them came past the homesteads. More and more of them went to other, farther towns to trade, no matter how poor their wagon ponies were.

By now the broader outlines of the murder were generally known. In a saloon at Mullen, some said in the back room, Hamilton was struck on the temple with a Colt 44. His false teeth flew out and when he was struck twice more he groaned "Oh! Oh!" and sank into unconsciousness. Then he was dragged away by the arms into the cellar, the teeth taken to the outdoor privy and dropped down the hole. Afterward the saloon floor was scrubbed clean by the killer while a couple of the witnesses brought in a lunch and sat around to eat it. Toward morning three of the U.B.I. men got a cart, lifted

Hamilton, already stiffening, into it and started away, one carrying the shovel over his shoulder. Out at the stockyards, where the ground was loose and constantly trampled, they dug a hole. One went through Hamilton's pockets, took his money and watch and then, while the man who had planned this peered from behind a little hill like a buzzard at a dying, they dumped Hamilton into the grave and filled it up. After the bloody sand was scraped away in the cellar, everybody went home.

With all the talk a grand jury finally had to be called. There was a handsome relay of perjurers and tall-tale spinners, but finally one of the eyewitnesses turned state's evidence and told where the body lay. The jury went out to watch the digging and everybody agreed it was Hamilton from the clothing, hair, everything that was left. Someone shook the sand from the decomposed head so it could be brought into court and examined. The skull was crushed at the temple and those teeth were gone.

So there was a trial, in court along in June 1910, as well as around the livery barns and saloons and at settler gatherings. When things seemed to be getting pretty hot for one of the U.B.I. men, a second request for a look at the head of Hamilton was made. Once more it was dug up, from the cemetery this time. But the grave had plainly been disturbed very recently, and when the head was fetched in and examined, the temple was not crushed, the teeth were there, and the man had plainly been a Negro. So the case was dismissed.

It was an old, old dodge, but in the courts controlled by the cattlemen it still worked. Some recalled, openly and in loud voices, that Hamilton had been an unreliable man and had owed money. Probably skipped the country. Out of range of U.B.I. men the talk was different. There was that Negro killed by a train west of town some years ago and buried along the right of way. A couple of the curious, not planning to stay around the region anyway, went out to look. The Negro's grave was empty, the fresh earth barely spattered by rain.

Other locators had trouble too, these years, particularly those who had helped the government cases. Over in Sheridan County, Jules Sandoz was still alive, his 30-30 always on his arm, as it was the day a killer rode into the yard, soon after the locator's brother had been shot down while milking the family cow. The gunman had his hand on his open holster, but no killer worth his hire goes against a Winchester with a pistol, certainly not while in the saddle, and against a known crack shot. When the locator ordered him off the place, the man set his spurs and went, the Winchester unwaveringly upon him.

Richards and Comstock of the Spade were in jail too, at Hastings, where the Olive trial for killing and burning settlers had caused such a stir thirty years before. They were sitting in easy chairs, it was said, with their feet on red carpet and eating their own chef's cooking. But their power was gone and now it was suddenly the settlers who could do no wrong. The thieves among them, and some who had never stolen anything, robbed the ranches of practically everything that could be pried loose, even pulled some of the well piping. At the cookhouses the settlers were welcomed around mealtime, and well treated at the little stores many cattlemen had set up, to get them into debt and collect as soon as their homesteads were patented and could be sold. Sometimes it worked, for a man's children get hungry, and starting in a new country without capital is not for amateurs, but not everybody paid his bills.

Even when well managed few ranches had made money for their investors from free grass and now the range must be paid for. That meant that the cattle must be better—better stock, more pounds for the grass, meat worth more per pound. Most of the cattlemen had been buying blooded sires a long time, Herefords, usually, and some Durhams and later more and more black Angus to build up their grade herds. A few settlers and small ranchers had gone in for purebred stock, but it was difficult to make the arrogant ranchers keep up their bulls. Cutting his fences at night, throwing scrub bulls among his cows, or any sires not of the blood, was one way of getting the purebred stockman out of business.

As the vast Spade Ranch, the U.B.I. and the others disintegrated, new ones grew up like seedlings when the old oak goes down in a windstorm. Most of them were owned by ambitious, hard-working settlers, some located by the dead Hamilton or Sandoz or a dozen others—locators who often had to protect them with guns and other backing against the hired killers. Some of these settlers bought up a neighbor, then another, operating legally, not on grass that belonged to the public, or land that belonged to anyone who came to file on it. Not that the age of the big outfit was entirely over. The Abbott Ranch, with headquarters at Hyannis, spread northwestward, in chunks and joinings, fifty miles and more, including the Buffalo Spring on Deer Creek, to which the Sioux were hurrying their chief, Conquering Bear, after he was shot down, back in 1854.

Many of the new cattlemen got a start in the First World War, but meat prices fell afterward and were just beginning to come back when the depression of 1929 struck, with the great drouth following. Too many ranchers held their cattle for better prices next month, next year, adding this to the regular increase, at the very time when the rains failed and the range should have been relieved, not overstocked. Much of the region was soon in the hands of banks and loan companies who leased to any outfit trying to make ends meet by eating the grass roots out of the ground, until the hills, even the knobs, were bald and cupped into blowouts, the valleys stripped so there was nothing but weeds when the rains returned where the grass had once stood to the saddle skirts. After a little prodding by the federal government, even some of the careless ranchers undertook a pasture rehabilitation program. With intelligent management the sandhill range and hay flats came back, blossomed as none had ever seen them before. Now the hills produced the finest grass-fat beef of the nation, with sound bone and muscle, ready for fattening in the spreading corn regions and the market and processing at Omaha.

Then one day, under the Sower striding the sky on the capitol tower, the senate voted to call Nebraska the Beef State, with the brag plain on every automobile license plate and jeered as far away as *Time*. But the name stuck. Nebraska, the essence of the Plains, had become the Beef State in a protein-hungry, a meat-hungry world.

Abilene and Dodge and Johnson County were tamed, curried, law-abiding. The sandhills of the days when settlers were found face down were gone. Even at its worst the violence had been purposeful. The tradition of the cow country to Canada was largely Texan, which scorned fists as fit only for immigrant greenhorns and Yankees, the razor for Negroes, the knife for Mexicans. The proper Texan had two weapons, pride and his pistol, the latter used very sparingly. Brawling could get the ranch hands fired quicker than stealing calves from the boss.

The cattle country has become the most law-abiding region of the Plains. Spreading ranch houses, more naturally fitted there than in Westchester County, New York, stand in large groves, gay and handsome in fresh paint, cool, air-conditioned, with every electrical device that the dreams of a Senator Norris could run. One can still travel much of the sandhills and find practically every door open to the touch, every alfalfa patch with a wind sock. Sundays, instead of a gathering of wagons, buggies and saddle horses to indicate where the big dinner happened to be, there is a collection of airplanes—red, blue, orange, yellow, and silver—in this or that alfalfa patch.

Cattle, white-faced Herefords and handsome blacks, browse on the slopes with deer in the buckbrush patches and the white flag of antelope flashing in the farther reaches. The great lengths of meadow are dotted with haystacks and cut by an occasional ditch, to drain, to flood as the season and the place demand. Along the foothills are the trees that the white man brought in, some ranchers with half a million planted for beauty, yes, but primarily for profit—windbreaks, snow catchers, protection for cattle, to hold them from the endless drifting into lakes and bottomless snowbanks; for whatever man has learned to control, the blizzards still howl unhobbled out of the north.

Here men who would not have offended another even in word for profit once casually hired professional murderers to kill for the cow, for the deep-lying and ancient mystic symbol that the cow had become 20,000 years ago to the European and Asiatic. Now here in the sandhills man was once more working in his oldest partnership, with no need for bloody sacrifice.

Since the early 1930's the shrinking population of the Plains has been a serious problem, the loss always from among the young, the ambitious, the alert, the progressive and imaginative. It was so with earlier New England, the young heading westward, leaving the cautious, the set, the conservative, the afraid behind. New England's industry brought in the fresh and vigorous from Europe, but where is Nebraska, where are the Plains, to find their like?

And this was happening in less than a hundred years after most of the upper Missouri country was cut into territories, the region that voted for William Jennings Bryan. Not that Bryan was ever much of a liberal except when it was thrust upon him, never really in sympathy with the Populists. But he was a frightening radical to the East, with a fine and powerful voice developed while speaking from the back of a wagon against the northwest wind of fall, and there is radicalism in any voice that carries, no matter what the words. The day Bryan became great was the day he resigned from the cabinet, not because he was right, but because he was true, true as a die is true.

In those days the liberals of the nation were mostly in the Republican party, with Senator George W. Norris a force on the national scene. He had been a leader in the overthrow of Cannonism in the House, and in the Senate he sponsored progressive legislation, particularly the Tennessee Valley Authority that not only brought power and industry to a vast hopeless agricultural region but became the pattern for the whole power system of the West that made the tremendous industry required to win World War II possible and the construction of the atom and hydrogen bombs, not for themselves but for the vast new world they open to all who are courageous enough to enter.

George Norris is another of the many who disprove the notion that children must have secure, stable homes. He lost his father when he was not quite four and soon he was the only son left of a family that had been twelve. He saw his mother work in the fields, learned very early what real need means, and passed through that curiously formative experience of the pioneer teen-ager—he taught country school, at an age when many boys are still "My baby" to an overfond mother. He studied law, came to Nebraska in time to see the bursting crops of the wet years followed by the heartbreaking drouth of the 1890's that Willa Cather saw at Red Cloud, not very far from Norris' town. As district judge, Norris saw the power of the moneylender and the manipulator of farm prices. He acted to hold off foreclosure of settler lands, gave them the opportunity to make a crop or two to pay out—a sort of mortgage moratorium thirty-five years before those forced by the depression and drouth of 1933. But the men who would have become wealthy on the foreclosed lands of the 1890's never forgave George Norris.

From these origins rose the man who was the symbol so long for the progressive. From the middle of the 1920's into the 1940's, to say, "I am from Nebraska," anywhere over the nation and over much of Europe, brought the response: "Oh, yes, Senator Norris . . ."

Out of the drouth and hardship years grew the dream of a Little TVA for Nebraska, embracing the Platte, Loup and Republican River valleys, with great reservoirs, great lakes to water the parched earth, make electricity for every farm home. It was a long and dirty fight in which the senator was even accused of traitorously accepting money from Mexico to destroy the United States. The unlimited funds of the power companies were thrown into the struggle, with the press behind them, practically all but the little Lincoln *Star* and the editor, James Lawrence. Part of the fight was under the actual feet of the Sower on the capitol—a long struggle to break the enabling act that authorized the creation of Nebraska power districts and the sale of their bonds. None who saw this will ever forget the batteries of high-powered eastern attorneys operating around the hotels and the capitol corridors, on the very floor of the state senate, nor the stern fighting Scandinavian face of C. A. Sorensen, former attorney general of Nebraska, working to save public power, to ward off the stultifying hand of eastern control, eastern piracy, once more reaching out. There were stories of millions floating loose for anyone able and willing to deliver the state. Many sought out the faces of the stalwarts every morning, and of Sorensen, to see if the unicameral had broken. But they held, somehow they held. The fields to the horizon were dead in drouth, corn, if it grew, was not worth the burning, and dollars were like those of 1890, big as cartwheels, and still the men held.

Senator Norris didn't live to see the man-made lakes of his own Republican valley, but he saw some of his dream in actuality elsewhere and more in his remarkable mind's eye: the new Chain o'Lakes stretching from the North Platte down past Lexington, old Plum Creek, all watered from the reservoir called Lake McConaughy at the top, already seeming old as geologic time, huge. Here are stored the snow waters that once rolled down the valley with the bounding fur-loaded bull boats, and that helped spread the Missouri and the Mississippi over the lowlands all the way to the Gulf. Now McConaughy welcomes the cloudy flocks of the great flyway, and carries the white-sailed regattas racing before the wind. And in season its waters are nursed downward, mostly through canals along the bluffs, to soak the crops of the Platte valley where so many thousands walked westward to far bonanza lands, passing what has since been called the handsomest, most beautifully fruitful valley of the country, the valley of the North Platte and below.

Irrigation was not new to the region. Even before the Reclamation Act of 1902, pushed by that enthusiastic one-time emigrant to the Plains, Theodore Roosevelt, there had been small state and private projects. The real forerunner, however, seems to have been the fairly extensive prehistoric Stump Ditch, as it was called by the early settlers, near Cozad. This could be traced from the creek waters of the Loup region southward, with studied gradual fall to carry it far into the fertile Platte valley. But there are vast regions that can never be reached by canals and ditches, and in most of these Nebraskans have tapped the water tables with around 24,000 registered irrigation wells to 1961, and no telling how many unregistered. They stretch from the Wyoming regions across Nebraska to Richardson County, most concentrated in the region of the center downbend of the Platte valley and southward in a sort of sag. But they are scattered over large areas of the Plains. No wonder the water dowser, the water witcher, made such a fine reputation in the early days there. While the pessimists predicted that the extensive pump irrigation would lower the water tables, dry up springs and yard wells, run itself out, by the fall of 1960 the average of Nebraska's ground-water level was found up, not down. Still no one expects this to last forever, not on the Plains any more than elsewhere. Some day sweet water will have to be converted, made, the first great need in the Texas Panhandle, but northward too.

Through all of the story of water runs the story of George Norris, and like any good Plains tale it too has a wry, a rueful ending. By 1930 it was plain that the senator could not be defeated by ordinary means, and yet the Republican party was determined to get rid of him. The primaries seemed the place, and so they hired a poor grocer of the same name to run against him, cut the Norris vote in half and give the lead to some other Republican candidate. There was a sensational investigation, with a stink and humiliation that made it a little difficult to get first-class men into Nebraska political life. Reelected in 1930, Norris ran as an independent in 1936, but in 1942 his enemies managed a split in the liberal vote and the senator was defeated. He had been held in Washington by the poll-tax fight in Congress until the Friday before election. Perhaps the time was too short; anyway he was defeated. Like Jim Bridger, he had been run up a box canyon and "didn't get out." But who remembers the Nebraska senators since Norris?

One of the recurring sorrows and complaints of the early settlers was the lack of trees, of shade anywhere on the Plains except right at the waterways, which offered some protection against fires. A few territorial citizens fostered tree plantings. The first and perhaps the most effective was Robert W. Furnas. Orphaned at eight, he was soon shifting for himself. He tried one occupation after another and slipped into printing. In 1856 he came to Brownville on the Missouri and established the *Nebraska Advertiser*, with great influence south of the Platte in those harsh days. He was in the brawling legislature awhile and accused of accepting a bribe to keep the capital at Omaha. In the Civil War he became one of the Short Beards, the energetics. He organized three regiments of Indians from Indian Territory against the South and later the Second Nebraska Cavalry against the Sioux and Cheyennes. He was Indian agent for several years and governor for a term, but all this time his interest, his dedication, was what Nebraska had to have—improved agriculture. He pushed the board of agriculture and made the state fair a hobby and pride. He operated a large nursery awhile and was apparently the originator of the Arbor Day idea, but graciously let his promoting friend, J. Sterling Morton, crystalize it into a state day and get the credit for its international adoption, aided by Morton's fine plantings around Arbor Lodge, his home in Nebraska City.

Trees were planted to mark the early homestead lines, often as part of the live fencing. Mile after mile of eastern Nebraska was cross-barred by these rows of fine trees, but because they shaded the snowbanks and the ground, kept the section-line roads in the mud, they were cut down. Thousands of fine sound elm and oak and maple perhaps forty, fifty years old fell to the steam-saw man, the stumps often still there when the lines were replanted, whip-sized, after pavements came.

"Got to keep making improvements," an old settler said over his pipe to a newcomer. But he looked a little embarrassed by the old stumps of the trees of his youth.

In 1860 Stolley of Grand Island started one of the first tree cultures in the territory by planting 6,000 on his claim. Nine years later the U.S. Surveyor General had a typical Plains idea. He advocated dropping seeds of the honey locust in each stake hole made by the surveyors running the original lines—four trees to each mile corner, two on every half-mile all up and down the Plains. A real attempt to get some plantings was through the Timber Culture Act, in force from 1873 to 1891, giving the entryman 160 acres for setting out ten acres to trees and caring for them for five years. This was vastly abused. Sometimes only sticks were stuck into the breaking, or sunflowers were allowed to grow five feet over the seedlings, but on hundreds of miles of prairie the widely scattered loaf-shaped groves marked the spread of settlement during those times, groves standing a dark blue-green from far off, and unbelievable. They sheltered game, saved cattle and even men in blizzards, were picnic grounds for Fourth of July celebrations with the platform dances, the races and speechmaking, and for old soldier and old settler reunions, the occasional rendezvous of lovers or cover for fleeing bank robbers. Fifty, sixty years later the groves stood as evidence against those who scoffed at Franklin Roosevelt's whole shelter-belt idea.

The late 1880's had brought Dr. Charles Bessey of that fabulous group around the little university sprouting at the edge of a cornfield in Lincoln. Goateed like the physicians of his time, or gamblers like John Cozad, and heavy-browed in concentration, Dr. Bessey had walked through the great pine forests of Michigan and noticed that they grew on sand. When he came to Nebraska he covered the farthest reaches of the state in his little grasshopper buggy accumulating bundles of specimens to stick out the back—grasses, shrubs, trees. The sandhills interested him the most, particularly the ridges, where he found moisture close under the surface, even at the very crest. He ran down a few scattered native ponderosa pines and red cedar; he began to talk and write and hope for some experimental plantings in the hills. Washington was not interested, not with the powerful cattlemen lobbies working there and in the state legislature as well. Trees growing in the sandhills would draw settlers like flies to a sorghum boiling for sure, to the last free grass range, the last of the cattle country.

Even the scientists were against Bessey in the 1890's, on scientific grounds. Plainly trees would not grow in the region or there would be some. The good doctor knew the value of irritation and got attention if only to shut him up. In the meantime he had been offered a planting of pine seedlings—and had no ground. Professor Lawrence Bruner, called the region's bird man, and his brother in southwest Holt County, had ground—sandy ground. It was offered to Bessey. The plantings on plowed ground failed, died, blown out, but those set in grass grew and ten years later were eighteen to twenty feet tall, in a dense thicket of forest conditions, doing much better than similar trees on heavy soil.

This success in Holt County, as good for pines as for Irishmen, encouraged a thorough survey of all the light-soil regions, particularly the sandhills. Then came the luck of a Theodore Roosevelt in the Presidency and a Gifford Pinchot as chief of the Bureau of Forestry. Forest reserves were established, two in Nebraska, in the sandhills, one south of the Niobrara and the other between the Middle Loup and the Dismal, called the Bessey Division, or Halsey Forest. Here plantings were started, experimentation carried out, and although many trees died in the drouth of the 1930's, which killed so much native growth right at the creek banks, by 1960 there were 206,028 acres in trees at Halsey, the world's largest man-made forest, not in the deep fertile black dirt of the sandhill valleys but in the loose chophills, in the light sandy soil Dr. Bessey had seen under Michigan pines. At the end of the first half-century, twenty million trees were growing at Halsey and three million had been distributed elsewhere, some to shelter orchards slowly moving out from the tight little commercial fruit area of southeast Nebraska. There were a few out farther, like the Sandoz Fruit Farm, established by the early settler and locator. These orchards in drier regions grow fruit of heightened flavor, as desert flowers bloom sweeter, but they are few.

From scattered plantings to timber claims to Halsey and the miles and miles of shelter belts along the fields and roads is a tall tale of the Plains too. Through the work of two Roosevelts the idea of tree planting lived, grew, spread until the belts have changed the appearance, the look, of vast stretches of open country, changed O'Neill's home region so he would scarcely know it. They shelter homes and stock and fields from wind and storm, hold earth and snow, bring wild life and bird song, rest the eye.

But there is another tall tale growing, of a man who lived so long on the Plains he never died. Statistics do seem to indicate that a man who wishes to live as long as possible should manage to be born in a mid-Nebraska small town or plan to move there very early. The problem has been how to make a living during that long and healthy life. Not everyone could farm and, besides, living solely from a small farm has become practically impossible.

Land has been comparatively cheap in the Plains country and water usually plentiful, either on the surface or in the ground, sweet and plentiful. What many sections, particularly Nebraska, lacked was coal for industry. Now there is oil, great fields of it, first in Wyoming and Oklahoma, then Kansas and now Nebraska and the rest. Oil has brought in money, but there is no avoiding the realization that oil is a temporary asset, as everything that does not renew itself must be. Besides, fortunately or unfortunately, oil will be outmoded before it is used up, with electric power preferable and the possibilities for its production by no means exhausted. In Nebraska the Niobrara, with its three hundred miles of deep, narrow canyon and an average drop of ten feet per mile all that distance, could be harnessed for a great deal of power. Senator Norris once outlined a project for the river on his wife's dinner tablecloth—a dam thrown across the river every twenty miles or so, using that deep narrow canyon for the reservoirs.

"Water does not wear out just letting it fall," he said, "if electricity is what we want."

But now there is the great promise of nuclear power, starting at various plants, one at Hallam in Nebraska, with talk of perhaps a score of others over the Plains before very long. Oil and electric power have already freed much industry from the river and its old-time cheap coal barging. To be sure the Missouri has been put back to work, so harnessed that the barge terminals handle vast freight. Omaha disposes of 18,000 bushels of grain per hour for 250 member elevators in the surrounding seven states, with ten million bushels sent out from her terminal the first season.

The Plains were settled largely by people from Europe and America hoping to escape the unhealthful factory and mine of the nineteenth century—the Irish coal miners of Pennsylvania coming to O'Neill, the stomach cases to such places as Gordon, the lungers to every community. There should be no reason why their descendants must leave the region, not economic or cultural reasons. Culture, in the larger sense, has followed the routes of commerce, to Athens, Rome, Paris, London, New York. But that was in a time of long distances, impenetrable space. Now a farm-factory unit, adjusted so the seasonal work of the factory comes at the slack time of farm or ranch, can give the agricultural worker the additional economic insurance he needs against crop failures and disastrous farm prices, the factory worker the health of clean air, outdoor work, a pleasant prospect for the eye as well as some economic shoring against the tragedy of the layoff. With easy power available anywhere, now any level spot near the fields and grasslands can become the location of a small and pleasant farm-factory or ranch-factory community. There are some with considerable such work now, Scottsbluff, for instance, and others.

Such combination communities can have good schools, and avoid the appalling implications in the fact that in 1960 Nebraska was apparently thirty-eighth in the money spent per pupil in school—twelfth from the bottom. Many can recall when Nebraska was eighth from the top and thought it should be higher. The combination communities could also have good libraries and attractive parks in addition to the private gardens, orchards and fields, with blooded stock, fine dogs, good fishing and hunting, even deer and antelope—all within reach of the factory worker, the lens maker, the printer and the artist. There would be music as in the old days of the E-flat cornet man and his band, but with a new dimension from such organizations as the Sandhills Symphony Orchestra of North Platte, the fifty musicians living within fifty miles or so.

Any consideration of the future compels a little thought to the sky, a sky that must not be hidden by flying mechanical monsters outdoing anything imagined in the nineties in ferocity and in number, and thick as the old flights of buffalo gnats, but roaring giants, flying at almost invisible speed, colliding, crashing down on house and tree. They must not destroy the Plains dweller's most pleasant prospect —the sky of depthless blue, of blazing gold and red at sunset, or the velvet of night, the stars standing scarcely beyond the arm's reach.

With unlimited nuclear power there will surely be transcontinental travel tubes to carry all these wanderers in endless catapulting cars, the thrust and the automatic stand-off brakes compressed air, the passengers perhaps taking a pleasant nap from New York to Omaha, to South Pass and the coast.

The first of these tubes will probably follow the old, old transcontinental trail across Nebraska along the south bluffs of the Platte. One can imagine the artificial little sausage ridge landscaped with trees and fine natural growth to deaden the sound as millions are shot past underneath, the oriole's nest above scarcely swinging, the pheasant and quail and wild turkey feeding unconcerned.

Even then the Plains will lie like a golden hackberry leaf in the October sun, a giant, curling, tilted leaf, the veins the long streams rising out near the Rockies and flowing eastward to the Missouri.

BIBLIOGRAPHY—for the General Reader

(A comprehensive bibliography of the published material pertaining to the Great Plains would fill at least a volume; with the briefest word or phrase to distinguish the sources of value from the blatantly worthless and misleading, the list would run into thousands of pages. In addition there are the vast accumulations of unpublished documentary and other material in the National Archives and in related federal and local repositories. In no other region is the record, the story from stone age society to space man, as complete as on the Plains. Here one can see, can study, what modern man has done to a piece of his earth and what it has done to him.)

On the Region

DODGE, R. I. *The Plains of the Great West* (New York, 1877).

HIBBARD, B. H. *A History of the Public Land Policies* (New York, 1924).

KAPPLER, CHARLES J. *Indian Affairs, Laws and Treaties*, 4 vols., (Washington, 1903).

MALIN, JAMES C. *Grasslands of North America* (Lawrence, Kans., 1947).

POWELL, JOHN WESLEY. *Report on the Lands of the Arid Regions of the United States* (Washington, 1879).

ROBBINS, ROY M. *Our Landed Heritage: The Public Domain, 1776-1936* (Princeton, 1942).

SCHMIDT, L. B. "The Westward Movement of the Corn-growing Industry . . ." *Iowa Journal of History and Politics*, XXI, No. 1.

THWAITES, REUBEN GOLD (ed.). *Early Western Travels 1748-1846*, 32 vols. (Cleveland, 1904-1907).

CHAPTER 1 *Pathway to the Southern Sea*

ABEL, A. H. (ed.). *Tabeau's Narrative of Loisel's Expedition to the Upper Missouri* (Norman, 1939).

BARKER, B. B. *The McLoughlin Empire and Its Rulers* (Glendale, 1959).

BELL, C. N. *The Journal of Henry Kelsey, 1691-1692* (Winnipeg, 1928).

BOLTON, H. E. *Spanish Explorations in the Southwest 1542-1706* (New York, 1916).

BURPEE, L. J. (ed.). *Journals and Letters of . . . La Verendrye and His Sons* (Toronto, 1927).

——. *The Search for the Western Sea* (New York, 1908).

COUES, E. (ed.). *New Light on . . . the Greater Northwest: the Henry-Thompson Journals, 1799-1814*, 3 vols. (New York, 1897).

CROGHAN, GEORGE. *Journals, 1750-1765*, Thwaites (*q.v.*) Vol. I.

HANKE, L. *The Spanish Struggle for Justice in the Conquest of America* (Philadelphia, 1949).

HANSON, CHARLES E., JR. *The Northwest Gun* (Lincoln, 1955).

HENRY, ALEXANDER. *Travels and Adventures in Canada and the Indian Territories between . . . 1760 and 1776* (New York, 1809).

LONG, JOHN. *Voyages and Travels 1768-1782*, Thwaites (*q.v.*) Vol. II.

MACKENZIE, ALEXANDER. *Voyages from Montreal . . . to the Pacific . . . 1789 and 1793*, including *The General History of the Fur Trade* (Philadelphia, 1802).

MICHAUX, ANDRE. *Travels into Kentucky . . . 1796*, Thwaites (*q.v.*) Vol. III.

MORTON, J. STERLING, and WATKINS, ALBERT. *Illustrated History of Nebraska*, Vols. I and II (Lincoln 1905-7).

NASATIR, A. P. *Before Lewis and Clark, Documents . . . of the Missouri 1785-1804*, 2 vols. (St. Louis, 1952).

THOMPSON, D. . . . *Explorations in Western America 1784-1812* (Toronto, 1916).

CHAPTER 2   *A New Flag*

BRACKENRIDGE, H. M. *Journal of a Voyage up the Missouri . . . 1811*, Thwaites (*q.v.*) Vol. VI.

BRADBURY, JOHN. *Travels in the Interior of North America . . .*, Thwaites (*q.v.*) Vol. V.

BUTTRICK, TILLY, JR. *Voyages, Travels and Discoveries . . . 1812-1819*, Thwaites (*q.v.*) Vol. VIII.

CHITTENDEN, H. M. *The American Fur Trade . . .*, 2 vols. (Stanford, 1954).

COUES, E. (ed.). *The Expeditions of Zebulon Montgomery Pike 1805-6-7*, 3 vols. (New York, 1895).

CUMING, F. . . . *Tour of the Western Country . . .*, 1807-1809, Thwaites (*q.v.*) Vol. IV.

DAVIDSON, G. C. *The North West Company* (Berkeley, 1918).

EVANS, ESTWICK. *A Pedestrious Tour . . . through the Western States and Territories*, 1818, Thwaites (*q.v.*) Vol. VIII.

FAUX, W. *Memorable Days in America,* 1818-1820, Thwaites (*q.v.*) Vol. XII.

FLETCHER, ALICE C., and LA FLESCHE, FRANCIS. *The Omaha Tribe,* Bu. of Am. Ethnology, *27th Annual Report,* 1911.

FLINT, JAMES. *Letters from America* . . . 1818-1820, Thwaites (*q.v.*) Vol. IX.

FRANCHERE, G. . . . *A Voyage to the Northwest Coast of America* . . . 1811-1814, Thwaites (*q.v.*) Vol. VI.

GOETZMANN, W. H. *Army Explorations in the American West, 1803-1863* (New Haven, 1959).

JAMES, THOMAS. *Three Years Among the Indians and Mexicans* (Chicago, 1953).

LEWIS, MERIWETHER, and CLARK, WILLIAM. . . . *Journals of the Lewis and Clark Expedition, 1804-1806,* Reuben Gold Thwaites (ed.), 8 vols. (New York, 1904-5).

NUTTALL, T. *A Journal of Travels into Arkansas Territory* . . . 1818-1820, Thwaites (*q.v.*) Vol. XIII.

ROSS, ALEXANDER. . . . *First Settlers on the Oregon or Columbia River,* 1810-1814, Thwaites (*q.v.*) Vol. VII.

SCHNEIDER, N. F. *Blennerhassett Island and the Burr Conspiracy* (Columbus, 1945).

STUART, R. *The Discovery of the Oregon Trail, Robert Stuart's Narratives* 1812-1813, P. A. Rollins, ed. (New York, 1935).

WATKINS, ALBERT. *Notes of the Early History of the Nebraska Country,* 1808-1861, *Publications,* Nebraska State Historical Society, Vol. XX.

WERKMEISTER, W. H. *A History of Philosophical Ideas in America* (New York, 1949).

WILKINSON, ANN BIDDLE. "Letters of Mrs. Ann Biddle Wilkinson from Kentucky, 1788-1789," *The Pennsylvania Magazine,* LVI, No. 1.

CHAPTER 3   *Elysian Fields*

BULLOCK, WILLIAM. *Sketch of a Journey through the Western States* . . . 1827, Thwaites (*q.v.*) Vol. XIX.

CAMP, C. L. (ed.). *James Clyman, Frontiersman* . . . *His Own Reminiscences and Diaries* (Portland, Ore., 1960).

CHITTENDEN, H. M. *History of Early Steamboat Navigation on the Missouri River* (New York, 1903).

DALE, H. C. *The Ashley-Smith Explorations and Discovery of a Central Route to the Pacific* (Glendale, 1941).

DENIG, E. T. *Indian Tribes of the Upper Missouri,* Bu. of Am. Ethnology, *46th Annal Report,* 1930.

Fort Atkinson, Records, 1819-1827, A. E. Sheldon, ed., typescript in Nebraska State Historical Society Library.

JAMES, EDWIN. *An Account of an Expedition from Pittsburgh to the Rocky Mountains . . . under Major Stephen Long,* Thwaites (*q.v.*) Vols. XIV-XVII.

JOHNSON, SALLY A. "Cantonment Missouri, 1819-1820," *Nebraska History,* XXXVII, No. 2.

———. "The Sixth's Elysian Fields," *Nebraska History,* XL, No. 1.

KENNERLY, W. C. *Persimmon Hill . . . Old St. Louis and the Far West* (Norman, 1949).

KIVETT, M. F. "Excavations at Fort Atkinson . . ." *Nebraska History,* XL, No. 1.

LIBBY, O. G. ". . . Villages of the Mandans, Arikara and Hidatsa in the Missouri Valley, North Dakota," *Collections,* State Historical Society of North Dakota, Vol. II, 1908.

PATTIE, J. O. *Personal Narrative . . .* 1824-1930, Thwaites (*q.v.*) Vol. XVIII.

PAUL WILHELM, DUKE OF WURTTEMBERG. First Journey to North America . . . 1822 to 1824, South Dakota Historical *Collections,* Vol. XIX.

PORTER, K. W. *John Jacob Astor,* 2 vols. (Cambridge, 1931).

SIMPSON, GEORGE. *Fur-Trade and Empire,* F. Merk, ed. (Cambridge, 1931).

WESLEY, E. B. "Life at Fort Atkinson," *Nebraska History,* XXX, No. 4. (See also Chittenden's *Fur Trade*; Morton and Watkins, and *Publications* Nebraska State Historical Society, Vol. XX.)

CHAPTER 4   *The Golden Floods*

ABEL, A. H. (ed.). *Chardon's Journal at Fort Clark, 1834-1839* (Pierre, 1932).

CATLIN, GEORGE. *Letters and Notes on . . . the North American Indians* (New York, 1842).

COUES, E. (ed.). *Audubon and His Journals,* by Maria R. Audubon (New York, 1897).

DE SMET, PIERRE JEAN. *Letters and Sketches . . . among the Indian Tribes of the Rocky Mountains,* Thwaites (*q.v.*) Vol. XXVII.

FARNHAM, T. J. *Travels in the Great Western Prairie . . .* 1839, Thwaites (*q.v.*) Vols. XXVIII-XXIX.

FLAGG, E. *The Far West . . . 1836*, Thwaites (*q.v.*) Vols. XXVI-XXVII.

FREMONT, JOHN C. "A Report on an Exploration to . . . Missouri River and the Rocky Mountains . . ." *Sen. Doc. No. 243*, 27th Cong., 3rd Sess. 1843.

GREGG, JOSIAH. *Commerce of the Prairies* (New York, 1844).

McDONNELL, ANNE (ed.). "The Fort Benton Journal, 1854-1856, and the Fort Sarpy Journal, 1855-1856," Montana Historical Society *Contributions*, Vol. X, 1940.

MAXIMILIAN, PRINCE OF WIED. *Travels in the Interior of North America, 1833-1834*, Thwaites (*q.v.*) Vols. XXII-XXIV.

MERRILL, MOSES. ". . . Diary of Rev. Moses Merrill, a Missionary to the Otoe . . . 1832 to 1840," *Trans. and Reports*, Nebraska State Historical Society, Vol. IV, 1892.

SHELDON, A. E. *Land Systems and Land Policies in Nebraska* (including federal), Nebraska State Historical Society *Publications*, Vol. XXII.

TOWNSEND, J. K. . . . *Journey across the Rocky Mountains . . . 1836*, Thwaites (*q.v.*) Vol. XXI.

WARREN, LIEUT. G. K. . . . *Exploration in Nebraska and Dakota in the Years 1855-56-57* (Washington, 1875).

WYETH, J. B. *Oregon . . . 1832-1833*, Thwaites (*q.v.*) Vol. XXI.
(See also Chittenden, etc.)

CHAPTER 5   *Tall-Tale Country*

ABERT, J. W. "Journal of Lieutenant James W. Abert, From Bent's Fort to St. Louis in 1845," *Sen. Exec. Doc. 438*, 29th Cong., 1st Sess., 1846.

ALLIS, SAMUEL. "Forty Years among the Indians . . ." *Trans. and Reports*, Nebraska State Historical Society, Vol. II, 1887.

BEATH, PAUL R. *Feobold Feoboldson* (Lincoln, 1948).

BIDWELL, JOHN. *Echoes of the Past in California* (Chicago, 1928).

CLAYTON, WILLIAM. *Journal* (Salt Lake City, 1921).

COUTANT, C. G. *The History of Wyoming . . .* (Laramie, 1899).

DODGE, HENRY. . . . *Dragoons under Colonel Henry Dodge, to the Rocky Mountains in 1835, American State Papers*, Military Affairs, Vol. VI, 1835.

DORSEY, GEORGE A. *Traditions of the Skidi* Pawnee (Boston, 1904).

DUNBAR, JOHN B. "The Pawnee Indians . . . Their Habits and Customs," *Magazine of American History*, Vol. V, 1880.

HAFEN, LEROY R., and YOUNG, F. M. *Fort Laramie . . . , 1834-1890* (Glendale, 1938).

HASTINGS, L. W. *The Emigrants' Guide to Oregon and California* (Cincinnati, 1845).

IRVING, JOHN TREAT, JR. *Indian Sketches taken during an Expedition to the Pawnee Tribes*, J. F. McDermott, ed. (Norman, 1955).

MILLER, A. J. *The West of Alfred Jacob Miller*, M. C. Ross, ed. (Norman, 1951).

MURRAY, C. A. *Travels in North America . . .*, 2 vols. (London, 1839).

PALMER, JOEL. *Journal of Travels over the Rocky Mountains . . . 1845-1846*, Thwaites (*q.v.*) Vol. XXX.

PARKMAN, FRANCIS. *The Oregon Trail* (Boston, 1892).

POUND, LOUISE. *Nebraska Folklore* (Lincoln, 1959).

ROOT, F. A., and CONNELLEY, W. E. *The Overland Stage . . .* (Topeka, 1901).

WEDEL, W. R. *An Introduction to Pawnee Archeology*, Bu. of Am. Ethnology, *Bulletin 112*, 1936.

WILLMAN, LILLIAN M. *The History of Fort Kearny*, Nebraska State Historical Society *Publications*, Vol. XXI.

WINTER COUNTS, SIOUX. *4th Annual Report*, Bu. of Am. Ethnology, 1882-3.

(See also Nasatir, Morton and Watkins, Nebraska State Historical Society *Publications* II and XX, and Sorenson, Chapter VII.)

CHAPTER 6   *Friendly Earth for Hoof and Plow*

ANDREAS, A. T. *Andreas' Historical Atlas of Dakota* (Chicago, 1884).

——. *History of the State of Kansas* (Chicago, 1883).

——. *A History of the State of Nebraska* (Chicago, 1882).

BAUR, J. E. "The Health Seeker in the Westward Movement, 1830-1900," Mississippi Valley Historical *Review*, XLVI, No. 1.

BUTCHER, S. D. *Pioneer History of Custer County* (Broken Bow, Nebr., 1901).

CATHER, WILLA. *My Antonia* (Boston, 1918).

COWDREY, M. B. (ed.). *The Checkered Years*, by Mary Dodge Woodward (Caldwell, 1937).

GARLAND, HAMLIN. *A Son of the Middle Border* (New York, 1928).

GREEN, JAMES. "Incidents of the Indian Outbreak of 1864," Nebraska State Historical Society *Publications*, Vol. XIX.

HERTZLER, A. E. *The Horse and Buggy Doctor* (New York, 1938).

ISE, JOHN. *Sod and Stubble* (New York, 1936).

LARIMER, SARAH L. *The Capture and Escape and Life among the Sioux*, 1870.

O'GARA, W. H. *In all Its Fury, History of the Blizzard of January 12, 1888* (Lincoln, 1947).
ROENIGK, ADOLPH (ed.). *Pioneer History of Kansas* (Lincoln, Kans., 1933).
ROLVAAG, O. E. *Giants in the Earth* (New York, 1927).
SANDOZ, MARI. *The Buffalo Hunters* (New York, 1954).
——. *Old Jules* (Boston, 1935).
STEWART, ELINOR P. *Letters of a Woman Homesteader* (Boston, 1914).
WIK, R. M. *Steam Power on the American Farm*, American Historical Association (Philadelphia, 1953).
WILLARD, J. F., and GOODYKOONTZ, C. B. "Experiments in Colorado Colonization," University of Colorado Historical *Collections*, Vol. III.

CHAPTER 7   *Speculators—*

ABBOTT, N. C. "Lincoln: Name and Place," Nebraska State Historical Society *Publications*, Vol. XXI.
CAREY, FRED. *Mayor Jim* (Jim Dahlman) (Omaha, 1930).
DANKER, DONALD. "The Nebraska Winter Quarters Company and Florence," *Nebraska History*, XXXVII, No. 1.
HODDER, F. H. "Genesis of the Kansas-Nebraska Act," *Proceedings*, State Historical Society of Wisconsin, 1912.
OLSON, JAMES O. *J. Sterling Morton* (Lincoln, 1942).
New York Times. "Omaha Riots," Sept. 29-30, Oct. 1-15, 1919.
RIEGEL, R. E. *The Story of the Western Railroads* (New York, 1926).
SORENSON, ALFRED. *The Story of Omaha* (Omaha, 1923).
SYLVESTER, B. F. "Omaha's Floods, 1952," *Nebraska History*, XXXV, No. 1.

CHAPTER 8   *Moccasin Tracks on the Buffalo Grass*

ALLEN, C. W. "Red Cloud, Chief of the Sioux," an autobiography, *The Hesperian* (Hot Springs, S. Dak.), Vol. I, No. 5.
ARMES, GEORGE A. *Ups and Downs of an Army Officer* (Washington, 1900).
BOURKE, JOHN G. *On the Border with Crook* (New York, 1891).
BRONSON, EDGAR BEECHER. *Reminiscences of a Ranchman* (New York, 1908).
BYRNE, P. E. *The Red Man's Last Stand* (London, 1927).
CLARK, W. P. *The Indian Sign Language* (Philadelphia, 1885).
CRAWFORD, LEWIS F. *Rekindling Camp Fires* (Bismarck, 1926).

CUSTER, GEORGE A. *My Life on the Plains* (New York, 1874).

DELAND, C. E. *The Aborigines of South Dakota,* South Dakota Historical *Collections,* Vols. III-IV.

EVANS, JOHN. *Reply of Governor Evans* . . . Territory of Colorado. To . . . "The Committee on the Conduct of the War," headed "Massacre of Cheyenne Indians" (Denver, 1865).

GRAHAM, W. A. *The Story of the Little Big Horn* (New York, 1926).

GRINNELL, GEORGE BIRD. *The Cheyenne Indians,* 2 vols. (New Haven, 1924).

——. *The Fighting Cheyennes* (New York, 1915).

——. *Two Great Scouts and Their Pawnee Battalion* (Cleveland, 1928).

HEBARD, GRACE R., and BRININSTOOL, E. A. *The Bozeman Trail,* 2 vols. (Cleveland, 1922).

HODGE, F. W. *Handbook of American Indians,* Bu. of Am. Ethnology *Bulletin 30,* 1907.

HOLMAN, A. M., and MARKS, C. R. *Pioneering in the Northwest* (Sioux City, 1924).

HURST, JOHN. "The Beecher Island Fight," Kansas Historical Society *Collections,* Vol. XV.

HYDE, GEORGE E. *Red Cloud's Folk* (Norman, 1937).

MARQUIS, T. B. *A Warrior Who Fought Custer* (Minneapolis, 1931).

MILES, N. A. *Personal Recollections* . . . *of General Nelson A. Miles* (Chicago, 1896).

MOONEY, JAMES. "The Ghost Dance Religion and the Sioux Outbreak of 1890," *14th Annual Report,* Bu. of Am. Ethnology, Part 2, 1896.

Nebraska History Magazine, Crazy Horse Number, XII, No. 1.

——. Massacre Canyon Number, XVI, No. 3.

NEIHARDT, JOHN G. *Black Elk Speaks* (New York, 1932).

PAINE, BAYARD H. *Pioneers, Indians and Buffaloes* (Curtis, Nebr., 1935).

ROBINSON, DOANE. *A Comprehensive History of the Dakota or Sioux Indians,* South Dakota Historical *Collections,* Vol. II, 1904.

SANDOZ, MARI. *Cheyenne Autumn* (New York, 1953).

——. *Crazy Horse* (New York, 1942).

SCHMITT, M. F. *General Crook, His Autobiography* (Norman, 1946).

Sioux Indian Painting, Editions d'Art (Nice, France, 1938).

SPRING, AGNES WRIGHT. *Caspar Collins* (New York, 1927).

U.S. Army. *The Official Record of the Reno Court of Inquiry,* W. A. Graham, ed., 1951.

——. Congress, Serial 2165 ". . . Leases of Indian Lands . . . for Cattle Grazing and Other Purposes," 1884, *Sen. Exec. Doc. No. 54,* 48th Cong., 1st Sess., 1883-1884.

VESTAL, STANLEY. *Sitting Bull* (Boston, 1932).

WARE, E. F. *The Indian War of 1864* (Topeka, 1911).

WISSLER, CLARK. "Societies and Ceremonial Associations in the Oglala Division of the Teton-Dakota," *Anthrop. Papers*, American Museum of Natural History, Vol. XI, Part 1, 1912.

WRIGHT, J. W. *Chivington's Massacre of the Cheyenne Indians* (Washington, 1865).

(See also Coutant and *Publications*, Nebraska State Historical Society, Vols. II, XVI, XVIII, XIX, XX.)

CHAPTER 9   *A Few Bad Men and Good—*

Biographical and Historical Memoir of Adams, Clay, Webster and Nuckolls Counties (Nebr.) (Chicago, 1890).

BENNETT, MILDRED R. *The World of Willa Cather* (Lincoln, 1961).

BROWN, JESSE, and WILLARD, A. M. *The Black Hills Trails* (Rapid City, 1924).

COZAD, ROBERT HENRY (ROBERT HENRI). "Personal Diary of Robert Cozad," early section, *The Cozad* (Nebr.) *Local*, Nov. 27, 1950.

(HICKOK, JAMES BUTLER). "Wild Bill-McCanles Tragedy," *Nebraska History Magazine*, X, No. 2.

HICKS, JOHN D. *The Populist Revolt* (Minneapolis, 1931).

JOHNSON, ALVIN. *Pioneer's Progress,* an Autobiography (New York, 1952).

LANGAN, SISTER MARY MARTIN. *General John O'Neill,* Master's thesis, University of Notre Dame, 1937.

LEACH, A. J. *History of Antelope County* (Nebr.), 1909.

MENNINGER, KARL. *The Human Mind* (New York, 1930).

O'NEILL, JOHN. *Northern Nebraska as a Home for Immigrants* (Sioux City, 1875).

PALMER, FREDERICK. *John J. Pershing, General of the Armies* (Harrisburg, 1948).

SANDOZ, MARI. *Son of the Gamblin' Man* (New York, 1960).

WALSH, RICHARD, and SALSBURY, M. S. *The Making of Buffalo Bill* (Indianapolis, 1928).

WILSTACH, FRANK J. *Wild Bill Hickok, Prince of Pistoleers* (Garden City, 1928).

YARROW, WM., and BOUCHE, L. *Robert Henri, His Life and Work* (New York, 1921).

YOST, GENEVIEVE. "Historical Lynchings in Kansas," *Kansas Historical Quarterly*, II, No. 2.

CHAPTER 10   *The Water, the Grass and the Tree*

ABBOTT, E. C. (TEDDY BLUE), and SMITH, HELENA HUNTINGTON. *We Pointed Them North* (New York, 1939).

BABER, D. F. *The Longest Rope*, as told by Bill Walker (Caldwell, 1940).

BENSCHOTER, GEORGE E. *Book of Facts*, concerning . . . Sherman County (Loup City, Nebr., 1897).

BRATT, JOHN. *Trails of Yesterday* (Lincoln, 1921).

BYE, JOHN O. *Back Trailing in . . . the Short Grass Country* (Everett, Wash., 1956).

CLARK, J. S. *The Oil Century*, Drake Well to the Conservation Era (Norman, 1958).

CLAY, JOHN. *My Life on the Range* (Chicago, 1924).

COLLIS, JOHN S. *The Triumph of the Tree* (New York, 1954).

COOK, ROBERT C. *Human Fertility: The Modern Dilemma* (New York, 1951).

DOBIE, J. FRANK. *The Longhorns* (Boston, 1941).

GORDON, SAM. *Recollections of Old Milestown* (Miles City, 1918).

HALL, BERT L. (ed.). *Roundup Years, Old Muddy to the Black Hills* (Pierre, 1954).

HOFSTADTER, RICHARD. *The Age of Reform: From Bryan to F.D.R.* (New York, 1955).

HYAMS, EDWARD C. *Soil and Civilization* (London, 1952), Jacquetta Hawkes, gen. ed., *The Past in the Present*.

JENKINS, A. O. *Olive's Last Roundup* (Loup City, Nebr., 1930).

MERCER, A. S. *The Banditti of the Plains* (Cheyenne, 1894).

MILLIGAN, E. W. "John Wesley Iliff," Denver *Westerners Brand Book*, 1950.

The Mullen Roundup, The Local History of Mullen, Nebr., 1884-1917, Mullen Public School.

NORRIS, GEORGE W. *Fighting Liberal*, The autobiography of . . . (New York, 1945).

OSBORN, FAIRFIELD. *The Limits of Earth* (Boston, 1953).

PAINE, BAYARD H. "Decisions Which Have Changed Nebraska History," *Nebraska History Magazine*, XVI, No. 4.

POOL, RAYMOND J. "Fifty Years on the Nebraska National Forest," *Nebraska History*, XXXIV, No. 3.

Progress, Missouri River Basin, U.S. Dept. of Interior, Billings.

Theodore Roosevelt; an Autobiography (New York, 1913).

RUSSELL, CHARLES M. *Good Medicine* (Garden City, 1930).

SANDOZ, MARI. *The Cattlemen* (New York, 1958).

SHANNON, F. A. *The Farmer's Last Frontier, 1860-1897* (New York, 1945).

STUART, GRANVILLE. *Forty Years on the Frontier*, P. C. Phillips, ed., 2 vols. (Glendale, 1925).

UMLAND, RUDOLPH. "Phantom Airships of the Nineties," *Prairie Schooner*, Winter 1938.

U.S. General Land Office. *Report*, 1886 (illegal fencing of public lands).

——. *Sen. Exec. Doc. 181*, 48th Cong., 1st Sess., 1883-84 (foreign ranch holdings).

——. *House Exec. Doc. 267*, 48th Cong., 2nd Sess., 1884-85, Nimmo, Joseph, "Range and Ranch Cattle Traffic."

——. *Sen. Doc. 189*, 58th Cong., 3rd Sess., 1905, "Report of Public Lands Commission" (range lease laws and overgrazing).

WEAVER, J. E., and ALBERTSON, F. W. *Grasslands of the Great Plains* (Lincoln, 1956).

WRIGHT, ROBERT M. *Dodge City . . .* (Wichita, 1913).

Wyoming's Pioneer Ranches, Burns, R. H.; Gillespie, A. S.; Richardson, W. G. (Laramie, 1955).

Acknowledgments

The Sioux Indians believed that a people without history was like wind on the buffalo grass, and looked with some scorn upon the early Americans to the Plains because these pale faces seemed to have few stories of their past and carried no historians to record what happened.

The white men who stayed changed that, and now one can spend a lifetime working through the records and stories of the Plains, from the History Center at the University of Texas and the Panhandle-Plains Historical Museum to the historical societies of Oklahoma, Kansas, Colorado, Nebraska, Wyoming, the Dakotas and Montana. Then there are the collections at the University of Wyoming Library and at the Denver Public Library. Beyond, there are the vast accumulations in the National Archives. In one way or another I am indebted to the staffs of all these institutions, and to those of the New-York Historical Society and the New York Public Library. Most of all, perhaps, I am indebted to the old-timers on the Plains, to those who kept their records, put down their stories, sensing, somehow, that in their experiences lay the essence of what the region could become.

M. S.

Index

ABOUT THE AUTHOR

Mari Sandoz was born at Sandoz, P. O., Sheridan County, Nebraska, on the Niobrara River. She is the eldest of the six children of Jules Sandoz, a medical student who emigrated from Switzerland to western Nebraska in the middle 1880's and became a lifelong friend of the old buffalo Sioux of the region. Miss Sandoz can recall the tense and exciting times of her own childhood during the later years of the cattleman-settler troubles, when her father, as locator, surveyor and star witness in the cattleman land fraud cases, was in constant danger from the hired killers of the ranchers. She experienced the usual rigors of a pioneer childhood, fought prairie fires, survived May blizzards (including six weeks of snow blindness), taught country school and finally attended the University of Nebraska as an adult special.

Miss Sandoz began writing on the sly—to her father's intense disapproval, both in her childhood and during college. In addition to her many books, listed in the front of *Love Song to the Plains*, she has written stories and articles for many magazines, and has received numerous awards for her knowledge and contribution to the history of the Plains.